UP ALL
NIGHT

UP ALL NIGHT

MY LIFE

—

AND TIMES

—

IN ROCK RADIO

CAROL MILLER

An Imprint of HarperCollinsPublishers

HarperCollins books may be purchased for educational, business, or sales promotional use. For information please write: Special Markets Department, HarperCollins Publishers, 10 East 53rd Street, New York, NY 10022.

FIRST EDITION

Designed by Leah Carlson-Stanisic

Library of Congress Cataloging-in-Publication Data has been applied for.

ISBN 978-0-06-184524-6

12 13 14 15 16   OV/RRD   10 9 8 7 6 5 4 3 2 1

To the memory
of my father, Hyman I. Miller, M.D.,
and the memory of Elaine Kaufman

PREFACE

"Would you be interested in writing a memoir?" the letter read.

Unbelievable! Me? I'm no household name. Just a radio DJ. Who would care?

I was in the air studio opening a promotional package from Ecco/HarperCollins, which contained a copy of their latest offering—a biography of Warren Zevon—and uncharacteristically for this type of mailing, a personal letter from Abigail Holstein, an editor at Ecco.

"Considering that you're . . . a fixture on the New York airwaves . . . you probably have several volumes' worth of great rock stories . . . ," the letter continued.

Oh, so they want me to dish some dirt? No way, I thought, but for weeks I mulled over this most generous invitation anyway. A once-in-a-lifetime chance to—maybe—write a book.

"OK, I'll give it a shot," I told Abigail and Ecco's associate publisher, Rachel Bressler, over drinks, "but it won't be what you expected."

And so I sat down at the kitchen table with my laptop, composed and clunked out every word of this volume by myself. My wonderful editor fortunately removed a few of them.

Everyone's life, including yours, reflects a place in time, and can be charted as a cultural chronicle, a small piece of a much bigger historical picture. Everyone's life is a story.

This one's mine. I hope you like it.

UP ALL
NIGHT

1

I thought Steven Tyler was dead.

Waking up fully dressed from a three-hour nap, I glanced across the vast expanse of hotel bed, where the childlike lead singer of Aerosmith, the world-famous rock group, lay in a motionless huddle under the floral spread.

Upon assessing this peculiar situation, my first question was "Well, how did I get here?" The snappy answer: "By limo, of course." The real answer was more complicated. And what was I doing here? Actually, my job.

I have an evening radio show. I talk and play rock music, rock artists drop by for interviews, or sometimes I broadcast from their concerts. I've been on the air professionally since the end of 1971, and since 1973 in New York. Some people would just say I'm a DJ, but that doesn't mean what it used to mean. Nowadays, a DJ is a traveling music mixer with his own collection of tracks. In the late fifties and early sixties, a DJ was a fast-talking older guy from your local AM radio station who often wore a loud plaid jacket and spun "platters" in the high school gym for the big sock-hop.

Even though we grew up with these lively entertainers, some of us who started on FM radio early in the rock era found that image to be a little bit cheesy. At that time, we took ourselves more seriously, so we coined the term *radio personalities*. I consider myself a professional lifelong friend. I play the music we both love, and we've had a running conversation for years now. Mundane but important stuff—the weather, sports, some news, definitely bulletins too. Almost any given weeknight, you can count on my being there. An audio version of a stable relationship. As of writing this, I'm on Clear Channel's WAXQ-FM: "Q104.3—New York's Classic Rock." Also heard nationally on SiriusXM Satellite Radio and through United Stations.

But back to Steven Tyler. Summer of '77: The Blackout. Son of Sam. The demise of Elvis. Heat. Garbage in the streets . . .

It was a Monday night, and I had just finished my radio show on 95.5 WPLJ, New York's Best Rock, which ran from 10 P.M. to 2 A.M. Taking a cab from the ABC building on Fifty-fourth and Sixth to my block on West Seventy-second Street, I stopped off at Trax, the late-night club on the southwest corner of Columbus. Through an unmarked doorway and down a steep, narrow staircase was a dark basement firetrap of a venue crowded with banquettes, chairs, and tables, with a stage for performances in an adjacent room. Pick a night, and someone famous (whose records I was playing) would be there—Led Zeppelin, Peter Frampton, Kiss, and on that particular night, Aerosmith.

"Someone would like to meet you," said Phil De Havilland, one of the club owners. I had barely made it through the entryway, self-consciously wondering whether my dark hair was still straight and my Fiorucci jeans, which I'd recently bought at their flagship store on Fifty-ninth Street, fit just right. No doubt Phil had already pointed me out to Steven Tyler as a DJ on the big rock station who played his records. I was yet another good reason for Tyler and company to frequent his establishment when in town. Tyler, in a gray T-shirt and jeans, sat sideways with his feet up on a far corner chair and warmly extended his hand. "We're working on the new album," he said, "and I could play you some of the stuff, but it's back at the hotel. You wanna hear it? You don't have to do anything."

What this meant was "You don't have to sleep with me," and although a normal guy might consider this invitation a bit presumptuous, coming from a rock star it was downright gentlemanly! I agreed, and took the five-minute ride in Tyler's limo back through Central Park to the Hotel Navarro, on Central Park South.

In the two-room suite, Tyler produced a large silver cassette device and played some of the tracks-in-the-making for "Draw the Line." *Da-da-da-da-da-da-dah!—Dah! Dah!* Joe Perry's opening guitar salvo on the title track bounced off the walls. Tyler watched my face for a reaction. I concentrated, silently nodded my head to the music, and punctuated with "Yeah, great . . . You got some great stuff here!" My favorite was the funky "Get it Up," which when finished I thought sounded overly complicated, with too many layers of extra riffs and flourishes.

After about twenty minutes of this listening party, Tyler abruptly stopped the tape. "Well, I'm going to sleep," he said. "See, I told ya you wouldn't have to do anything! But you can stay here, on the couch, if you want." Tyler immediately rummaged through a bag for a large brown bottle, jumped on the bed in the adjoining room, and shoved a handful of red capsules down his throat. Within seconds, he was out cold.

It was now close to 5 A.M. I had to make a decision. In just a few hours I had to be five blocks down Sixth Avenue, back at 1330, the ABC building, for a WPLJ music meeting where new releases would be presented, discussed, and voted on for airplay.

The practical move would be to stay, dust myself off, and just walk to work. I would get more sleep, and save the cab fare. Tyler wouldn't be up that early anyway, so I could just disappear. I felt guilty and a little uneasy just at the prospect of staying in a strange man's hotel room. But who would find out? Tyler could probably sleep through the apocalypse. I was perfectly safe here.

But what was the point of all this reasoning if I couldn't get to sleep? I tried the couch in the main room, but the spaces between the cushions made lying down a miserable experience. I walked over to the bedroom: a huge, comfy-looking bed, which could have fit five Steven Tylers, and Mr. "Dream On" himself curled up on the extreme left side. Silently, I slipped under the covers on the opposite edge, which seemed like an ocean away, dialed the hotel operator for a wake-up call at 9 A.M., and stiffly settled in for a nap.

But the next morning, tiptoeing to the bathroom, there was no sign of movement from my sleeping host. I began to poke Steven Tyler. If this guy was breathing, I couldn't tell, and where was his pulse? A wave of

horror and dizziness swept over me. "Don't panic! Don't panic!" I repeated, and tried to collect my thoughts. If I simply slipped out of the
hotel now, I might be tracked down by the police as the last person to be
seen with a deceased rock star, and that couldn't be good. Better to face
the music.

Maybe some water would do the trick? I filled the little glass next to
the faucet. Not wanting to soak the bedding, I made sure to drizzle the
water squarely on Tyler's face. Nothing.

The phone began to ring. Perhaps it would be someone who could
help. "Mr. Tyler's suite," I answered crisply, doing my best secretarial
impersonation. "No, he's not available at the moment." The phone rang
again. "Good morning, Mr. Tyler's suite." It was *Rolling Stone* magazine
calling to confirm their appointment for the Aerosmith interview. "No,
he'll get back to you shortly. I'll be happy to take a message." I grabbed
a pen and hotel notepad.

It occurred to me that I had spoken to someone at the club during
the night who was part of the Aerosmith entourage. A protective secu-
rity guard of some sort, but what was his name? Michael. Michael
Cohn, or Cohen. Yes, I remembered, because it seemed odd to find a fellow Jew in that line of work. I asked the hotel operator to connect me
with his room. "We have three people under that name," she said.
"Which one do you want?" I picked the one closest to Tyler's room.
"Hello, is this Michael Cohen with Aerosmith?" Bingo! "My name is
Carol Miller. I'm a DJ. Do you remember me from Trax last night?"
Thankfully, he did, even though I felt embarrassed to admit I was still
in Steven's room. "I don't know how to tell you this, but—Steven doesn't
seem to be breathing."

"Oh, he did that again," laughed Michael. "Here's what you do. Order
a hot breakfast from room service with eggs and coffee. Make sure it's
hot. When they bring up the tray, stick it under Steven's nose." And
when I did, sure enough, Tyler grunted vaguely, still asleep. Extreme
relief! I called Michael back: "Okay, he's all yours." And there were still
twenty minutes left for me to freshen up and get over to ABC.

But what was the social etiquette in such a situation? How do you
leave an unconscious rock star you barely know but in whose favor it

would be wise to remain for business reasons? Besides, he seemed like a genuinely nice guy! I pulled one of my promotional WPLJ postcards from my purse. Everyone on the air staff had them. I scribbled something like "Hope you're okay, nice to meet you, the new album sounds great." Then I signed it and left my number, in case Tyler ever wanted to know what happened.

That evening, as I was getting ready to go on the air, my phone rang.

"Hi. It's Steven. Want to go to Martinique with me for the weekend?"

"Hey, glad you're okay, you had me scared there," I said.

"Yeah." Steven chuckled, as if to gloss over a usual occurrence. But I had no intention of ever flying anywhere with anyone, no matter how famous, who would inflict his near-death experience on me like that. "Thanks, but maybe another time," I said, and went on to do my show.

Turns out there would be another time, many more, and I did go, but no one went comatose on me again. And it was a lot better than sitting home alone.

2

The horseless carriage sputtered along the dirt road as it made its way from the Kalishman family home in Yedenitz, Romania. Or so I had always imagined. Papa Kalishman had hired this newfangled automobile to take his quiet, suffering wife to Vienna, in the hope that a doctor there could treat her deteriorating condition and save her life. Alas, there was nothing to be done, and upon Mama's passing, at about thirty-nine, Papa took the children, boarded a ship for America, and made a new home on New York's Lower East Side. This was a good plan; conditions for Jews in Russia and surrounding areas were getting dangerous anyway. The three Kalishman sisters would all be stricken by a similar ailment in their late thirties and, like their mother, die shortly thereafter. One of the sisters, Kate (Katya), had a daughter named Hilda. As Kate was dying, her physician told Hilda she should not have any children, as she was sure to pass along the family's unfortunate fate. But who would want to hear that? And who would listen?

There were stories Hilda, my mother, told me, in dribs and drabs, when I was a baby. Mommy never talked baby talk; she always spoke to me as if I were a little adult. And she only had adult stories to tell—mostly of hardship, loss, fear, and sickness. We lived on the army base in Fort Bragg, North Carolina, having come there from New York while my father served and prepared for deployment at the start of the Korean War. Whatever it was that had taken the life of Hilda's mother and aunts would surely take hers too. "My turn is coming," she would say. Early on, I came to believe that my turn was coming as well. There were no old people in our family. I didn't know what old people looked like. The family's fatal condition had no name. Mommy never referred to it directly, calling it "You know." That and the stories were all I knew of it.

Mommy's melancholy radiated throughout our small barrack. From my earliest memories, I remember Mommy not being happy. Somehow I knew that it wasn't my fault, and that I couldn't blame her—but I felt sad too. I began to sense that there was more to it than the dreaded illness. Something involving her other stories. As a brilliant Depression-era schoolgirl, Hilda had gotten herself a scholarship to NYU, where she had graduated first in her class with a major in chemistry and then taken a job with Allied Chemical. During World War II, she had also worked in a factory making bullet dies. But Hilda had aspired to something greater; she sometimes talked about becoming a doctor. Once, when we were back in Brooklyn staying with Daddy's sister Aunt Mildred, Mommy ran into an old college professor, Harry Tarr, on Coney Island Avenue. "Hilda!" he had exclaimed, "I expected great things of you, but what have we here?" as he nodded down at me in my uncomfortable blue metal stroller. (There were sliding colored beads on the handlebar. Mommy had explained that the beads made an abacus.)

Mommy didn't seem any happier either when we'd head up to the Catskills for the summer, several years later. She did not socialize or play mah-jongg with the other mothers. Instead, she engaged in her usual joint pursuits of smoking and reading the *New Yorker,* or any intellectual tome available. One morning as I headed for the children's campground, I caught "Uncle Ed" Stevens, the camp's *tummler* and head children's counselor, climbing the three gray wooden steps to our bungalow. He knocked on our screen door, and my mother let him in. Through the side window, I heard the loud voices and saw Mommy's apparent distress. Then Uncle Ed left. Not long after, I learned that Uncle Ed had been a boyfriend of Mommy's back in Brooklyn, with whom she had broken up to marry my father. What a chafing, uncomfortable way it must have been for Mommy to spend her summer vacation, a few bungalows down from her ex-boyfriend and his wife. Add to that the company of a group of women who did not share her enthusiasm for Adlai Stevenson, or for that matter, anyone else who hadn't yet appeared on the *Lucky Strike Hit Parade*.

But in Fort Bragg, Mommy was far from the Jewish enclaves of New York, alone with a baby, waiting for the phone call that could be sending her husband, Captain Hyman I. Miller, M.D., overseas. Just the ring of the heavy black appliance would cause her instant panic; the phone only brought bad news. Conversely, any call she made would be sure to disturb the recipient. "I'm sorry, is this a bad time?" was her standard refrain. I inherited this peculiar syndrome, which I later labeled *phono-phobia*. Not the ideal fear for a radio host to have.

Sometimes, as she chain-smoked Chesterfields (she upgraded to Kents when I was about four) and read in our tiny house, Mommy's doom and gloom seemed overwhelming. Sadly, I wasn't helping her, so I plotted escape. Not to be mean, just for fun. Once, having crawled over a window terrace, I managed to toddle several barrack blocks away, to be found by Joe, our neighbors' huge Great Dane, who was my best (and only) friend. Another time, on a day off from the base with Daddy, I ran into the large, muddy field at Mr. Potter's chicken farm. Mommy screamed for me to return, which I did, but only after attempting to pet a chicken. Later, back in Queens, while Mommy was very pregnant with my sister and couldn't run, I took off down Metropolitan Avenue toward the Interboro Parkway. As if by magic, who should appear at the traffic light of the service road, in his black '52 Buick with the Dynaflow transmission, but my father, en route from making the rounds at Kings County Hospital. With his typical never-panic, matter-of-fact authority, he stopped and asked what I was doing there. "I came to see you" was the first excuse that came to mind.

"Good! Where's Mommy?"

"Over there. She can't walk fast." I pointed to a location nearly a block and a half away.

"Oh, okay, Nanny [my nickname from my middle name]. I'll see you later." And Daddy happily drove off. I trotted back down Metropolitan to my mother, to report the successful rendezvous.

Mommy's radio was another escape. In North Carolina, it only picked up that hillbilly music she hated. But soon I had a first favorite song, a ballad by someone called Hank Snow, who mournfully wailed, "I went to yer weddin' although I was dreadin' the thought of l-o-o-s-ing you." At which point I would always burst into tears, imagining that I couldn't find Dorothy, my one doll, whom I was constantly dragging around, punishing her for her disobedience. (Once, her head actually came off, and Dorothy had to be sent away for repairs. I couldn't wait for her to get back. I figure a shrink might have a field day with that one.)

When my father was finally tapped to go to Korea, his overseas assignment was changed at the last minute because of his rank. As an army captain and physician, he would travel by ship and ice-cutter to Thule, Greenland, to head up the construction of a new military base. The Cold War was rapidly heating up, and we had to keep an eye on those Russians. Hyman had actually been drafted during WWII, but since he was chief medical resident at St. John's Hospital in Queens, Sister Thomas Francis, the head nun, had requested he remain to keep things running.

When Daddy was leaving, he gave me the first present I remember, my first book, a large illustrated volume about a cat, *Pussy Willow.* He also gave me very explicit instructions: "Keep an eye on Mommy." No matter how seriously he meant it, this statement confirmed what I already felt—that Mommy was somehow fragile. Watching her became my job. And I never let down my guard. When Mommy was learning to drive, lying down with a migraine, or paralyzed with fear because a phone call had not come, I perceived myself to be in charge. And whether giving directions from the backseat of the car, or trying to calm her down with reason, I would be my father's advocate, and therefore my own. When my sister arrived, I thought I'd gained yet another responsibility.

To say I was my father's girl would be an understatement, although I saw little of him when I was very young. He spent those six months in Greenland, then returned to long hours of medical residency and a budding practice in Queens. I tried my best to copy his levelheadedness and practicality, and the calm with which he handled even the most overwhelming emergencies.

When I was four, I became fanatically interested in driving a car, and Daddy gave me an actual driving lesson while I sat in his lap at the wheel. One Sunday, Daddy brought me and my sister along while he checked in on a patient at Jamaica Hospital in Queens. In the early to mid-fifties nobody thought twice about leaving small children in a car for half an hour, so he parked us by the side of the hospital, on Eighty-ninth Avenue, which sloped gradually downhill. No sooner had he disappeared from view toward the hospital entrance than a bullish blue car bumped us from behind, and our Buick began rolling. Scrambling over the driver's seat from the backseat where I sat with baby sister Jane, I crawled under the dashboard and threw myself on the brake. The car stopped its descent, but my sister continued to wail. I sat under the dashboard pressing on the brake for what seemed like hours, until my father returned. "What's going on, what's the problem?" he laughed, in Yiddish and English, opening the driver's seat door. I told him how the car had started to roll. "Nanny, look, next time if that happens, just pull the emergency brake over here," he said, showing me yet another intriguing aspect of the automobile. "Okay, now who wants ice cream?"

Another time I got on the wrong school bus home and nonchalantly told the driver to let me off in front of my apartment, explaining that my mother would be overcome by panic if I failed to disembark. I wasn't frightened; I knew I could get home from anywhere. (Like Daddy, I have some kind of implanted sense of direction.) But the driver refused to let me off, and as we traveled past Lefferts House, I could see Mommy anxiously waiting, turning her head back and forth. I did what I thought Daddy would do. I refused to get off the bus at any of the subsequent stops, and sat in my seat until the end of the route. I yelled at the driver, an ignorant-looking "JD" (juvenile delinquent), and told him he'd be in big trouble because I would tell the school what happened. Grudgingly, he drove me home. Mommy was still waiting in the street, obviously frantic.

Daddy and I shared the same black hair and olive Sephardic complexion and features, which routinely got us in a bit of trouble during our time down South. I looked nothing like my fair-skinned mother. "Your little girl is mighty dark," said the counter waitress to my mother, as she asked us to leave the diner. Supposedly, the butcher refused to deliver meat to my father's barrack, and so my parents ate a lot of tomato herring instead. "I'm related to my father's side of the family," I would quip, when no one recognized Hilda as my mother on parent-teacher school nights. As a teenager, similarly complexioned Aunt Mildred, Daddy's sister, who worked in a beauty supply house, would introduce me to facial fade creams like Porcelana and Esoterica. She would also get me Lilt home permanent, which I would use "backward" to straighten (and of course fry) my frizzy hair.

As he told it, Hymie was a rascal of a boy, who spoke only his native Yiddish until he was about five. His father's last name was Mehter, which I only recently learned is Israeli or Turkish in origin. His family motto was "Pack light and keep moving." The Mehters had eventually migrated (or escaped) into Russia before arriving at Ellis Island, whereupon some of them were given the name Matter, and my grandfather was given the name Miller. Hymie learned English at school and by reading his favorite childhood stories, *The Adventures of Frank Merriwell.* He loved to read locked inside the bathroom, fully clothed in the empty tub. He had many odd jobs as a child, including outdoor sign painting with his father in Brighton Beach. Hymie expected to learn the sewing and garment business along with his cousins, but his father had something else in mind. A copy of a letter Hymie was instructed to write to a neighborhood doctor, asking how to become one himself, still remains tucked in the pages of his high school yearbook.

Like my mother, Hy was the only member of his family to finish high school and go on to college, and then he went on to medical school. In the late thirties and early forties, many of the local New York medical schools were not too keen on admitting Jews, and so Hy worked, scrimped, and traveled up to Massachusetts, to Middlesex Medical college, which later became Brandeis. It was at a summer job as a busboy at the Hotel Regal, in the Catskills, that the wisecracking, practical-joking Hymie would meet the quiet, intellectual teenager Hilda, who was there earning money for school as a children's governess. They married in 1942.

In my first memory of Daddy on the army base, he was in the middle of yelling instructions at my mother on where to stand for a photograph, lambasting her in a combination of English and Yiddish. Mommy seemed frozen with fear, taking his yelling personally. It didn't take me long to recognize Daddy's denigrating humor, but I would have to wait until I was an adult to be able to dish it out in return. And yes, it was often hard not to take some of it personally. My father could have skewered Don Rickles with insults, minus the apology.

Some of Doctor Miller's more memorable insults (in English) include:

"What's that stuff on your eyes, honey? It looks like bird shit!" (Daddy commenting on the Revlon icy green/brown eye shadow that I wore as a teenager. For years thereafter, he would silently mouth the words "bird shit" and tap his eyelid when seeing me with makeup at family functions.)

"You look like a Seventh Avenue whore in that outfit, so since we're on Seventh Avenue, you can walk in back of me!" (Daddy disapproving of my Mary Quant minidress and dangle earrings when the family went to a Broadway show for his forty-eighth birthday.)

"What? They're selling a square inch of the Beatles' bed sheets for a dollar? Do they even wash it? How about the used toilet paper?" (Daddy hating the Beatles and all that crappy noise from the get-go.)

"You wanna be a kindergarten teacher? Your mother's cousin Ellen is a kindergarten teacher, and she's a moron! No, wait, maybe she's a low normal." (Daddy's opinion of my first expressed career choice.)

"Nobody could be this ugly, especially my daughters!" (Daddy surveying the number of shampoos and other necessary beauty potions in the bathroom I shared with my sister.)

"Everyone's on a date on Saturday night except you. What are you doing, playing records in a closet?!" (Daddy getting concerned that I wasn't married yet by the old age of twenty-three, and wasting my life doing a radio show.)

And most recently, nearing age ninety-two in his hospital bed, as he tried to eat with plastic utensils: "What kind of forks do they give ya in this place? The food—it falls right off! How much are we paying for this?"

ƧƧƧ

I missed Daddy terribly when he was in Greenland, and being his representative at home, I was even more aware of his absence. Prior to his return, he moved Mommy and me back up to Brooklyn, where we stayed with Aunt Mildred, Uncle Saul, and their daughter, Ruth Gail, in their small apartment on Avenue N, right off Coney Island Avenue. When at last Daddy's ship came in, we moved back into our apartment in nearby Queens. I never went off duty as his deputy, even though he was home.

3

"Knife Man!" "Scissor Man!"

It was a Friday afternoon in October, almost Erev Shabbos. From across the street, on a large lawn fronting an old apartment residence, I watched Mrs. Biederman adjust her head scarf. Mrs. Levine was already wearing her *sheitel* (wig). They and another woman came down the slate steps of my building, Lefferts House, and approached Knife Man's small open-backed truck. He would sharpen their cutlery on his wheel, right in the open on Lefferts Boulevard.

Earlier that day, the I Cash Clothes Man had made a rare appearance. Here it was, the 1950s, and he was still making his rounds at the rear courtyards of the apartment buildings, apparently a lingering holdover from the turn of the century. The I Cash Clothes Man would holler up at the windows, "I pay cash for clothes!" encouraging the housewives to trade in a few old items in exchange for grocery money. Yet another truck visited on a semi-regular basis. Two men would pull out a large rectangular object from its back and carry it to the sixth floor. Rumor had it that someone still had an icebox, although all the kitchens I had seen in our modern (1937) building had Kelvinators.

As I watched Mrs. Biederman, a group of kids was now assembling near me on the lawn. Moishe Halberstam, in long pants, yarmulke, and *peyos* called out, "I make a *schlimilechel* and somebody sticks it in," tracing the shape of a circle on the back of a kid named Hesh, whom I didn't know. Hesh was now officially designated the "little fool." Someone ran up and stuck his pinky in the target and everyone ran to hide. Now it was up to Hesh to find the perpetrator. I had wanted to join in, but frequent illness and breathing problems that I'd had since birth made it difficult for me to run.

Instead, I walked just a few steps north, past the cleaners with the flashing red-green neon sign, to the luncheonette on the southwest corner of Lefferts and Metropolitan. The luncheonette was owned by the Razzlers, a neighborhood family. For a dime, you could get an egg cream and a pretzel stick. The beverage, made of milk, seltzer, and Fox's U-bet chocolate syrup, was a treat, although it always gave me stomach pains. From my perch on the round, backless, twisting bar stool with its red cushion, I would contemplate my nearly eight-year-old universe. And as I saw it, there were very few mysteries, and everything was very serious.

There was never a time that I didn't know about "the War." WWII was, and still is, the defining standard of my life. Nothing I would encounter, or have, could ever be that horrific. Relatives were still coming over in the early 1950s, mine and so many others: camp survivors, escapees, displaced persons, each with a story too horrible to tell. So they didn't. But I could piece a narrative together from the bits and pieces of overheard comments, mostly in Yiddish, and their perpetually covered arms hiding the tattoos, always referred to as "the numbers."

Although my parents had lived in Brooklyn, their childhoods too, mainly my mother's, seemed tainted by tragedy and early death, and the War must have added to it. Perhaps another reason why our household was so somber. It wasn't anyone's fault. No one was trying to be mean. But because others had suffered so much, I shouldn't complain about anything. Not surprisingly, I remember thinking that any tall oblong buildings looked like giant gravestones, although I had never been to a cemetery. And it made me all the more certain that my turn at suffering would come one day too. As sobering as that seemed, at least then I would be worthy of having "a story" and joining the ranks of my people.

ʃ ʃ ʃ

School was PS 90, Richmond Hill, on 108th Street, right near the El on Jamaica Avenue. It was (and still is) one of those formidable prisonlike stone fortresses of education built by the City of New York in the 1800s. Ancient sagging wood floors, wooden flip-top desk-bench contraptions with now empty inkwells and black metal grilles that were bolted to the floor, and teachers seemingly just as old who were constantly admonishing us to stop playing with the inkwells, which made a metallic clinking sound when you opened and dropped the lids. From the start, my parents made it clear that nothing less than an A in every course would ever be acceptable throughout my scholastic career.

Public school was a trip to the outside world. Most of the kids there had different holidays than we did in my neighborhood. There was one where a man came back to life after being killed and horribly hung up on wood. They would celebrate his reappearance by coloring the outside of hard-boiled eggs, eating chocolates, and hanging up pictures of bunnies. Then they had the other holiday, equally curious. A woman had a magical baby in a barn, but there was no real father; her husband, however, was there with her. "Who's that man?" I had asked Mommy as I pointed to a greenish billboard of a tubby, bearded, white-haired man in a red suit and stocking cap drinking a bottle of Coca-Cola.

"Oh, that's Santa Claus," she said matter-of-factly. "He's an imaginary man who brings the Christian children presents on Christmas."

"Well, if he's imaginary, then who do they say thank-you to?" I remember asking. The children would get these presents under a dead pine tree, which had been brought into their apartments and covered with pretty lights to coincide with the birth of the magical baby.

None of this concerned me until my best friend at PS 90, Alice, went off to something in the afternoon called "catechism class," and then permanently rejected me for being a "dirty Jew who ate Jew food." This despite the fact that we ate Campbell's tomato soup together, and Daddy had helped Alice's mother, a Czechoslovakian immigrant, to get a nursing job at a local hospital. Well, so much for the catechism class and the strange holidays; why would anyone want one of those presents anyway?

$$\text{\textbf{✈ ✈ ✈}}$$

In my matter-of-fact world, I had two favorite mysteries, which I loved to mull over while I sipped on my egg cream. One concerned my father's outside phone-answering service, which he simply called "Service." Daddy would call to let them know at what phone number he would be in case there was a medical emergency when he was not at home or at the office. "Service" would somehow interrupt the incoming calls en route to our phone, and so, I reasoned, these operators would have to be sitting outdoors. I first imagined three old ladies sitting in chairs clustered atop the telephone poles at the intersection of Metropolitan and Jamaica avenues. But no, I decided, they would have to be somewhere indoors, in case of bad weather. Probably a special building where lots of ladies interrupted calls on lots of phones. That would have to be it!

The far more complex mystery concerned the Elmhurst Gas Tanks, two monolithic structures located at Seventy-ninth Street and Grand Avenue, near Horace Harding Boulevard, which was to officially begin its transformation into the perennially congested Long Island Expressway, or LIE, in 1956. Whenever we passed the gas tanks in the car, Daddy would speed up, because according to him, they were a potential Hiroshima. This from a man who never panicked about anything made the tanks all the more fascinating, and my fascination would last for decades.

The two huge circular metal canisters with a diameter of 275 feet could rise to a height of about 200 feet, and then appear to lower nearly to the ground within their stationary steel frames. They housed "natural gas" for heating and running the whole city of New York! (I was sure.) There was reportedly a little man, in a rowboat, who periodically checked the circumferences of the canisters for possible leaks. So, were they full when they were all the way up, or were they then empty? Did they merely descend into two holes each 200 feet below Queens, or did they collapse, kind of like a travel drinking cup, slightly below the ground, where they would be repeatedly filled and then expanded? And how did the rowboat man really fit in?

I ultimately went for the travel cup theory. Places could leak when they scrunched in, and that's when the little man in the boat would come in handy. Aha!

During the various meetings of SIMS (the Student International Meditation Society) and the Buddhist Nam Myoho Renge Kyo sessions to which I was dragged during the late sixties and early seventies, the gas tanks became my mantra. "Gas Tanks, Gas Tanks," I would mentally respond in my cosmic surroundings. Up and down or collapse?

To my dismay, the Elmhurst tanks were rendered obsolete in 1995, and were dismantled. They had been there since 1910. A library trip, and then a subsequent Google revealed that their mechanism was in fact similar to a collapsing drinking cup, but in an inverted position. Ingenious! And the little man in the rowboat, yes, he had periodically patrolled the tanks' perimeters, until the sixties, when leakage could be monitored electronically.

In addition to the phone service and the gas tanks, my two other major interests were the New York Yankees, and driving a real car. That was until a riveting new sonic phenomenon began one night below my bedroom window. The alleyway beneath the first floor of Lefferts House, where they allowed the deliverymen passage and stationed the garbage cans, was an unexpected place to find my future.

4

Actually, the TV had arrived before the singing started. Mommy had postponed the inevitable arrival of the "dreaded box" as long as possible, but one afternoon, most likely in 1953, a huge, heavy carton was delivered to apartment 1B in Lefferts House. I watched as the men wheeled it in on a dolly, set it down, inconveniently, in the middle of the hall, and left. And there it sat, for many hours, maybe even a day, until the clunky Zenith with the rounded (but not circular) screen and the light beige exterior was set up in my parents' bedroom.

The first black-and-white moving presentation that came on when the device was activated was a newsreel of our boys with machine guns slogging victoriously through what looked like Korean snow, keeping things under control. Ordinarily, people would see such a newsreel as a short in a movie theater before they showed the feature film. Later television news broadcasts, featuring "The Most Trusted Man in America," Walter Cronkite, would invariably elicit a Yiddish insult from my father, and then: "Why should I trust him? What makes him such a *gantseh k'nacker* (big shot)? I don't trust him no-how!"

Of course, we only turned on the TV for specific shows, especially in order not to run up the electric bill. There were so many funny regular people on the TV who made jokes, at least half in sort-of Yiddish. Obviously, the whole world (outside of my public school classmates) understood! Uncle Miltie, Sid Caesar, Jack Benny, Groucho . . . so many regular grown-ups having silly slapstick fun, filled with clever innuendo. I didn't know grown-ups could be anything other than serious! (No, I didn't exactly understand the innuendo, but I knew something funny was going on that only adults were supposed to know about.) And then, another favorite, who didn't seem to speak Yiddish: Ernie Kovaks. You could just tell that Ernie must be saying really sharp things, slipping them in, with a deadpan delivery. Plus, he used camera tricks, like Pinky Lee, the children's-show host. Pinky, with his signature checkered coat and hat, would be sitting on a stool, and then the stool would disappear, and Pinky would still be sitting there, in midair. Obviously impossible! Many later shows like *Rin Tin Tin, Lassie,* and *Bachelor Father* would introduce me to this foreign culture that supposedly also existed in America. A place where "Dad" "came down to breakfast" wearing a sweater, and ate bacon. Unheard-of.

I wanted to be part of all this excitement coming from the outside world, out of the ether and right into apartment 1B. And so I had Mommy send a collection of my drawings of swans to Miss Francis for *Ding Dong School,* another popular children's show. My father had taken me on a long drive on a Saturday, after his office hours, far away, out to Long Island, and we wound up at a place called the Roslyn Duck Pond. This setting had deeply impressed me, and became the inspiration for my first public artistic endeavor.

Usually, the stout (actually you could say a little *ungeshtupt,* or overstuffed), dark-haired Miss Francis directed the camera around her playroom, showcasing one work of art for each of several different children on any given day. I never missed a broadcast, waiting for one of my drawings to be shown. And when the big day came, there was triumph, and then, tragedy. "All of today's drawings are from Miss Carol Nan Miller of Queens, New York," said Miss Francis, as she began to verbally point out each of my duck pond drawings on her wall. But I couldn't see them! I was stunned. "Mommy," I called, "fix the TV!" Alas, the lady above us in 2B was running the vacuum cleaner, which, like any plane flying in or out of nearby Idlewild Airport, would reduce the television transmission to noisy black-and-white static.

Another major media revelation would come in December of 1954. It was a sunny, cold Sunday, most likely the twenty-sixth, when Daddy took Mommy, me, and baby sister Jane along with Mommy's brother, Murray, and his wife and daughter, Karen, to see a demonstration of the new color television at Rockefeller Center. On the way in, for the first time, I saw the huge Christmas tree by the ice-skating rink. Outside the GE Building, maybe on Sixth Avenue, a TV screen beamed a live black-and-white transmission of the crowd, taken by an actual television camera. Daddy put me up on his shoulders to see myself, and there we were, bunched in with everyone else, but not backward, like in a mirror. Inside the demonstration hall, several different large televisions showed the same color presentation simultaneously. It was Errol Flynn starring in *Robin Hood,* but the colors were all wrong! On one TV, Flynn's face was beet red, and on another, it was green. Clearly, color television would have a long way to go before it was "perfected." According to my father, it never was. Jane and I finally bought my parents a Sharp color set in 1984 as a present.

But it was the singing that ultimately left a bigger impression on me. "Earth angel, earth angel / Will you be mine?" The voices of the three teenage boys blended and ricocheted off the cement walls of the garbage entrance alleyway of Lefferts House. I couldn't see them as they sang, about ten feet below and directly under the window of the bedroom I shared with baby sister Jane, and I could only momentarily glimpse their faces sometimes as they arrived. Several evenings a week they would show up to practice their harmonies, about seven o'clock—luckily for me, my bedtime. Even as a child (who became a lifelong night person), I could never sleep at such a ridiculously early hour. Mommy would take care of the baby, cover me, close the door, and disappear for the night. That was my signal to run to the window and peer through the slats of the blinds, hoping to get a glimpse of the singers. The boys sounded wonderful, even if their words made no sense; didn't angels have something to do with flying dead people? What could be so special about "only you"? And what about all the gees, doo-wops and sh-booms? This seemed like something just made for kids; no busy adult would have the time to waste singing these silly nonwords.

Any exposure to music I'd had up until then (outside of that hillbilly music Mommy hated back on the army base in North Carolina) was serious. Daddy lay down and took a nap listening to the opera every Saturday afternoon. I was enrolled in Ruth Ettinger's ballet classes right off Austin Street, for some mandatory purpose related to my one day becoming a cultured young lady, and I would study classical piano for ten years. But maybe some of this other fun music was on the radio. I had been introduced to that remarkable, portable appliance on the army base, and was fascinated by the blinking towers off in the distance that sent in the sound from the sky.

On a late afternoon before supper, I got hold of the table radio in the hall, near the chartreuse couch where the coughing patients would sit waiting to see my father at his home office during his evening hours. With a turn of the brown dial on the left, the radio crackled to life on Mommy's station of choice, WNYC, sober public radio. Of course I'd heard other stations when we went in the car, usually WQXR with its somber chamber music. Once in a while, we'd get to hear something a little less sedate, like WOR, with the chatty Fitzgeralds or *The Shadow*, and WABC, with Martin Block's *Make Believe Ballroom*, but I was looking for something different. I found it on 1050 WMGM.

At which point, I heard a key turn in the front door and Daddy entered, carrying his black medical bag and taking off his hat. "What's that you're listening to, Nanny?" he said, surprised. "It's bebop, Daddy, bebop." That's what I'd heard the boys in the alleyway call it. My father winced at the sound, in a humorous way. "That noise? Why don't you listen to JZ, or what do they call it now?" he suggested, referring to the newly renamed WABC. My mother appeared, to add her dismissive, well-educated opinion. "If you really want to listen to garbage, you can find more down the dial." Embarrassed at my obviously poor taste, I turned the radio off. My fate was sealed. If I wanted to hear any more of this inferior crap, I would have to do it privately, on my own time. And I wouldn't be proud of it.

Soon, this garbage made its way to the television. But somehow, watching it with other people because it happened to come on didn't seem as much of a personal statement as selecting it on a small radio did. Frankie Laine's TV show had many of the popular music stars on, including a group called Frankie Lymon and the Teenagers, who sang the same kind of music as the boys under my window.

One musical television appearance of the time remains vivid in my mind.

Sunday, September 9, 1956, as I recall, was a cloudy, maybe rainy day. Daddy had taken all four of us to visit the family of one of his fellow young physician buddies, a Dr. Julie Gewirtz, at their private house in nearby Brooklyn. I had hardly, if ever, been in a private house (what we called a single family house), since everyone I knew lived in a building. Not only did the Gewirtz's have a private house; they had a screened-in front porch, where they kept a dark brown wooden television set. Their friendly eldest daughter, several years older than I, excitedly informed us kids, "Elvis is on *Ed Sullivan* tonight!" With my limited access to frivolous popular music, I had never heard of Elvis Presley before. But I wouldn't admit to that, wanting to seem in the know. Sullivan was not working his own show that night due to an injury, and he had a guest host. Presley performed twice in the show, but what I remember best is the camera zooming in to capture him from the waist up, as he began to jump around and dance, singing "Ready Teddy." This was a strange, but exceedingly memorable angle, and I had no idea why they did that. Later, of course, the public was informed that the network had not wanted to show Elvis's "indecent" wiggling hips. As for Elvis himself, I thought he had a really nice voice, wasn't crazy about his music, and was struck by his sometimes rather blank expression, which I had never seen before on a performer. Elvis didn't look very intelligent to me, as if that mattered. I was not old enough to read anything else into his performance, yet curiously, I still remember being riveted to the set.

5

Very sadly (for me), within a few years we had moved to a newly built private house in suburban Nassau County, right outside of Queens, about twenty minutes away by car from my father's office, which remained on Austin Street. Although it was part of a tract development of similar dwellings, Daddy reviewed and supervised every inch of the construction of the new house, from the thermal insulation to the contours of the specially raised dining room ceiling. I missed the Lefferts apartment building very much, but didn't want to hurt Daddy's feelings. And it was, and remains, a very nice house. At least I could stay somewhat in touch with the old neighborhood when we went to visit Daddy's office. I knew he regarded the new house as a crowning achievement, intended, as everything was, for my benefit and Jane's. I wasn't really sure if Mommy liked the idea of the new house, on the muddy, flat, quiet street under construction, but she did a masterful job of decorating it in her modern midcentury way. The original sofas and chairs that my parents had gotten in 1947 were reupholstered for the new decor in a bright dark blue, with complementary colors, to contrast with the light beige grass-cloth-textured wallpaper and matching wall-to-wall carpet. All of it is still there, in near-perfect condition. (Okay, they did replace the carpet once.) The lesson here: Always buy quality furniture. That way you know you'll never have to do it again.

The relocation to the new private residence, or "The House," represented kind of a culture shock for me, as a grade-schooler. I jokingly referred to the whole experience as "moving to America." No more knife man, seltzer man, or endless parade of noisy merchants and Orthodox neighbors in the street. Actually, hardly anyone came to our new street at all. It was too quiet, and there was nothing moving when you looked out the window. It was a scary idea that a criminal could possibly break in to The House from the outside, and we would be the only ones there. This was a dangerous situation, and I developed what I call *housophobia,* or fear of private houses. When my sister and I were home alone, I would "take action" and confront my fear directly, patrolling the split-level premises from the top floor to the spooky basement, loudly announcing, "I have a gun!" to scare off any possible intruders. When we got our beautiful big white dog Hunter, he would accompany me on my rounds. Everything, even the grocery store, was beyond walking distance, so unless a parent was driving, I was trapped. And now my mother would have to learn to drive, which required (I thought) my backseat direction and assistance. Mommy's nerves kept her from ever driving on the "big roads," but she did learn to navigate slowly on the local streets to the new, large supermarket. As a reward for her motoring mastery, Mommy was given her own car, a state-of the-art deep-red Pontiac Tempest.

Our family's connection to our former universe was certainly not severed, although it seemed that way from a residential point of view. Major purchases of lighting, home fixtures, clothing, etc., etc., especially underwear, were still made on the Lower East Side. Daddy would take us on a Sunday, before it was time to study, to Orchard Street, near Delancey, where the prices were close to wholesale, and you weren't going to get clipped or have to pay through the nose. Also, there was plenty of room to *hondle* (bargain) them down, which was the commercial expectation.

Mr. Machlis was a patient of Daddy's, and so would give us an extra-special deal on the ladies' foundations, girls' undergarments, and other assorted *gatkes* (underpants) he sold from his small, crowded, walk-down tenement shop. "Machlis," as Daddy called him, a short, middle-aged man, labored behind a packed glass display counter with numerous plastic drawers stacked directly behind him. Each drawer was stuffed with universally white, indistinguishable folded merchandise. "A girls' twelve for you," Machlis would assess, after throwing me a quick glance. And so a new rayon slip for the school year, along with several serviceable cotton undershirts and panties, would be tossed into a bag. I didn't know anything about wearing a bra until I asked one of the girls at summer camp about it because my chest hurt. After the underwear excursion, we would have a special treat: handpicked Kosher dills from an outdoor wooden barrel at Gus's Pickles of Hester Street. Once in a while, maybe knishes from Yonah Schimmel's on Houston, or a delicacy from Ratner's on Delancey. Between business and family, we stayed connected to our former world. But now that we were installed in The House, my new school and surroundings were gaining ground. I had begun a process of assimilation—to this day it remains unfinished.

6

"We're here because we're here because we're here because we're here! We're here because we're here because we're here because we're he-e-e-re!" Nietzsche? Hegel? Schopenhauer? No, just a little ditty shrieked to the tune of "Auld Lang Syne" by a bus of high school and preteen New York kids on the way to summer sleepaway camp. This musical masterpiece of simple, elegant philosophy would usually be a follow-up to the mathematically correct and impeccably logical "Ninety-nine Bottles of Beer on the Wall." (Yes, if one of those bottles should happen to fall, there would be precisely ninety-eight bottles left.) If all song lyrics were as universally meaningful and self-explanatory as these, I probably wouldn't be writing this book. But as a serious girl who spent most of her time following a strict regimen of study, my overall impression of the complexities of any future social life and relationships came from musical poetry far more enigmatic in meaning.

"I want to be Bobby's girl / That's the most important thing to me" "And I pray that someday he'll love me / And together we will see how lovely Heaven will be" (Again with the flying dead people, and their destinations, heaven and paradise!) "I love him, I love him, I love him, / And where he goes I'll follow, I'll follow, I'll follow." "You didn't want him when he wanted you . . . / And there's not a single thing that you can do" "Don't they know, it's the end of the world? / It ended when you said good-bye" "True love means planning our lives for two, / Being together the whole day through." "It's my party, and I'll cry if I want to / Cry if I want to" "(Eight) your crazy clothes / That's just half of sixteen reasons why I (why I) love you!" And the strangely aggressive "I know something about love / You've gotta want it bad" All that is just a very small sample of contemporary social mores according to popular music of the fifties and early sixties, as sung by the girls.

The guys of the day, the Fabians, Jimmy Clantons, Bobby Vees, etc. all reminded me of our school bus drivers, the JDs—only now we called them "hoods." They all wanted to "make time" (some kind of fooling around) with the neighborhood girl who was "fast," but eventually "settle down" with a nice girl like you. There were really only two of these serenaders whose voices I liked, for no particular reason, Ricky Nelson and Dion.

The current music was just about my only source for the alien but evidently essential information about socializing, since such things were never spoken about at my house. This love stuff, you seemingly would fall into it, have no control over it, but it would decide the rest of your life. Apparently you couldn't live without it, and everyone was in it: how many songs had women wailing, "I'll die without your love!" Only I didn't see any evidence of this behavior in my regimented little world, just always-married parents, relatives, and their families, whose matter-of-fact marriages, if not actually arranged, might as well have been. No "tears on my pillow" or "watch out, here comes that play-y-y-boy!" for us. As for my old friends in Lefferts House—their parents' marriages were certainly arranged according to custom, and I knew they would be obediently married parents themselves by the age of nineteen.

And so, in the manner of an aural tourist, I would visit the "real world" of love on my red Minato AM transistor radio with the all-important personal earjack (to avoid the embarrassment of publicly revealing my poor musical taste), which I had gotten as a requested birthday present. The Minato would be followed a couple of years later by the additional beige Fleetwood AM 6 transistor in the brown leather case. One of the good things about moving to The House was that I got my own bedroom, where I could interrupt my long hours of study and frequent headaches with brief forays into an alternate universe, Radioland.

Radioland was all around you, all the time, even if you couldn't see it. But you could hear it, secretly, just by flicking a little round dial with your thumb. It was even more exciting than television, because Radioland would get directly into your head, right through your ear. All these catchy, revealing songs, the fast-talking and often goofy DJs, the high school contest reporters, the fans on the request lines, the singers harmonizing on the latest commercials for Keds, the guys with the sports scores, even the straitlaced newsmen with their authoritative voices—they were there in my room having a big invisible party every night, just waiting for me to join them! Cousin Brucie, B. Mitchel Reed, Gary Stevens (who took over when BMR left), with his imaginary pal the Woolyburger, Murray the K with his Swingin' Soiree, who had followed in the footsteps of the "first" rock and roll DJ, Alan Freed—all of them were my friends, and I would look forward to being with them. With the many hours of studying, I wasn't exactly spending too much time with actual people. Besides the invisible music parties, my childhood favorites, the New York Yankees, would hammer away at their rivals, right there in my head, with their smooth-talking, confident play-by-play guys like Mel Allen and Red Barber calling the scene.

I began collecting hit 45s (singles) with money from my small allowance and the nickels and pennies I'd saved by not eating the whole school lunch: a piece of two-cent cake and milk were enough. I stored my prized 45s in a red box with an index especially made for that purpose, and added a tan box as the collection grew, more or less to match the colors of my two radios. Along with the index in each box, I filed a series of "surveys," or listings of the top-selling recordings, put out on a weekly basis by the three major New York radio stations playing the hits: WABC (with their Silver Dollar Survey, which became the All-American Survey), WMCA (home of the Good Guys), and 1010 WINS.

Once, when I was invited to an actual party (where there were going to be boys), thrown by a junior high schoolmate, I carefully transported my prized record boxes around the block. It occurred to me that I just didn't want anyone else touching them! Inside were the perfect record sleeves, which could be torn or frayed, and the records themselves could be scratched, broken, or misfiled. So I assigned myself the job of selecting and playing the 45s on my hostess's folding portable record player.

This provided an important additional advantage: I could avoid the inevitable germy game of spin the bottle. The idea of having to kiss any of my fellow classmates was unappealing, and laden with consequences. What would I say to them the next day at school? No advice for this situation had been given in any of my favorite songs. Here, as the DJ, I could be at the party on my terms! No one could force me to kiss anybody, or play that other game, seven minutes in heaven, where someone turned the lights out and the boy nearest on the couch was supposed to grope all over you. I was the maître d', controlling the music. And no one could lay a finger on my 45s. Since there were no complaints from my classmates, I figured I was making some pretty good choices. It never occurred to me that one day I could do this on the radio: all my hosts in Radioland were guys with the zany fast-talking shtick. I never thought about the future anyway.

⸘ ⸘ ⸘

It was at this time that the pains started. My "curse" had arrived, which caused excruciating internal stabbing sensations two weeks before every monthly event. Although this was certainly something of a medical nature, and Daddy was a doctor, "women's problems" were not something you would ever discuss with your own father. His specialties were heart and lungs anyway. Mommy said the stabbing pains were called *middleschmerz*, or middle-of-the-month pain. She said the mother of one of my friends had it so badly that she would take to her bed. Well, I couldn't do that—there was school, and there was no way I could miss a day. When my "friend" (as we called it) actually showed up, the visit would last up to a gripping, painful week. In addition, there would be an accompanying fever, and about five days prior to my "friend's" arrival, I would experience that most special day of the month, which I secretly named my "crisis day." My head and my body just didn't seem attached, and I would be overcome by some sort of nervous affliction.

I had to be very, very careful never to let any of this internal mayhem out to the public, and almost in the manner of an alien observer from another planet, I would practice acting like a normal human being so I could escape detection. And "normal" is the way I described my one good week of the month, which immediately followed my "friend's" departure. Nothing helped to alleviate any of this cycle, no Midol, no hot water bottle, no nothin'. How did all the other girls manage to get through lunch and gym class without seemingly suffering? Certainly, I thought, they must be overcome by the same monthly lunacy. Women in government, how did they address Parliament feeling like this? "Guess I'll never be the prime minister," I used to joke to myself, when Indira Gandhi and then Margaret Thatcher took office.

At the same time, my chest began to hurt. Though not as sharply painful, this ache was certainly more consistent and would prove to be equally sinister. This new "young woman's body" I was developing was apparently composed of hard marbles. It hurt when I walked, when I ran, even when I breathed. Except for that same one week of the month I called "normal," when my chest was sort of okay too. This growing up was a bad business. I got used to dragging around in pain, pretending I wasn't, but it tired me out. All I wanted to do was get home from school and fall asleep in my chair, pretending to read so as not to appear lazy. After all, reading gave me a headache trying to focus on the words on the page. Was it the same for everyone? I didn't know. I would save the reading energy for after supper. I looked forward to the days when I could just go home from school and sleep in my chair without attending any of those after-school "extracurricular" clubs or sports in which I had to participate "to make it look good for my college application." Of course, my invisible friends from Radioland, like Scott Muni or Dan Ingram, were waiting for me at the flick of a dial, and often I would drift off listening to their late afternoon preparty.

But one such afternoon, I came home from school, and there was no party for anyone. The whole world had changed, and not for the better.

7

It was the second announcement that caused Henry Levine to fall forward out of his chair. The first had been made somewhere after two o'clock. The timid Mrs. Vitale was lecturing us on some aspect of music, or health, but I couldn't tell you what. After all, these classes were mandatory, but commonly regarded as trivial. I always found it extremely hard to concentrate during Mrs. Vitale's period; not because of the subject matter, which was a piece of cake on the intellectual difficulty scale, but because it was after lunch, and unfortunately for me, Nap was not offered as a course elective. The southwesterly sunlight streaming in from the half-opened window blinds on the left side of the room didn't help either. The P.A. buzzed me out of my stupor, as the principal, Mr. Olmstead, tapped the microphone for his announcement, which was roughly this: "Attention all students and teachers, this is the principal. We interrupt your classes to report that three shots were fired at President Kennedy's motorcade in Dallas, Texas. The president has been taken to Parkland Hospital. We will keep you informed of any further details."

Mrs. Vitale tried to restore order to her agitated swarm of eighth-graders. The P.A. system buzzed again within the half hour: "Attention all students and teachers: All classes and after-school programs today have been canceled. Please report to your homerooms." And then, the exact wording immediately, indelibly etched on my memory: "Our president . . . is dead."

That's when the academically precocious Henry, always interested in matters of government, who was sitting about four seats to my right, gasped and fell forward, taking the lightweight combination chair and folding desk with him.

Although it only took a few minutes to return to homeroom, Mrs. Dickerson was ready. The elderly social studies teacher from the Deep South had already wheeled in a television, plugged it in, and adjusted the antenna for the grainy black-and-white transmission. Walter Cronkite was presiding over the harrowing drama. "Now I want you-all to pay attention, class," Mrs. Dickerson drawled, strangely unemotional. "This is history in the making! Hi-i-story in the ma-aking." As if that were the only thing we should be thinking about. The teacher had an uphill battle on her hands. Since classes had been officially canceled, students were up, out of their seats, nervously chattering and milling around. The school buses to take us home would not be around for anther twenty minutes or so. I had a pit in my stomach and wanted to cry, and maybe throw up, so I left for the girls' room down the hall.

Inside the gray lavatory, Kim was giggling at something; I had no idea what. Who could be giggling at anything at a time like this? Suzanne was applying the newly invented cosmetic Revlon Blush-On, a powdered sort of rouge to be applied with a brush. Suzanne admired the plastic compact as she plastered her cheeks with a light apricot. Wasn't everybody horrified? Weren't they taking this personally?

I boarded the bus, shocked and in tears. Opening our back door to the kitchen, I found Mommy slumped over her little desk, crying, but she had still remembered to set out my after-school cookies. Hunter, our recently arrived puppy, tentatively walked back and forth, obviously sensing that something was wrong. I remembered what Mommy had told me about when FDR died; she had found her mother crying in front of the radio set. And now here it was, her turn again to personally mourn a president. We thought the president was perfect, despite the contemporaneous dinnertime stories Daddy told us. One of his patients, Walter, was the headwaiter at the '21' Club in midtown, where the president often dined when he was in New York. I couldn't decide which was more controversial, the secondhand story from Walter that they would sneak President Kennedy through some kind of tunnel system into the Waldorf-Astoria Hotel for visits with Marilyn Monroe, or the fact that a hamburger cost five dollars at the '21' Club. Five dollars for a hamburger! Then there was Daddy's contention that the Kennedys were a bunch of rum-running drunks; that the president's father, Joe Kennedy, had made his money during Prohibition.

I climbed the split-level stairs up to my room, closed the door, and sank into my chair. I positioned the earjack in my left ear and flicked on the red Minato. Only news and somber funereal music filled the airwaves. So then everyone felt the way I did, right? I went to the closet and picked up our current issue of *Look* magazine, with the pictorial feature on the Camelot family in action at the While House. They had just taken these photos: little John-John crawling under his father's desk, the president's favorite rocking chair. No, all this was just impossible. And where was the Deity? Why didn't God step in if he was so great? I kept the *Look* magazine, and started a President Kennedy picture collection. The assassination left me with no appetite and depressed for weeks.

Several days later, I pored over our December 2 issue of *Newsweek*, with its profile portrait of JFK against a dark blue background, and the words "John Fitzgerald Kennedy 1917–1963" on the cover. I always liked the Letters section, because you could find out what regular (but smart) people thought about things. Under the top of the right column of page 8, next to the ad for J&B rare scotch whiskey, the minor headline ran "There'll Always Be . . ." and then the body of the letter from a Nicholas LaMotte, of Wimborne, Dorset, England, responding to a story about The Beatles. He explained how the article barely captured the insanity the group inspired. He described how a cancelled concert in Portsmouth caused hundreds of girls to collapse and weep, and extra police had to be called to the scene.

A photo of an unusually long-haired male singer bore the caption "Head Beatle: Croon, Swoon."

I couldn't imagine crying over a postponed music show or, at this time, frankly, anything other than President Kennedy and his seemingly endless televised gut-wrenching funeral. I parked the Beatles information in the back of my head, as a curiosity. This whole Kennedy story was getting fishy anyway. If you just looked at the pictures, you could see the president being shot, horribly, from the back, but they were blaming it all on this one guy Oswald. I developed my own theory: that when Oswald's first shot missed the president, the Secret Service guy behind his car tried to fire back up at the Book Depository, but in a panic he shot too low, directly hitting Kennedy above his shoulder. Since it was a terrible accident, they didn't want to let it out that the Secret Service screwed up, because then no one would trust them anymore. Also, there was the weird creepy rumor about the president's brain being missing. Maybe it was for our own good that they were keeping all this stuff private. The president was dead; nothing could change that.

After dinner on January 3, 1964, I sat brooding as usual in my room. I thumbed through our local newspaper, *Newsday*. The TV listings reported that Jack Paar, "another neurotic chain-smoker," as my father called him, would be featuring a film clip of the Beatles, a "pop vocal group" from England. I scampered down the steps to warm up the Andrea TV in the den. Since it was the weekend, I could put on the TV without an inquisition as to why I wasn't studying. My parents and sister joined me, and I braced myself for the criticism that would surely be heaped upon these unknown singers of "garbage," which of course would reflect badly on the taste and character of anyone who might enjoy the performance. Paar showed a clip of the Beatles singing a song with the chorus "She loves you . . ." at a command performance for the queen. My parents didn't disappoint me. "They look like a bunch of hoods," exclaimed Daddy, happy to have yet another bone to pick with popular culture. "Probably Eton boys, earning money for school," Mommy offered disparagingly, "but they're not very good."

Jack Paar's guest, a British commentator named Malcolm Muggeridge, heartily agreed with my parents. Muggeridge commented something to the effect that if you called the Beatles' wailing "talent," what would be next—an audience applauding for someone starting a lawn mower on stage? I didn't see it that way, and was fascinated by the Beatles' performance in somewhat the same way I had been by Elvis Presley's on *Ed Sullivan* a few years earlier. But there was just something else about these Beatles, and the way they looked and sang, that wasn't, well, "greasy" like Elvis. Not as threatening. No exaggerated bodily gyrations. They were cute, especially the one who held his guitar in the opposite direction from the others. The Beatles looked wryly intelligent, and their song was really catchy too; I could kind of sing it already after hearing it only once. The next day I inquired at the Floyd Bennett store for the "she loves you" song by the Beatles as a 45, but the salesman had never heard of them. He would soon.

8

"Okay, my little chickadees," Ed Sullivan droned, stiffly taking a step sideways on the stage. "Now when the applause light comes on, I want you to scream for Gerry the way you do for the Beatles!" Blasphemy! Only the Beatles deserved screaming, which I stoically refused to do anyway, considering it to be undignified. Plus, then you couldn't hear their music. Hearty cheering was certainly more grown-up. And there was no way I was going to pay Gerry and the Pacemakers a fraction of the respect and admiration I reserved for the Beatles. But Gerry and his friends were part of a whole new world, as I perceived it: with-it, now, British, mod, pop, smart, fresh, fun, "gear," go-go, and radically differ-ent from my day-to-day life, rooted in an ethnicity of dutiful study and preparation for a future that was still vague, but undoubtedly bleak.

It was Mother's Day, 1964, and I was my classmate Lillian Littman's guest at an *Ed Sullivan* preshow rehearsal, featuring Bobby Rydell, Dusty Springfield, and Gerry and the Pacemakers. Lillian's father had a friend who played in Sullivan's Ray Block Orchestra, and unable to get enough passes to include me with his daughters when the Beatles played *Sullivan,* he had come up with this next-best substitute. (I seem to remember some-thing about Lillian's sister Judy having her mouthful of metal braces removed for the occasion. My mouthful had been even worse, but that's a tedious story.) For this special occasion, I wore my "green outfit" (all my clothes had names): the light green cotton A-line skirt and accompanying green and white striped poor boy sweater. Under the sweater, my chest with its bags of marbles hurt badly, but as usual I figured that was normal, and what's a little throbbing pain when you're at *Ed Sullivan*— merely twelve rows from the stage?

Bobby Rydell was one of the many talented singers who were now unknowingly caught on the dwindling cusp of the Elvis/bobby-soxer era as it slid into the sea of Golden Oldies. It would be irrevocably overtaken by the topsy-turvy Beatles Youthquake, from which we still have not emerged. Bobby had that back-combed semipompadour hairstyle that now suddenly screamed "old swinger." In fact, Bobby was actually younger than a couple of the Beatles, but his waning popularity and American status relegated him to third on Sullivan's bill of popular musical acts.

The excitement was palpable as the first Brit of the afternoon took the stage. It was Dusty, of the soulful voice and beehive hairdo, which made her look a bit top-heavy, if not matronly. Although she was a "new" artist, she too seemed caught in the sonic seismic shift, but at least on the ascending plate. If no one had told you Dusty was English, you would never have known it by her singing, which was as smooth and bluesy as that of her American counterpart, Dionne Warwick.

When it was finally time for Gerry and the Pacemakers, the latest minstrels from Mersey to take the stage, the applause lights flashed on and off, and most of the girls in the audience instantly did Ed's bidding, jumping out of their seats, squealing, and waving their arms. Instead, I couldn't take my eyes off the lead singer's receding hairline, which itself seemed to be screaming—for negative attention. Gerry must have realized that this unfortunate bit of genetic inheritance would ultimately sabotage any hopes he might have harbored for ever entering the pantheon of teen idols. Nevertheless, he and his Pacemakers were from Liverpool, and even had the same manager as the Beatles! The group, in their black-and-white checked suits, did a very faithful-to-the-record presentation of their hits "I Like it" and "Don't Let the Sun Catch You Crying," before taking their "Beatle bow" in unison.

As Lillian and I exited the CBS television theater (now named the Ed Sullivan Theater, from which David Letterman does his show), a crush of teenage girls planted themselves at the Fifty-third Street stage door exit. How childish, I thought, as I glanced back while crossing Broadway. Suddenly, the deserted front doors of the theater opened, and out came Gerry and his crew, to pile into a waiting limousine. "Hey Gerry," I impulsively yelled and waved. "Good show!" Gerry waved back. How very much more dignified than being a "stage-door Johnny," I thought, as Lillian and I scampered down the steps of the IND subway station for the E train.

Of course, the *Ed Sullivan Show* was a mere warm-up for my first Beatles show, at Forest Hills Tennis Stadium, later that year on August 28. (I don't recall the term *concert* being used to describe a pop music presentation until the Beatles played Shea in 1965.)

My father, surprisingly swallowing his contempt for any of this type of "noise" just once, went above and beyond any expectations by purchasing the tickets in advance for sister Jane and me. Of course, I had nagged him, and at $2.95 apiece, the ticket price was somewhat reasonable. Daddy had pulled his dark green Buick up to the front of the ticket office, in a movie theater on Continental Avenue, flipped down his sun visor with the Doctor on Call permit, and cut ahead of hundreds of girls as he zipped in and out of the box office. He was loudly booed by the entire crowd.

Much has been written about Beatles concerts: the brevity (thirty-five minutes), the screaming girls, and the near impossibility of actually hearing anything the Beatles performed. August 28, 1964, was no different. It was a sweltering ninety-degree, mostly sunny day in New York, but that didn't stop one long-haired, bleached blond woman, obviously emulating John Lennon's wife, Cynthia, from wearing a complete black leather ensemble: pencil skirt, vest, jacket, and newsboy cap, to Forest Hills. She stood directly in front of, yet slightly below, Jane and me, in the sloping outdoor amphitheater. People were talking—Who was she? Was this mystery woman part of the Beatles entourage arriving early? Was she going to see them right after the concert? Was she sorry that John was already married? How could she wear all that leather in this heat and not even take off her jacket? My outfit (the "black and red"), if not as glamorous, also had a purpose. Black cotton skirt (seats could be dirty) and sleeveless stretch helenca top in red—so in case the Beatles looked at the audience, Janie and I might be more noticeable when I waved hello.

Rumor ripped through the crowd that the Beatles would arrive via helicopter, just like they did in their brand-new movie, *A Hard Day's Night*. Since the stadium was located relatively near the New York airports, the World's Fair Grounds (with the 1964–65 fair in full swing), and major traffic thoroughfares, the sky was abuzz with transit and traffic choppers. Each one would elicit a wave of pointing and screaming in anticipation of a possible Beatles landing. "The next time there's a helicopter, while everyone's looking up, we'll climb over this fence," I said to Jane, nodding in the direction of the waist-high metal barricade that separated our section of the stadium from the one below. And so we did, but in my rush to make it without being caught, the inside of my left thigh got momentarily stabbed by a sharp part of the metal, and started to bleed. A small price to pay for getting a couple of feet closer to and in the proximity of the stage, where, I overheard a couple of girls gushing, "We're breathing the same air as the Beatles!"

And suddenly, there they were, bounding onto the stage, skipping around the tangle of electrical wires and other sonic paraphernalia. Yes! We were breathing the same air as the Beatles! It was simply hard to believe. Over how many photos, trading cards, and articles from any newspaper or magazine available had I pored? I knew everything about the personalities of these four light-hearted, yet articulate, totally adorable guys from thousands of miles away, who were saving the world from descending into a murky post-JFK depression. And now, they were really here, in person, just yards away. If only I could just . . . meet them, especially the gorgeous Paul McCartney. He was the one I had the real crush on. So smart, so sophisticated, so talented, and so sweet. He would be such a great boyfriend, or dare I imagine it, husband? We would have so many things in common, and I'd already learned so much about his intriguing English culture. No boy from school would ever be able to come close in comparison. I knew the logistics of the relationship at the time seemed pretty impossible, but I could dream, right? Or maybe obsess was a better description of my constant focus on the imaginary conversations we were already having. And there he was, in the moment, singing . . . so close, and yet so far away.

As for the music, what with the primitive P.A. sound ricocheting off the cement amphitheater and dissipating into the air, I couldn't exactly discern what was being said or played. (That would not be the case at Shea Stadium.) But according to my parents, who were having coffee at a diner a few blocks away, the event sounded "just like a bullfight!" Apparently it was the massive high-pitched squealing of thousands of girls, and not the twang of George Harrison's guitar, that reverberated up Queens Boulevard.

"Okay, *genug* [enough] with this, you girls had a good time with this nonsense?" Daddy said as he drove us home. "That's the end of it, right?" But of course, the door to my brave new world was just opening wider.

9

And through that door to the world of mod Beatledom I went, always dressed in my inexpensive version of mandatory mod miniskirts, ironed hair, bangs, and eyeliner, and of course carrying my baggage—emotional, educational, cultural, and physical—at all times. No problem there, for the most part. Of course, my parents strongly disliked my fashion sense, and Daddy had no problem telling me all about it, and what it made me look like—a tramp. In my naïveté, I made absolutely no connection between my makeup and apparel, and any moral inferences one might draw from my appearance. I didn't want to be a rebel, but I was drawn to this totally different and "fun" culture. I usually managed to keep the two worlds separate. There were frequent silent breaks into Radioland with my transistor earjack, often including the perusal of fashion and music articles in magazines that I kept hidden in the back of my loose-leaf binder. But sometimes the two worlds would collide, with unfortunate results.

"Hey, Janie, look over there, it's Cousin Brucie!" I whispered, pointing to the legendary DJ from 77 WABC radio in New York. We were in London, respectfully watching the changing of the guard at Buckingham Palace. I was (and still am) extremely grateful to my father for deciding that in additon to ski trips to Canada, and later Colorado, the Millers should broaden their intellectual horizons in 1965 with a short trip to Europe. Even though school was out for the summer, this was astronomically better than memorizing facts. And now I couldn't believe our good luck. For weeks, I had heard about, and even entered, the Revlon Natural Wonder Makeup contest, with its grand prize of a trip to swinging London with Cousin Brucie. And there was more! The winner, who turned out to be from Huntington Station, Long Island, would accompany the Cuz and the Dave Clark Five to the Brands Hatch auto races, the Ad Lib nightclub, and the popular British *Ready Steady Go* TV show, hosted by Her Modness, Cathy McGowan!

I took Jane by the hand, slunk through the crowd to the very tall radio legend, and with smiles galore, introduced the two of us. Brucie's face lit up as well; although I didn't realize it, being spotted in Europe, for a local New York DJ, is rather a big deal. Excitedly, I recited the list of announced contest prize experiences the winner (and where was she?) would enjoy, and to my absolute astonishment, Cousin Brucie said, "Why don't you girls join us?"

"And who are you?!" my mother said belligerently as she approached Brucie, no doubt unsettled by the sight of her daughters talking to a strange man, in a foreign country.

"I'm their Cousin Brucie-e-e-!" he trilled, with his famous radio inflection.

Dead silence from Mommy, who had never heard of this person. And then, coldly, her exact measured words: "I wasn't aware that we had a Bruce in the family."

More silence. Had she only sensed that the DJ was a gentleman and a fellow Jew from Brooklyn, perhaps she would have been a bit nicer. We could have been related, right? I did the explanation and introduction, and Brucie assured Mommy that her girls would be well chaperoned along with the contest winner for the incredibly fab upcoming afternoon and evening events. Mommy softened a bit, but her answer was no. We had tickets to the ballet at the Royal Albert Hall, graciously arranged by a relative of one of Daddy's patients. I thanked Brucie, and sulked away. Later, at the ballet, I could actually feel the steam coming out of my ears.

The rest of our European trip was fascinating, in a strictly educational way, and I finally saw the inside of a church; actually, some of the world's most famous cathedrals, with their musty smells and giant scary statues, which looked as if they could fall over at any moment and randomly crush any unsuspecting parishioner or tourist.

That October, right after the school year started, when my issue of *Seventeen* magazine arrived, I was treated to, or should I say taunted by, a story and photo essay by the Natural Wonder Makeup contest winner, describing her superfab, once-in-a-lifetime British bash with Cousin Brucie. I ran down to the kitchen to show it to Mommy, who was frying fish over the stove with the noisy exhaust fan on high. Of course, she couldn't be bothered.

As life would have it, I met up with Cousin Brucie again the next year, 1966, in front of the ABC building on Fifty-fourth and Sixth. The Beatles were staying directly across the street at the Warwick Hotel, and I had artfully faked two contest passes to crash their press conference, but never got in. About a decade later, I would actually work on a voice-over commercial with Cousin Brucie, and now, forty-five years later, I see this lovely fellow just about every Saturday night, since we both work at SiriusXM Satellite Radio. Brucie always gives his "little cousin" a big bear hug, and has had me as a guest on his show, telling our London story.

ζ ζ ζ

Nineteen sixty-six was also the year that I got an unpleasant preview of the Summer of Love. "Under My Thumb," from the new Rolling Stones *Aftermath* album, was echoing from above as I climbed the twisty narrow staircase to the photographer's studio on West Fortieth Street between Fifth and Sixth avenues. The painted white walls were adorned with a number of framed black-and-white photos of—well—I had never seen anything like this displayed before—one specific part of a naked woman's body—below the waist! Actually, it must have been several different women, because each individual photo was different. Sophisticated, artsy, avant-garde (I wasn't exactly sure if this qualified as "intellectual"), and . . . intimidating. Exactly what my parents must have been afraid of when I announced that my summer job was going to be—

modeling. At first, they had vehemently objected, but I was able to convince them that this would be a daytime activity, and after all, who was
more responsible than me? What trouble could I possibly get into?

For a summer job, modeling seemed better than typing or working in
a fish shop. I had hated the extra touch-typing class, and swore that
whatever might become of my future, it wouldn't include clunking away
on a Smith-Corona, or anything like it. And none of that steno stuff
either. "if u cn rd ths u cn gt a gd job & mo pa," trumpeted the subway
placards for the Katherine Gibbs secretarial school. No, after a year or
more of assorted Saturdays combing Greenwich Village, frequenting
the Café Wha and Le Figaro with my dear friend and Beatle Buddy
Ronni Stolzenberg, sneaking into Sybil Burton's disco Arthur (named
for one of George Harrison's quirky lines in "A Hard Day's Night"), and
trying on dresses I could never afford by Mary Quant and Betsey John-
son at the new shop Paraphernalia on Madison Avenue, there was no
way I was going to be tied down to a dull summer job. Who knows,
through modeling, maybe I could meet the Beatles and get in on all the
mod excitement!

And so I decided to visit a couple of top New York modeling agencies
by myself, as a fifteen-year-old, in hopes of getting signed. At the time,
the teen modeling business was nothing like what it would become, and
it seemed as if one or two American girls, most notably someone named
Colleen Corby, were in all the pictures. But all of a sudden, these new
British "birds" like Jean Shrimpton and Pattie Boyd appeared on the
scene too.

I was immediately but politely rejected at my first stop, the big gun,
the Ford Agency, because the representative told me I was "too ethnic."
This was a novel phrase at the time, and I wasn't sure what ethnicity
they were talking about. But it reaffirmed my suspicion that indeed, I
did not look American, or WASPy. I promised myself to somehow rectify this failing by making "adjustments" in the future, but right now
maybe another agency would take me on for testing. And one of them
did—I think it was called Frances Gill. They got me the gig on West Fortieth.

"Come in," a man's voice said from somewhere in the room with the blaring Stones record. "I have an outfit for you from Pier One." The bearded young photographer produced a pretty green-patterned, floaty minidress and matching floppy hat, and pointed toward a barely private, makeshift dressing room. I hurriedly changed and stood on the broad white photographic background paper, which was hanging from a roll. After taking several shots and muttering the now clichéd "That's it!" "Beautiful!" "Now turn your head slightly to the left," the photographer handed me a long-stemmed glass and filled it with white wine. Now here comes trouble, I thought. I had never so much as been on a supervised date, and here this smooth talker wanted to get me drunk! "I'm not old enough for wine," I announced responsibly, and to my surprise, he said, "Okay, you don't have to drink it, just put the glass up to your lips for some poses." I escaped unharmed, and still have some color slides from the session, which look like they were just taken (that is, if anybody takes slides anymore).

My last session was at a fab, gear, swinging studio, this time on East Twenty-third Street, in a tenth-floor loft. I had taken a freight elevator up around 6 P.M., and since this was to be an evening event, my parents insisted they would be waiting for me in the car in front of the address at eight o'clock to take me home. The bearded, young, sweaty photographer wore a large collegiate-type ring and was playing some kind of hillbilly fiddle record when I came in. He was drinking a beverage called Mountain Dew, which had recently been marketed across the United States, although I had no idea what it tasted like. We chatted during the first few shots. He told me that just that week he'd gotten married. Then he stopped and said that my underwear was "reflecting through my dress" and had to be removed. This sounded odd, but what did I know about professional photography? I ducked into the makeshift dressing room, removed my slip and bra, leaving on my white cotton panties and garter belt, which held up my white fishnet stockings (panty hose were not readily available yet) and reemerged in my dress.

Mr. Sweaty Photographer instructed me to sit on the floor, and proceeded to arrange the folds in the top half of my dress, from the inside, "accidentally" brushing against me with his hand. All of a sudden, he grabbed me, pulling me forward with his right hand, and shoved his tongue down my throat as he ripped aside my underpants and painfully violated me with two fingers of his left hand and that large collegiate ring. "Hey!" I yelled. "Hey! Leave me alone!" Kicking and pushing the photographer, I rolled to the side, grabbed my bag, and ran toward the elevator across the wooden floor of the loft. The photographer scrambled after me. I pushed the button, and immediately realized that the power had been cut off for the evening. I spotted the open door to the left, and raced down the dark stairway. "Come back here!" the creep shouted. "You come back here!"

I frantically ran down the ten long flights of stairs, petrified that I was going to trip, as my pursuer trailed me by about half a flight. Arriving at the bottom of the steps, I threw myself at the large door, and to my great relief, it flung open onto Twenty-third Street . . . right in front of the dark green Buick with my parents and sister waiting for me. No sooner had I breathlessly appeared on the sidewalk than the photographer showed up right behind me. Daddy got out of the car.

In less than a second, I realized that there was no way in hell I could tell my parents what had happened; I would surely be blamed with an "I told you so" for getting involved in such a shady business, and who knows, I might never again be allowed to go anywhere on my own. Daddy had already begun a campaign of veiled morality stories, in which the kinds of girls who became airline stewardesses or had anything to do with show business were out-and-out tramps. I wasn't exactly sure what that meant, but it couldn't be good to be one of them. I also was afraid that my father, who was a very strong guy, might impulsively haul off and deck the photographer. So I paused, and graciously introduced the beast, and they shook hands. Daddy thanked him for seeing me downstairs, and shaken, nauseated, and humiliated, I got into the backseat of the Buick, alongside my sister.

No one would ever know what happened, and I silently took the responsibility, blame, and disgrace for my actions. There were several major lessons to be learned here. Avoid potentially dangerous situations, trust common sense (underwear doesn't "reflect"), and—what has become a very important MO for me ever since—"When in doubt, get out!" It would be at least ten years before I could set foot on Twenty-third Street again without feeling sick to my stomach.

Several minutes into our journey home, I announced, "I don't know if I'm going to do this modeling anymore. I don't really like it that much. I'll get a different job."

"I'll tell you what," said Daddy, perhaps pleased that I was leaving this all behind. "If you do really well in French, *min de leben* ("We should be lucky enough to be living"), we'll see, maybe we can help you a little with the finances so you can take a school class in France next summer." That was all I had to hear. I won a French award, and spent July of 1967 at Cité Universitaire, at the American University in Paris. It was one of the best trips of my life. I knew enough to be on guard for questionable situations, and there were plenty, as the Summer of Love was in full swing. Although I still wanted to be part of the mod scene (which was rapidly transforming itself into the Age of Aquarius), there would be no more modeling or show businesses for me.

꿍 꿍 꿍

The next year, upon my graduation from high school (tied for second in my class), I got a job at Deepdale General Hospital in Queens, where my father was on staff. All very on the level. I worked in the medical records department filing death certificates, became very skilled on the telephone switchboard, and handed out visitors' passes in front of the elevators. It would have been an uneventful summer, but I was repeatedly propositioned and groped, this time by one of Daddy's colleagues, the chief physician on the hospital board. But this time I came up with a plan. "Maybe we can get together outside the hospital sometime," the redheaded director whispered into my ear, while patting my upper thigh as I sat at my post greeting the visitors. "Maybe you'd like to talk it over with my father," I said politely. "You know, your friend Dr. Hy Miller." With that, the tall physician's face turned as red as his hair, and that was the last of his advances. Not wanting to jeopardize my father's position or create a problem at the hospital, I never told him, or anyone else.

And now, prepared with this wealth of experience, I was ready to be dropped into the center of the brewing melee of absurdity that was the Ivy League college campus in the fall of 1968.

The morning of Saturday, November 15, 1969, broke sunny and cold in West Philadelphia. At 5:30 A.M., I stood on Forty-second and Chestnut throwing stones at the front ground-level window of Dave's three-story gray apartment building. Dave had not answered his requested wake-up phone call at 5 A.M., which I had made from a pay phone in the Hill Hall girls' (whoops, I mean women's) dorm on Thirty-fourth and Walnut. I had trudged west and north up the moderately dangerous periphery of the University of Pennsylvania campus to meet up with Dave, a college senior, and his apartment mates for the roughly two-hour drive down to Washington, DC. No one had answered the doorbell, so here I was, throwing stones. Until, at last, Dave peered through the shades and buzzed me in. The blond, popular prelaw student had more or less assigned himself to be my first school date a year earlier, when I was a freshman, and I had nervously sat with him, glued to the radio, as the draft lottery numbers were read. His was low, and he would wind up substitute teaching in Philadelphia and postponing his graduation and entrance into law school in order to keep his student deferment.

Although Dave and his friends were of the frat-house pre-hippie era, and my generation was from an alternate universe, no one would disagree about ending the war, and we planned on joining the more radical masses for the March on Washington to Bring the Boys Home Now. (At the time, I privately harbored my own view of how this could be done:

The U.S. military should fly around Vietnam dropping leaflets and making bullhorn announcements, urging the civilians to vacate one large ground area at a time within twenty-four hours, after which we would bomb the shit out of it, as only we could. Then we could spare lives, bring our boys home, and prevent the fulfillment of the Domino Theory, thus halting the spread of communism.)

When we arrived in Washington, we were immediately directed here and there for parking and marching positions by the student equivalent of safety patrol monitors. Actually, the atmosphere reminded me more of arrival day at sleepaway camp. And yes, there they were, old acquaintances and their comrades from throughout my nearly nineteen years on the East Coast, waving and shouting across different assembled lines, until we were urged by the monitors to be quiet and begin walking. As usual, I did not feel well, but while rounding the Capitol, I glanced up and noticed an armed rifleman on the roof corner making the two-fingered peace sign as he steadied his gun. Later, I saw a nearly identical photo in *Life* magazine, and wondered if it were the same guy. Two and a half years later, a giant metal sculpture of the circular peace sign was installed in front of the Van Pelt Library as our Class of 1972 gift to the university. Since it carried political overtones, I wasn't sure if it was the best choice, but in retrospect, the now overly commercialized symbol perfectly represents the era.

"It's very hard to convey to students today the palpable sense of revolution that was in the air," said my classmate Richard A. Clarke in the November/December 2008 issue of the *Pennsylvania Gazette,* of his arrival at the university in the fall of 1968. Yes, that Richard Clarke, presidential security adviser, world-renowned counter-terrorism expert, and author. No, I didn't really know him personally—it was a very large class—but I do remember seeing him. He was in the student government. And there he is, grinning, in a wide-lapeled, striped jacket, in my 1972 college yearbook. His words echo my sentiments. "Penn itself was changing and very significantly and very rapidly, and we were part of that. And then the world was changing, very significantly, very rapidly— and very negatively. Because it was such a tumultuous experience, it was hard, frankly, to have a calm academic experience."

I had gone on to college for what I hoped would be a "calm academic experience" to prepare me for whatever was to be my next step in life (which I was still somehow convinced would be short, and would probably not contain any element of fun). I had wanted to stay at home in New York and go to Barnard or NYU, but my mother didn't want to worry about me as a commuter student driving in traffic every day, and there was a residential distance requirement that would prevent me from staying in the dorms. So I was to be sent away and miss my family, my dog, and New York City, the Center of the Universe, where I wanted to be. Case closed. With my 4.0 academic record, I chose the closest urban Ivy League co-educational school to New York City. Having spent most of my time alone with my radio, and coming from my old-world background, I was aware of my lack of social and dating experience, and was hoping to acquire it in some kind of a "normal" fashion at college. Hah. Fat chance.

᚛ ᚛ ᚛

I smelled smoke. It was around nine o'clock at night, and I stuck my head out of my dorm room. A collective commotion was gaining steam. My suitemates, some in their bathrobes and hair curlers, ran screaming for the stairs. I immediately retreated, opened the windows in my single third-floor room, called out, "There's a fire in here," and then slipped out of the room again, closed the door, and blocked the bottom with a rolled-up towel, to have a safe breathing area if necessary. Really, what could the catastrophe be? There were fire extinguishers around Hill Hall, a common telephone in each suite, and the thick cement walls of the building just didn't seem flammable.

Suddenly, three women in trench coats and stocking masks darted around the suite corner, one of them carrying huge, sharp pinking shears. *Snap!* and the metal-encased phone wires for our common telephone were severed. "Hey! Hey!" I yelled, starting to run after them, but the smoke was getting stronger. The muffled siren of a fire engine wailed up Walnut Street as I made my way into the narrow, cement-walled stairway leading down to the ground floor. In the lobby, the front doors had been chained shut. Chaos, as my classmates gathered at the entrance and shrieked. *Thwack!* A fireman slammed away at the thick chains with an ax. Then several of them, carrying a large hose, burst through the door amid the shouting and cheering of my classmates. The firemen grinned broadly, perhaps enjoying the sight of a mob of coeds running to and fro in their nighties.

When the smoke cleared, we were told that the perpetrators anonymously claimed to be Black Activist students in the dorm, and to the best of my recollection, no one was ever charged. But I was tipped off by a couple of friendly "insiders," who weren't keen on these tactics, that there would be further acts of rebellion.

Several months later, I wound up confronting several activists personally, and I delivered a blockbuster oration that surprised even me. (Had it been broadcast, I'm sure, in retrospect, no doubt it would have rivaled Nixon's "Checkers" speech in its notoriety.) I had stayed on a week or so after the school year ended, and the dorm was pretty much empty. There was chattering in the hall one afternoon, and I heard what I thought was the sound of my wooden laundry-drying rack scraping the floor, as if it were being dragged away from outside my room. I was in the midst of changing clothes, and came out a minute later to investigate. Obviously the thieves had thought my room was empty, and now my clothes rack and laundry were gone. Four black girls sat on the suite couch, and when I asked, one of them told me in a mocking tone that no one else had come through, that they themselves had been there for at least half an hour, and so they had no idea what I was talking about. But if no one else had been there, one or all of the girls had to know the whereabouts of my recently disappeared property.

"Are you accusing us?" the apparent ringleader taunted. "Yeah, I am," I said, and went on to lecture them that as Blacks and Jews, neither of us was probably really wanted here by the old guard of Ivy League universities. Most schools in 1967 had 8 percent quotas for Jews, to keep my people out, and now some had obligatory quotas for Blacks, to make sure some of them got in. Either way, we didn't exactly get a welcome mat. (I had interviewed at schools such as Brown/Pembroke and Vassar, which had Jewish quotas, and had then refused to entertain the idea of going to such places. My interviews had been filled with subversively inappropriate questions. U of P did not have such a quota.)

So here we were, Blacks and Jews, and it seemed to me the only way to get more of us into school and maybe change things was to set an example and not play into everyone else's shifty stereotypes of us, which I spelled out in detail. "C'mon, this isn't news," I said. I told them that I had overheard a dormmate, Muffy, who was the daughter of one of the major deans of the university, saying she would never socialize with a Jew or a Black because we "smelled funny." I had then marched up to her, stuck my arm under her nose, and asked her if I smelled funny . . . and she said, "Yeah."

"Alrighty then, girls," I said. "They're letting us in, we're all in the same dorm, so what's the problem?"

Shocked silence. I marched back to my room and slammed the door. Within minutes I heard the sound of my clothes rack being returned, and I opened the door to find one of the black girls in tears. I started crying too, and gave her a hug and kiss. I thanked her for having the guts to stand up for herself. I don't recall seeing her, or any of them, again. Probably because I'd already had enough of this ridiculous community dorm business and moved out after my freshman year. I had discovered a strange guy in our bathroom several days earlier when I went in to take a shower. Since when were they allowed in here? We had "parietals" including the "matchbook rule," where no young lady could entertain a college gentleman in her room without the door being open at least the width of a matchbook. In any event, all the "gentlemen" had to leave the dorm by 10 P.M. Apparently the university had decided to "update" the regulations at the end of the semester. What a pain in the ass! Now I would have to come out of the shower all covered up.

Between the good-natured winks and nods of my favorite pop music over the years, the sneak preview from the photographer on Twenty-third Street, and the medical director at my father's hospital, I had an idea of what guys were after. But was all this bad, or good, or both at different times? What did this have to do with romance? Presumably I would find out for myself when I got married.

During a dorm meeting my freshman year, a university nurse displayed and explained various birth control objects; I couldn't tell if she was warning or encouraging us. She probably didn't know either. And odd objects they were: round rubbery discs with jellies, an especially painful-looking twisty metal thing, and the usual butt of jokes, that small round Trojan guys kept in their wallets, removed from its wrapper. All of these were to be inserted into your body! There was a tentative mention of "the pill," still fairly new, which could lethally screw up your hormones. And you had to take this pill every day.

Perplexed, I raised my hand. "Wait, so we're supposed to do all this torture so the guy you might go out with can have fun?" I asked, having little grip on the societal upheaval in the making. Chuckles and snickers from a few dormmates. The nurse, stunned for a moment, pointed out the obvious—the prevention of pregnancy—and then noted that "we" girls would want to enjoy the experience too. Was she crazy? With all those weird contraptions? She then suggested that all freshmen coeds pay a visit to a gynecologist. When I presented this as an isolated piece of information to my parents, my father replied, "What? You don't go to a gynecologist until you're married!"—confirming the unspoken cultural tenets of my upbringing.

In the end, no amount of fun could possibly offset the constant oppressive worry over such serious consequences. Abortion was not yet legal in Pennsylvania or New York, and there was certainly no way I was ever going to have to deal with such an emergency in my home state anyway. My parents would find out somehow. The only other place was Mexico, where you could die because they used coat hangers. Jokingly, I thereafter kept a savings of several hundred dollars in my small bank account, designating it the Mexico Fund, for use only if the unthinkable ever happened.

At least I did have an idea of how this unintended pregnancy could be accomplished. My friend Marsha did not. As we took notes in Dr. Waldron's physiology lecture one day, Marsha poked me and whispered, "What's she talking about?" The professor had used the phrase "involuntary sexual responses," and Marsha was stumped. "Well, what are they?" she said, anxious, as we all were, to get an A on the forthcoming exams. "I'm going to ask," and she waved her hand frantically at the prof. "Don't do it, don't ask! I think I know . . . tell ya later!" I hissed, but it was too late. I don't remember how Dr. Waldron actually answered the question, because the lecture hall exploded in laughter.

Of course, there were other questions—answered in overheard, hushed conversations in the dorm. During my freshman year, I had a roommate Rona (not her real name) who by all accounts was the only girl on our floor who had "done it." A lot. With, reportedly, an entire frat house or football team, or maybe riflery club. Sometimes, she would sneak a "gentleman" into our room. Then I would proceed downstairs to a cushioned bench in the lower cafeteria for a night's sleep. Rona's description of the act, which she relayed to a group of us in hair curlers having nighttime tea, did not sound very appealing. Especially the part where the guy sweats and grunts all over you.

Then there was (lesser) talk of the "big O." But only your husband could give you the "big O"! As a premedical biology major, I could not understand how legal status could possibly effect a physiological function. Nor why any other person would actually be necessary for the manifestation of the "big O." Inquiring minds wanted to know. But not that badly. The whole thing just sounded like a hell of a lot of aggravation. No, I was only interested in romance.

11

I wasn't exactly sure how romance was supposed to fit in to what undoubtedly little was left of my life. After all, it wasn't just my mother and me; her younger brothers, the twins Murray and Seymour, didn't think they'd be alive for a long time either—they'd mention it jokingly on occasion. I really didn't know how to feel about this. Sad? Cheated? I'd lived with it my whole life, so by now it was just a given. I'd had plenty of practice living with physical pains, and I knew how to slog through them. But here I was preparing for a lengthy career in medicine, a rigorous career at that, and when my usual ailments slowed me down and kept me in bed with an ugly red rubber hot water bottle and painkillers, I had trouble seeing just how this was going to work. Certainly the idea of helping and curing others was an aspiration I had inherited from my father, but I frankly didn't think I could physically accomplish the training. Also, I feared hurting someone. And what room was left for romance with this arduous career choice? And the end goal of romance—marriage? When would I do the housekeeping? I certainly didn't see my mother using any of her advanced scientific knowledge while cleaning the kitchen, and she never appeared too thrilled about her chores, although she became a wonderful cook. What was the point of all this if I had to get married? If I wasn't going to be here anyway?

And then again, what about fun? Would I ever see any more of that? There had to be answers to these questions, but I wouldn't find them at home. What else was out there that I didn't know about that might, like the songs of my early radio days, clue me in to how this was all supposed to work? The musicians, writers, designers, spokesmen of our increasingly vocal generation—they had to know something.

Whoo hoo! Whoahhhhhh! Twang twang! Dah dah dah dah dah dah dah dah! Thump thump! Big Brother had taken the stage at the Spectrum, banging out the instrumental opening of "Combination of the Two." *Thump! Thump! . . . Thump! Thump!* . . . And now . . . the arrival . . . of the lady herself! . . . "That one crazy broad! . . . Miss Janis Joplin!" A fluster of motion at one of the side entrance ramps, and there she was, making her entrance—feather boas flying, microphone in one hand, bottle of Southern Comfort waving in the other. The metal railings to Joplin's left tipped dangerously toward her as the crowd pushed for proximity, and the floor moved in waves. Taking a swig of the whiskey and tossing the bottle aside onstage, the blues-rock diva let out a piercing shriek, matched equally by the intensity of the audience's roar of approval. Now here was Excitement! With a capital E. And Freedom. Maybe this wasn't an answer, but at least it was an escape. I imitated Joplin's abandon, leaped up on my seat, and began jumping and dancing to her music like an un-self-conscious child who hadn't a pain or a care in the world. I'd done the same at Murray the K's 1967 Easter show featuring the first New York appearance of the Who, along with (the) Cream, Wilson Pickett, Phil Ochs, and the Jackie the K dancers. No thinking allowed! Just singing, whooping it up, arms in the air, letting the music totally take me on a "magic carpet ride," as the song said; what could possibly be more fun than that?

𝄞 𝄞 𝄞

The invisible party in my room with my wacky AM radio companions was still going on, but there had been some new arrivals on the soundscape. Back in New York, I had started listening to a guy named Steve Post, on listener-supported FM radio, WBAI. Steve often had a strange guest, an A. J. Weberman, who regularly rifled, in the middle of the night, through the garbage Bob Dylan had thrown out of his Greenwich Village apartment. Weberman would report on his findings, and then attempt to use them as clues for deciphering Dylan's cryptic lyrics. The lyrics on the then newly released *Blonde on Blonde* double album, in particular, provided fodder for hours of discussion. I had actually seen Dylan riding on the downtown B train one Saturday, I was sure of it. He was wearing dark sunglasses and looking at the floor.

I had also started listening to WOR-FM and WNEW-FM, as they began to assemble their new casts of eclectic DJ personalities, including the smooth, poetic Rosko, the glamorous Alison Steele, in her "Night Bird" persona, the youthful literary raconteur Jonathan Schwartz, and the authoritative, gravel-voiced Scott Muni. All of them had jumped over from AM to usher in the airing of album cuts from the likes of the Blues Project, Vanilla Fudge, and Country Joe McDonald. The FCC had decreed in 1966 that the FM band could not simply duplicate and broadcast what was on AM, so there was plenty of room for experimentation. Of course, I didn't know about that at the time, but was aware that the music "sounded better" on FM. This had required the addition of an FM transistor radio, and so the portable Panasonic with its black case joined the Minato and the Fleetwood.

At school in Philadelphia, it was difficult for me to receive FM in the dorm, but nevertheless I'd tune in FM 93.3 WMMR-FM fading in and out, which had begun the evening *Marconi Experiment* with host Herman, also playing what was now being called "progressive rock" album tracks. Around the same time, there was this other guy on WDAS-FM, who called himself "My Father's Son." He casually chomped away on gum while he talked. His father was actually a prominent AM Philly DJ, Hy Lit. More invisible friends, imparting loads of information about "the new direction," as the line went in "A Hard Day's Night." If there were only some sort of record club, where I could trade info about the musical landscape with other people. Also maybe quote dialogue from *Star Trek,* the TV series that had just come on a couple of years earlier. (In fact, I had immortalized my enthusiasm for the show by noting "likes Star Trek" as well as "pop music" under my name in my Class of '68 high school yearbook.)

These fellow enthusiasts would most likely be guys, as I had noticed only a limited interest in the music scene from my coed dormmates, and none whatsoever in *Star Trek*. What tastes the girls had ran mostly to mournful but beautiful dirges of love lost, expressed by other young women: Laura Nyro, Judy Collins, Joni Mitchell. You could really get depressed listening to that stuff! No, I liked loud, dramatic, angry music, usually performed by rambunctious, angry young men, maybe the kind you'd be afraid of, but who cared? It wasn't like I knew them or anything. Their music took your mind off things, and you could just get angry at anything or nothing along with them and be happy about it. Blow off some steam.

I took to visiting Jerry's Records, near my Hill Hall dorm on Walnut Street. There was an air of safety in the small cluttered shop that I did not feel elsewhere. No real feeling of safety in the dorm, the student halls (which underwent random sieges, sit-ins, and even bombings), the student health infirmary (where I was ordered to remove all my clothing so that several medical students could check all my "pulse points"), or even the hushed stacks of Van Pelt Library.

Things were definitely getting weird in the library, which was steps away from Jerry's: There was the lesbian who constantly stared, as if boring a hole into me—it seemed like every night. Once, a male student, apparently on acid, had broken the nerve-racking silence of collective concentration by jumping out of his chair, twirling around on one foot, and becoming . . . Ed Sullivan. "Tonight, ladies and gentlemen, right here on our stage," he intoned with Ed's signature style and herky-jerky body language, " . . . the Beatles!" With that, the impersonator twirled around again, and dropped back down in his chair to study, as quickly as he had arisen. The next year, when we were all studying for finals, there was a bomb scare at Van Pelt right after the Kent State shootings, to show solidarity with something. Of course, everyone had to be evacuated, and some of the finals were postponed.

No, it was definitely more comfortable at Jerry's. There was even a turntable with headphones where you could check out an LP by yourself before you bought it; I had only seen that once before, in 1967, at the Sony store on the Champs-Élysées in Paris, when I was studying abroad that summer. Although I never purchased anything at Sony, not having the money to do so, I made repeated visits to listen to a new group called the Jimi Hendrix Experience, whose album was not yet released in the United States. Now, here at Jerry's, all the amazing new stuff was showing up: the Steve Miller Band (who played on campus), Sly and the Family Stone, Jeff Beck, Blind Faith, new Stones, and of course, the Beatles. I even made two new "music friends" at Jerry's, one of whom would deliver a culturally transformative future masterwork right to the lobby of Hill Hall.

"It's here!" Glenn Fong announced, as he breezed into the Hill Hall lobby with the Jerry's bag. Glenn, an Asian-German aspiring architecture student, who also claimed photography as a serious hobby, had become my main music friend. I would go with Glenn to see acts like Procol Harum at Philadelphia's Electric Factory, where he would snap away with a professional air. My other music friend was a student named Chris Dolmetch, who shared my appreciation for the British band the Move. The Beatles on steroids. Energy, melodies, a free-for-all! Getting you out of your own head and stomachache while jumping around! "Lettin' it all hang out!" as the song went.

Glenn carefully removed the much-anticipated new Jimmy Page album from the Jerry's bag for my inspection. Page, the virtuoso guitarist from the Yardbirds, had assembled a new crew, and called them Led Zeppelin. The grayish white cover, with its ominous photo of the doomed *Hindenburg* zeppelin, had already been opened. I raced upstairs to check it out on my small portable phonograph. Heavy, thunderous chords, and an angst-ridden, ethereal male voice wailed, "In the days of my youth, I was told what it means to be a man" I had never heard anything of this intensity ever before. A descending pattern of guitar notes opened another cut: "Been Dazed and Confused for so long it's not true / Wanted a woman, never bargained for you" the voice railed, as the notes seemingly slid down into the depths of Dante's *Inferno*. No woman could be that confusing, I immediately thought. These Led Zeppelin guys had to be conveying something way bigger, way more cataclysmic than some girlfriend problem. It didn't matter what it was; this was the fiercest display of emotion ever recorded, I was sure. I pounded my fist in the air. I had to have my own copy of this album immediately.

It would inspire my decades of devotion to Led Zeppelin's music, which could never be bested by any other group for sheer sonic cohesion, bombardment, and otherworldliness. And also, for me, danger. Even Zeppelin's ballads had a threatening edge, which somehow made them all the more powerful. Unlike the Beatles, whose lives I'd followed, and whom I had always wanted to meet, the members of Led Zeppelin seemed way too dark and alien to socialize with. I did not view them as cultural gurus; rather, as incendiary entertainers. Wherever they were going, I wasn't sure I wanted to be there in real life, but, like *A Clockwork Orange,* I sure did want to see the movie. Regardless, Led Zeppelin's music was spellbinding, and their first album would be well worth the $2.63 price tag.

Whatever spending money I had came mostly from my summer or holiday jobs. Obsessively, I agonized over even the smallest purchase. And of course, most of my few purchases were records. If I didn't like every song on an album, I wouldn't buy it. I had actually returned the Vanilla Fudge album because not all of it was to my liking; then later reconsidered and repurchased it. The Zeppelin album was a perfect match for the new heavy brown headphones that plugged into the phonograph. Night after night, I would go to sleep with Led Zeppelin blasting its way into my brain at maximum volume, the tone arm picking itself up at the end of "Dazed and Confused" on side one or "How Many More Times" on side two and swinging itself automatically back to the first cut. Sometimes I would wake up in the middle of a side and try to calculate how many times it had repeated while I was sleeping. Proof that peace and quiet were not necessary for proper rest.

The first time I tried to see Led Zeppelin in person, on January 31, 1969, I'd only catch the tail end of their boisterous set. They were playing the Fillmore East, and my buddies and I got caught in traffic driving up from Philly to New York. Too exhausted after the ride to muster up the composure necessary to deal with these potential demons, I decided not to attempt to meet them after the show, but it would have been easy.

I also wanted to see an upcoming summer festival. Posters were popping up around campus for a three-day music and art fair to be held in Woodstock, New York, a quaint bohemian artists' colony a couple of hours

north of New York City. I had visited the town with the family back in
'63. Talk of this Woodstock event was picking up, but I already knew I
would have to miss it, because my summer plans were set. First, I would
again be working as a salesgirl at A&S department store in Manhasset,
Long Island, this time in the sunglasses department. Then I would take
my earnings with me to France, where I would receive college credit for
a month-long language and culture course at the University of Grenoble. That summer, I watched Neil Armstrong and company set foot on
the moon from a television in the front window of a French department
store. I cheered loudly in English, so the rest of the crowd would know
that they were witnessing U.S. history in the presence of an American.

Two of my dormmates from U of P (now referred to as UPenn) were
also taking the French course in Grenoble. We had traveled overseas
separately, but we were all assigned as boarders to the home of an elderly French couple. Not realizing my more than adequate understanding of French, they began to speculate out loud whether or not the three
of us girls were Jews. Only two decades after the War had ended, and
there was plenty of residual anti-Semitism. On my previous stay in a
French dormitory in 1967, I had graciously permitted my Christian
roommates to inspect my scalp to locate the horns that we Jews were all
alleged to have.

The old couple in Grenoble concluded that the three of us were Jews,
and began serving us separately at meals (there was another, apparently
Christian girl staying at the house) and cutting down on our food, eventually reducing our lunch to mere green beans, which we had in the
dining room. Unfortunately, the meals had been paid for in advance,
and each of us had very limited funds. So we drew up a budget for bread,
ice cream cones, the occasional pizza, and traveling money. Having already decided that the university's weekday French language course was
too elementary and would be of little use except for the academic credits, I took more and longer weekend excursions with my two girlfriends
around the French countryside.

It was on a rickety bus ride south to Cannes over a precipitous route
through the French Alps that I saw the headline of the newspaper *France-Soir*:
"Brian Jones Mort!" It was Friday, July 4, 1969, and I read over a strange

shoulder that Jones had been found the day before in his swimming pool. He had either recently quit or been kicked out of the Stones, depending upon which account you heard. Amazingly, the London Hyde Park Stones concert that had been scheduled for Saturday, July 5, to introduce Jones's replacement, Mick Taylor, would still go on, according to the newspaper. I fleetingly thought of "popping up" to London (after all, how often would I be right next door in France!) but quickly realized that from the interior of the French Alps, the last-minute expense and logistics would be a bit ridiculous. I would save my trip to London for a few weeks later, as I had planned, after my course was finished. I would be visiting my longtime British pen pal, Carol Silverstone. And, I could not pass up any opportunity while on that side of the world to again visit my musical Mecca, walk the streets I had seen in *A Hard Day's Night,* and just maybe, bump into a Beatle. The Magical Mystery Tour was waiting to take me away.

Upon arriving in London by myself, my first destination was Hyde Park, to catch a leftover vibe from the Stones concert. Although painfully aware that I had missed a huge cultural event, I was very happy to at least survey the premises, walking the paths and watching the nannies push their prams in the afternoon sunshine. I had just exited the park's northeast corner at the Marble Arch when something—a small rock, I realized—hit the right side of my head. And then another one. A group of three young boys chanted, "Paki! Paki!" and began to chase me. I started to run, and it dawned on me that because of my very dark, suntanned Sephardic skin and nearly black hair, the bigoted little lads had mistaken me for one of the many Pakistani residents of London. "No, you're wrong, ha ha!" I taunted back at them. "I'm a Jew!" With that, they sped up after me. I rounded a corner off Great Cumberland Street to catch my breath, and lost them. As I stood gasping for air in my gray miniskirt and navy blue nylon top, a middle-aged man in a suit approached me. "Would you be interested in being cast for a mold as a mannequin?" he asked.

I stared at him, completely lost.

"I make mannequins for storefront windows, like Harrods, and you'd be perfect." He offered me his business card. "And of course you'd be paid."

"Wait a minute, you want to sort of use my body to make a dummy?" I was stumped. Moments ago, I had been attacked for my appearance, and now someone else wanted to immortalize it? As much as I could have used the money, my warning alarm was going off. "No, but thank you," I told the man, and paused, "but, uh, would you mind telling me, how does that work anyway? I mean, how would you actually make a mannequin out of me?" He explained how he would cover me with wax, which would harden and then be cut in half, and then the wax dummy would be reassembled and used as a cast for the plaster. Was he serious? It sounded insane. It didn't matter. I shook his hand, bid him a good afternoon, and hastily made my way toward the Underground, and back to my inexpensive hotel.

The next morning, I arrived at 7 A.M. on a particular London corner (the name of which I've forgotten, most likely because it was the wrong street to begin with) to meet Nicole Cadish, one of my classmates from the university course in Grenoble. She was a fellow music enthusiast, and I was to catch a ride with her and another friend to the Isle of Wight Festival. Bob Dylan, the Who, and Free were headlining, and I also wanted to see Blodwyn Pig, Mick Abrahams' band, and the Nice with Keith Emerson. I'd heard something about the festival through the music underground back at Jerry's Records, but the idea of actually going to it took shape in the back row of a musty-smelling lecture hall at Grenoble University, as I silently mouthed the words to "Dazed and Confused" along with Nicole. I was happy to meet another girl, a British one at that, who liked the same music I did, and I was thrilled with her invitation.

After waiting for about an hour at what I thought was the right spot, it occurred to me that there was more than one street with the same name, except that I should have been on the one that was a "Road" or a "Lane" or an "Avenue". . . . No doubt the girl thought I had changed my mind and taken off without me. I never heard from Nicole Cadish again.

Extremely disappointed at missing the festival, I went instead to visit the outside of Abbey Road Studios, where the Beatles recorded. Since they had not yet released their album of the same name, with its now-iconic cover photograph, most people, save for a few of my fellow fanatics, had never heard of the place. I was surprised to see several other fans wandering by, stopping and taking pictures. Understandably, I thought, we were not allowed inside.

My next stop was Paul McCartney's house, which I had read was located on Cavendish Avenue, nearby. Turning the corner from Circus Road on to Cavendish, I saw a small mob of noisy girls in front of the short driveway, and knew this must be the place. How awful, I thought, to have these people constantly loitering around like busybodies, but . . . I wanted to see the house too. I had come all the way from New York! I began to walk toward the McCartney residence, but on the opposite side of the street, so as not to appear to have anything to do with the cluster of hangers-on. No, I walked quickly and purposefully, as if I had an important destination elsewhere on the block. Several paces into the walk, however, I realized that Cavendish appeared to be a dead end, so my visit up and down the block was very brief. How embarrassing, I thought, if Paul McCartney actually, say, pulled into his driveway and saw me there.

♪ ♪ ♪

Back at the University of Pennsylvania that fall, I presented my French course document at the registrar's office to receive the appropriate credits. Being home from Europe and headed for another grueling year of study, it was becoming clearer than ever that I just didn't want to give up this totally different life of music and culture, especially if I didn't have much time left. After all those years of hiding out in my room with my music, experiencing the actual "scene" had been exhilarating. My parents would never understand my choice, a burden that sadly weighs on me to this day. But years later, my father would say, just once, "You never really got to be a child, did you?" At first, I was surprised that he got it. About ten seconds later, I wasn't surprised at all. Daddy was right 99 percent of the time.

12

"Get into Radio!" urged the red poster, affixed to a tree on the campus quad. It featured a cartoon of someone crawling into the back of a table radio, and an open invitation to join the University of Pennsylvania's school radio station, WXPN. Eager to check out new music and meet other enthusiasts, I attended a meeting in a brownstone walk-up on Spruce Street. I knew that the rock director, Michael Esterson, who would come to call himself Michael Tearson, was a hyperintense whirlwind of a guy, and he might need a secretary to help file albums. But he was not there that day. I was, however, immediately and informally recruited (since I was the only girl) to provide the high-pitched voice of a little princess in a radio play based on one of my favorite sci-fi novels, *The Phantom Tollbooth,* by Norton Juster. My parents had given me the book as my birthday present, shortly after its publication in 1961, and I had never met anyone else who had heard of it. This was a good sign. I rigorously rehearsed my tiny part, in a tiny voice, and spent the remainder of an entire night studying for a microbiology exam. ("I pulled an all-nighter booking it" was actually the correct terminology.) The radio play would take place before the exam, and as I rushed out of my room and down the cement stairs in the new Superblock apartment dorm, I tripped on my red print granny skirt and smashed my left hand into the cement wall to avoid falling. The hand hurt badly, but the show must go on! After the play and the exam, I finally took myself to the student health facilities at the UPenn hospital, where my broken forefinger was put in a splint.

That spring, I had my wisdom teeth pulled, my face swelled terribly, and it was the end of the semester before I could really speak normally again. This prevented me from further participation on WXPN. However, it didn't stop me from attending a march and politically star-studded rally featuring consumer activist Ralph Nader and poet Alan Ginsberg, marking the end of Earth Week, which had been put together by some Penn grad students to raise awareness of environmental concerns. That event, with its sister events held in other cities, sparked the subsequent yearly designation of Earth Day every April 22.

But the significance of the first Earth Day paled in comparison to the unthinkable declaration that had been issued on April 10: Paul McCartney's announcement that the Beatles were breaking up. I was convinced the news media had it all wrong. What force could sever the greatest musical and cultural collaboration in modern history, which had fueled my "other life" for all of my teen years? I refused to believe this nonsense, and regarded it as another "Paul Is Dead" hoax. But ten days later, when McCartney released his first solo album, the unlikely story appeared to have merit. I felt hurt and betrayed. The Beatles' last album, *Let It Be,* then came out just as quickly, on May 8. I fell into a state of melancholy and could not enjoy listening to any of these post-mortem recordings.

No, I would rather listen to the new artist who'd recently released an album called *Elton John,* and another new group Argent, with a haunting song called "Liar" on their first LP. The Move had just come out with a great album called *Shazam.* I tried to take my mind off my beloved Beatles by seeing some shows at the Electric Factory on Arch Street: the Kinks, Miles Davis, and the increasingly popular late-night, spacey-sounding group Pink Floyd. But none of this alleviated my state of depression over the Beatles. "I miss you like I miss the sun," a line from a new Dave Mason song, struck a sad commemorative chord, even though I was not sure of the literal meaning. Even my fond memories of the recent Led Zeppelin show at the Spectrum failed to cheer me up.

ϟ ϟ ϟ

I spent the summer of 1970 back on the A&S sales floor, this time working in the boys' wear department. I remember even more pain from my "curse" that summer than usual. I had to take painkillers, and napped (more like passed out) on a pile of corduroy pants. I observed the young mothers and housewives, some of whom were my age. I wondered about the merits of my path to academia, independence, and uncertainty. Maybe the A&S shoppers had the right idea. They'd given up studying, and would each be taken care of by a nice man for the rest of their lives. Not entirely unlike my old Orthodox friends from Lefferts House. Very different from the "dangerous" university life, with its sociopolitical freakfests, unpredictable violence, and oppressively lecherous professors. I had already switched out of three different courses after being propositioned and groped by instructors. One of them had grabbed my hands and put them all over hard parts of his body, and another one told me that I had no idea how to write a paragraph and would require his after-class personal tutelage just to pass the course.

With the new school year under way, I paid another visit to the brownstone house on Spruce Street. The ground floor housed SIMS, the Student International Meditation Society. The whole concept was incomprehensible to me. How could a chant do anything? But a floor above SIMS was WXPN, an institution of engineering and logic, which also housed an amazing record collection. I felt safe there, like I did at Jerry's Records. The radio station had an AM side, which was "carrier current" only, and available just in the dorms and other school buildings. They ran Ivy League sports, in addition to a Top 40 format where the student DJs would hurriedly yammer on about the "platters," mimicking the wacky radio friends of my youth. I didn't know anybody who actually listened to the AM. The FM counterpart, however, with its mixture of eclectic programming, was available throughout the Philadelphia area at 88.9, and did have an audience. That afternoon, Dave Parris, the slide-rule-wielding student chief engineer gave me the tour.

After a short visit to the AM studio, where a hyper male student was playing a "super 73" jingle, we arrived at the FM studio. Beyond the heavy door was a lengthy metal apparatus, which I was told was called a "board," with colorful round knobs called "pots," short for potentiometers. The pots would be turned to certain audio volume levels to permit a recording or other transmission to be heard. A large microphone extended over the board, and the board itself was flanked on one side by several turntables, which could be operated in both directions in order to allow a record to be "cued up" to exactly the right start. The entire side of a nearly half-hour classical symphonic record was being played, as Dave showed me the large adjacent music library, with its subdivisions of rock, jazz, folk, bluegrass, and classical music, as well as other types of recordings. Oddly, it was a girl who sat silently behind the board that day. I had not seen any others at the radio station. I watched as she prepared another entire record side to be played on a different turntable, moving it backward to make sure it would be up to speed when the music started. If not, Dave explained, it would make a "wowing" sound, called a "wow."

Suddenly, Dave called for quiet in the room as the girl flipped on the horizontal microphone switch and simultaneously turned up its volume pot. I had no idea she was going to talk. "This is WXPN, Philadelphia. My name is Ethelea Reisner, and you're listening to the *Classical Hour*." Then she flipped the start switch on the next recording, turned up its pot, turned off the microphone, and resumed her silence. I was flabbergasted at what I'd seen, as the proverbial lightbulb went off over my head. Maybe I could actually talk on the radio too, I thought, but about rock records. Would they let a girl do that? This could be even better than filing the albums!

13

"If you want to play that kind of music, why don't you go out and get a job—at WMMR." That was Andy Baum and Nick Spitzer good-naturedly snickering over the phone as I played a cut from *Led Zeppelin II* on my eclectically oriented college radio show, *Phase Two*. WMMR was the newly minted Metromedia progressive rock station in Philadelphia, which was winning listeners with a free-form diet of Hendrix, Fairport Convention, Joni Mitchell, David Bowie, and just about any album that was released under the "rock" banner. Andy and Nick would probably have preferred something slightly more esoteric and less commercially successful, like Frank Zappa, Ramblin' Jack Elliot, or Pentangle.

It was summer 1971, and I had cajoled the student managers of WXPN into letting me complete their AM Top 40 training, which would qualify me to be on the air on their citywide FM station. Once I was allowed to try my coed hand at assembling programs of rock, folk, jazz, and blues, and commenting on the music, it was all over. I became intensely caught up in the medium. After all, how many hours of my youth had I spent listening to the radio? Although I was very nervous about this new venture, it was a huge thrill. Before my senior year at UPenn I arranged to take one of the chemistry courses during the summer so there would be plenty of time for me to study and "ace the course." And I could conveniently spend the rest of my time at WXPN. I clumsily illustrated a program guide with a hand-drawn flower and printed up copies. Then I got to work learning about every album in the varied library, even those that weren't exactly my cup of tea. Broadcasting was a public service, after all, so it was in everyone's best interests to attempt to entertain a variety of tastes. But my own invariably ran to the most melodic (to the Western ear), catchy, and therefore potentially commercial in pop and rock. As a biology student, this made perfect sense to me: it was logical that humans had a predisposition to finding certain sounds innately pleasant, while others could be more jarring. I was willing to defend my musical preferences, if necessary, by pointing out that ten years of classical piano lessons had at least given me a background knowledge of music that had commercially stood the test of time.

But I took my friends Andy and Nick's innocent taunt as a challenge. Well, maybe I would just try to get a job at WMMR; I'd show them! "Do you even think there's room on the air for a girl?" one of them said. "There's already an Alison Steele," referring to the glamorous, sophisticated, but a bit older, former AM hostess from New York who had reportedly been married to the big band leader Ted Steele, and who now ruled the overnight airwaves as the voluptuously toned "Night Bird." Why was only one woman allowed on all the airwaves? There wasn't one playing "our" music in Philadelphia anyway. I became obsessed with making this happen.

I set about studying WMMR from the black Panasonic transistor radio in my solitary apartment dorm room in Superblock. Herman, of the evening *Marconi Experiment,* had left and apparently taken a job at the newly rock-programmed WABC-FM in New York, under his full name, Dave Herman. Michael Cuscuna, another WXPN alumnus, was working there as well. I would hear them on my visits home to see the family. Michael Tearson, the elfin rock specialist from WXPN, had graduated from U of P and was now presiding over a spacey and creative late-evening shift. And a newly arrived, engaging English voice accompanied the earlier evening. I carefully listened to Luke O'Reilly on a nightly basis, while sitting on the floor heating up my frozen dinner with a hot plate and toaster oven combination. He certainly knew his music, and like Michael Tearson, Luke O (as he was called) kept the airwaves full of the latest music and concert information. Musicians would come up to the WMMR studios to be interviewed on his and other shows. I concluded that this British-accented personality had the added appeal of a gimmick, and it worked.

Well then, I decided, a girl would be a good gimmick too for this new format, and I was sure that none knew the music better than I did. I had never even seen another girl poring over the bins of vinyl offerings at Jerry's Records, or checking out the latest on their turntable with the attached headphones. I could identify any progressive rock release since *Meet the Beatles.*

Whether I could do one of these radio shows was another matter. Totally lacking in confidence, I attempted to cure my stage fright (I could barely get up in class to answer a question) and honed my imaginary craft over WXPN throughout that summer of '71. So what if I felt nauseated and short of breath when it came time to open the microphone? I would just have to force myself to do it, or the idea of ever joining WMMR would remain just that.

By the time the fall semester of 1971 got under way, my plans to cook up a job and convince whoever was in charge of WMMR that he or they should hire a college girl were in place. Easier said than done. I would have to find a way to meet someone who worked there, and then, with any luck, be personally invited up during business hours to deliver a sample audition tape to the director, at which time I would suggest the idea of putting a girl (me) on the air as a gimmick. Then I would surprise them with my musical knowledge of every rock record ever recorded. My ears were up for contacts, and by chance, my first actually walked into WXPN.

WMMR midday personality Ed Sciaky, who had recently graduated from Philadelphia's Temple University, came to the brownstone house on Spruce Street one late afternoon with his wife, Judy, in order to meet with one of the Beach Boys, Bruce Johnston. Bruce was evidently into Transcendental Meditation, and had been frequenting the SIMS headquarters downstairs. Since they were in the same building as the radio station, Ed and Judy brought their guest up to the WXPN-FM studio, where the surprised student on the air was—me. I put Johnston on briefly, as he acknowledged that the purpose of his visit was SIMS, and he wasn't there to promote music.

Afterward, Ed and Judy kindly invited me along with them to Artemis, the dark-interiored "happening" club on Sansom Street where all the interesting people coming through town gathered. A record company was holding a promotional buffet dinner with drinks, and as anyone who knew Ed would tell you at the time, he never missed a free meal. The bartender, with short hair in front, long hair on the back of his head, and a beard, was curiously costumed in a pink dress. I had never had alcohol, and was underage anyway, so it was just fine when this Rick Nielsen guy brought me a diet soda. He told me he was a musician, and was putting together a new group. Within a couple of years, it became Cheap Trick. (Coincidentally, I would soon meet his friend and future Cheap Trick bandmate, a guy named Tom Petersen, who was working at his girlfriend's hippie clothing boutique, Asta De Blue. Tom sold me a pair of shoes and a purple scarf.) A Philadelphia Top 40 AM DJ, Jerry Blavat, nicknamed "The Geator with the Heater," was also at Artemis. Although I had grown up in New York, and had never heard Blavat on the radio, I was told he was a very big deal. This was definitely an impressive party. I would have to come back to Artemis on my own sometime—that is, if they would let me in. Graciously thanking Ed for inviting me, and not wanting to appear overly pushy about my agenda, I waited for him to casually suggest that I come up to visit at WMMR sometime, and he did.

Now that I had an invitation, I decided not to act on it until I had a solid audition tape and maybe some more new "friends" at the station to bolster my credibility.

Soon after, I met Jonathan Takiff and Dennis Wilen at the popular soda shop / pinball machine parlor nicknamed the Dirty Drug, right near Jerry's Records. Both Jonathan, an aspiring and already published journalist, and Dennis were affiliated with WMMR; Jonathan had a once-a-week specialty show on Sunday nights. Dennis mentioned that he was going to catch a performance at the suburban Main Point folk music club in a few days—I think it was Randy Newman and Ralph McTell—and I casually said, "Yeah, maybe I'll be there too." The fact that I had no transportation out to Bryn Mawr wasn't going to deter me from appearing to be in on the Philly music scene.

So I hitched a ride out to the countrified vicinity of the Main Point, and walked the rest of the way until I found it. Once inside the small, crowded venue (more about the Main Point later), I located Dennis, and mentioned my interest in WMMR. He told me that the program director's name was Jerry Stevens, and that Jerry would surely be at an upcoming WMMR radio concert that Dennis was producing at Philadelphia's Sigma Sound Studios. The station had already broadcast concerts from Sigma that summer with Todd Rundgren, the Flying Burrito Brothers, and Bonnie Raitt.

I remember telling Dennis that I had actually met Bonnie recently at WXPN. One afternoon while I was on the air, a shy girl with red hair, carrying her promotional recording in a plain white jacket, came through the door. "My name is Bonnie," she said. "I wonder if you could play my record?" One of the guys in Bonnie's band, who called himself Freebo, was going out with one of my dormmates, so I had heard about the young blues singer. I was happy to play her music, which showcased her smooth voice and guitar playing. Here was a girl my age, at the front of her own band—clearly she had a foot in the new era of women's empowerment! Bonnie was singing about real "adult relationships," of which I was all but totally ignorant. I listened intently to the lyrics, many written by older blueswoman Sippie Wallace. Most of her songs were about women suffering and twisting themselves into pretzels to hold on to their men. (Too many years later, I would conclude that this behavior was anything but empowering, and although I still liked Bonnie's voice, I was very sorry to have wasted my time following her lyrical suggestions.)

When I met Jerry Stevens at the radio concert, he said, "Oh, Carol Miller . . . I've heard about you on WXPN. . . . You should get me a tape." I was flabbergasted. Had the shortish, midthirtyish, salt-and-pepper-haired Evans actually heard of me, or was he just making it up to be polite, or perhaps for some other reason? It didn't matter. It was Showtime, and I promised to get him the tape. At the concert, I also made the acquaintance of two of Sigma's top engineers, Jay Mark (Snyder) and

Carl Parullo, who later allowed me to sit in on some important recording sessions, most notably David Bowie's *Young Americans*. A crowd of
several hundred fans had parked themselves on line in the evening chill
at the door of the Twelfth Street studios, and were furious as I cut ahead
and was buzzed in over the intercom. Upstairs, Bowie stood alone behind a glass wall in the recording area, as Jay Mark soloed his vocals
over the control room speakers. I watched and listened intently. Suddenly, a large security man appeared and said I would have to leave.
Pushing his talk-back button, Bowie interjected, "No, it's all right. She
can stay." How generous, I thought. As he prepared to leave, Bowie asked
if I would come back to the hotel with him.

"Oh, no thank you," I said. "I have to go on the air." I figured he
would have asked any girl who was there, and didn't take the invitation
personally. I just wanted to see him sing.

                              ʅ ʅ ʅ

I labored over my audition tape, taken from reel-to-reel recordings I made
of my WXPN shows. At the end of that November in 1971, the little tape
was as ready as it was going to be, so I nervously called WMMR, asked
for Dennis, and requested to drop off the now officially solicited reel
with him. More good fortune, as Dennis told me to bring the tape up to
the WMMR studios myself, and he would give me a tour. When I arrived, shaking, at the gray Rittenhouse Square building on the northeast corner of Nineteenth and Walnut streets, Dennis took me into the
small windowed air studio on the third floor, where Ed Sciaky was
broadcasting, and I received a warm hello. Dennis then brought me,
clutching my red box with the small audition tape, to the door of Jerry
Stevens's dimly lit office. Jerry took the tape, and handed me a couple of
printed pages of public service announcements. "Go in the production
studio and record these," he said, pointing to a door across the hall. I
did my best. Seemingly satisfied with the recordings, Jerry concluded
the visit by saying, "I'll call you. Oh, and I'll listen to your tape." I
thanked him and Dennis, and left, thinking, Okay, that's it, there's
nothing left to do but wait, and to continue my shows at WXPN.

"Jerry Stevens called," read the pink While You Were Out note affixed to the WXPN bulletin board a little over a week later. The note had not gone unnoticed by some of the other WXPN student staffers (all guys), who again humorously snickered. "What does Jerry want with you?" one of them asked, unaware of my secretly conducted efforts. I didn't answer, and hoped that they would find out if and when they heard me over the big-time airwaves. When I returned the call, Jerry asked me to come back to WMMR, whereupon he offered me a Saturday overnight program slot, with additional shifts as a fill-in host when the mainstays were on vacation. A sharp breath of shock. Of course I agreed, flustered with enthusiasm, and shortly thereafter remembered that I was still a college student, and had classes during the day, which could possibly coincide with some of these fill-in shows. That probably won't happen anyway; cross that bridge when I come to it, I thought. "And we have to make up a name for you," enthused Jerry. "How about Cinderella? That's who you are!" Jerry must have been thinking about the Night Bird in New York.

"Uh, no, really, I just want to go by my name," I blurted out. The thought of a stage name or alter ego had never crossed my mind. I didn't think of this progressive radio stuff as "showbiz." It was all part of the New Direction. "I mean, I'm just a college kid talking to my friends. I don't have an act. Um . . . I'll just be me, if that's okay." But who was I anyway? I sure had never thought about it. What would I want people to think about me on the air, if they ever even did? All I cared about was presenting the music. I had better come up with something soon.

Jerry showed me to the door and handed me back the little red box with my audition tape. The box had never been opened.

14

The young fortune-teller spread his cards out before me on the Great Lawn in Central Park, and the forecast wasn't good. It was the summer of 1972. "Would you like a tarot reading?" he had said, approaching me as I wandered semi-aimlessly in the heat, absorbed in thought. Why the hell not? I thought. Who knows, maybe this voodoo nonsense will help me sort things out. Nothing else is working.

It was a little over six months since I had done my first overnight radio show at WMMR, and I had been working steadily ever since, doing fill-in shifts as well. Michael Tearson had preceded me in the air studio that December 11, with what was a typical greeting, if you knew the elfish Michael, who often lacked a verbal censor. "We won't be needing a girl around here," he said authoritatively but grinning. "Don't worry, you won't last long." With that, he popped on the air, while opening the switch and turning up the pot of the two attached stereo microphones. "Carol Miller is next. . . . Carol, this is a microphone," he said in a baiting tone. "Ever seen one of these before?" "Does it bite?" I had replied, faking confidence, and then delivered the station's slogan —"At FM 93.3, we're WMMR, Philadelphia . . . the Radio Station!"— simultaneously hitting the start button and potting up my first record, "A New Day Yesterday," by Jethro Tull. "It was a new day yesterday," lead singer Ian Anderson crowed, "but it's an old day now." A fitting way to start in the middle of the night, I had thought.

The minute I was left alone in the pitch black of that little corner-window studio, with its equipment board and colorful blinking lights, not unlike those of an airplane cockpit, I felt strangely at home, even though I was petrified. Why, it was exactly like being in my childhood room with the radio on at night, only better. This time I was on the other side of the radio, with all the records! I pictured the people listening through the airwaves, other kids in their rooms, maybe at a party, maybe in the car. I would be an invisible friend, just like the ones I'd had. Maybe even better, or at least different. My invisible DJ friends had been "wacky, zany" guys, most likely a good deal older than myself, who were kind of masters of ceremony with comedic acts. Some of the new FM personalities, especially those in New York, seemed like ultra-hip, cool, over-the-top sophisticates. None of them had just been a contemporary, a friend. Certainly none of them were girls, except for the mega-womanly beautiful Alison Steele.

Yes, a friend you could just hang out with, like some of the other guys at WMMR: that would be my approach. This radio friend would have certain qualities, I had reasoned, most of which I was sure I lacked. She'd be sociable, outgoing, caring, un-self-conscious, confident in an unpretentious way, always ready for fun, and wouldn't burden you with a bunch of heavy-duty problems. She wouldn't act overly sexy, because in real life, no one goes around like that all the time anyway. Of course, guys would have to like her voice in order to tolerate listening to it; they never cared for those chipmunk-chatterbox types, so I'd better make sure I never squeaked. True to the era, this radio friend would be on the laid-back side. Oh yeah, and she'd be smart; she'd know her stuff—you wouldn't be calling her a bimbo. The good thing about this girl, I thought, is that since she's just hanging out with you, she wouldn't have some sort of act you could get tired of. She wouldn't be earth-shaking. Your friends were supposed to mean more to you the longer you had them.

Out of all these characteristics, I figured I had about two, the pleasant voice and the smart part. I would have to pretend I had the rest. So it was, after all, going to be an act, but one that I wanted to become real.

Part of the act meant seeming happy and comfortable, when in fact I was often in my usual exhausting secret pain. But the radio broadcast studio setting made it all so much easier to deal with. When I flipped the "mike" on, all concentration immediately zapped into the front of my head, partly out of fear of flubbing, partly out of necessity (which is certainly not to say I never flubbed). It was as if there was no room left in my brain to pay attention to these other things. And then there was the matter of reading—on the air, it was usually in spurts—say for a news story, weather forecast, or commercial, so there was no accompanying vision headache, which would always arrive while poring over textbooks. (Of course, years later I would finally be fitted with strong prismatic lenses, which remedied the whole problem . . . blah blah blah.) In the studio, I could have my nice cup of coffee resting on a countertop (but never near the electrical broadcast board) and fidget with a Kleenex or whatever in my purse. I felt constant tension while the program was on, trying to speak well over the air and to keep everything running hopefully to the split second so as to avoid any "dead air," but the tension became energizing and familiar.

During those early months, I got to know the WMMR staff, which included (besides O'Reilly, Tearson, Sciaky, Takiff, and Wilen) David Dye and folk music specialist and impresario Gene Shay. A Temple University student, Shelli Sonstein, joined up as a public service director; she had come to WMMR along with her mother to meet me, a fellow schoolgirl, and see if she maybe wanted to get into broadcasting. (I currently work with Shelli all these years later.) University of Pennsylvania newspaper journalist Bill Vitka came on board as news director; and a bit later, WXPN's program director, my friend Nick Spitzer, joined as well. The production director was the creative Paul Messing. I had passed my FCC (Federal Communications Commission) licensing test, which permitted me to take power readings of the station's transmitter, and joined the union, AFTRA (American Federation of Television and Radio Artists). And then there was the stream of performers coming through the door of WMMR during those months, many of them early in their careers. To name just a few: Rod Stewart, Jackson Browne, Carly Simon, Jerry Garcia, Lily Tomlin, Todd Rundgren, David Bowie and his Spiders from Mars.

On July 2, 1972, Rod played a concert at the Spectrum, and I accompanied Ed and Judy, along with photographer Peter Cunningham (who was married to singer Janis Ian), back to Rod's hotel suite, where Ed recorded an interview. The four of us then proceeded into the very open-to-the-public hotel sandwich shop, which became overrun by gawkers, groupies on the prowl, and Rod Stewart look-alikes. Peter suggested we pile into his little car and head out.

Bizarre, I thought, being squashed in the backseat of what I think was a Studebaker, next to Rod Stewart, who was still wearing his gold lamé jacket. Rod fancied playing some pool, and the Sciakys knew just the place. Ed Sciaky's father-in-law answered the front doorbell of his modest suburban house, and welcomed us in. Ed introduced his friends, and of course, the father had no idea who the guy in the shiny jacket was. And downstairs we went to the semi-furnished basement with the pool table. At the moment, though, the table happened to be covered by packages and cans of foodstuffs, but this didn't deter Rod. He immediately began to clear it off. I wished I had a camera just to capture an image of Rod Stewart removing two sealed boxes of Streit's Matzos. Then it was up to the kitchen table for snacks.

As we got back into Peter's car to leave, Rod turned to me and said, "I'm going to Akron tomorrow. Would you wanna come with me?" So that was how these rock stars did it! It hadn't occurred to me: no date, no phone calls, no courting, just drop what you're doing, implicitly consent to everything ahead of time, and run off to a faraway place. Of course, I was flattered, but I thanked Rod and told him I had to be on the air the next day.

Comedienne Lily Tomlin was my first on-air celebrity interview on WMMR; her character was known to all as the "one ringy-dingy" switchboard operator on television's *Laugh-In*. Lily stood to my left as we spoke into the dual stereo side-by-side microphones, and she reenacted her switchboard persona, curling her tongue over her upper lip. When she was leaving, Lily insisted that I take one of her rather large vitamin pills, which I was dumb enough to do. I thanked her, said good-bye, and returned to the air studio to resume my regular routine of records and patter. Within minutes, the room felt like it was beginning to spin, and the walls and corner window were closing in, along with the rolling record bins. Freewheeling disorientation set in. What had Lily given me? Had I been dosed with acid? I'd sort of heard about that happening to people unexpectedly (when they stupidly took other people's "vitamins"). It was all I could do to pull myself together enough to pretend to act normal and finish the show. This was my first time tackling some hardcore excellent training for a task that faces all on-air people: to forcefully tune out any distractions, because "the show must go on." Afterward, I lay down on the lobby couch, where I clutched my purse and jacket, determined to ride it out.

By the summer of 1972 and my graduation from the U of P with a BA in Biology arrived, Jerry Stevens had appointed me music director of WMMR, although I had no music business experience whatsoever. I was also doing two weekend air shifts plus the fill-ins, and supporting myself in a sublet newly rented, oddly, from a niece of singer Eddie Fisher. Although I was shocked but certainly pleased about the appointment, the whole scenario made me very nervous. Things were moving faster than I'd expected; I hadn't thought all of it through. I had yet to receive a response from the several medical schools to which I had applied earlier in the year, and with all the new full-time radio work, I had all but put the thought aside, thinking perhaps they had forgotten about me as well.

But an acceptance letter finally came to my parents' house. I was to report in about three weeks' time to the State University of New York Downstate College of Medicine in Brooklyn. Rather than being overjoyed, which I should have been, I felt stumped, ashamed, ungrateful, and panicky. First off, whatever I did would mean quitting an effort I had already made in either direction, taking back my word, and insulting and inconveniencing people who had acted on my behalf. I couldn't imagine just dropping out of my new radio world, moving immediately up to Brooklyn, and entering the grueling, life-and-death world of a medical student. My new life was so exciting and totally different from anything I had ever experienced. And the hours and the sedentary work too made dealing with my physical pain and keeping a job possible. On the other hand, I knew it was a privilege to be able to enter such a meaningful career, for which I had studied, and which my family expected. This new FM radio fad wasn't any kind of "career," anyway, especially according to my family and upbringing. I should have anticipated my parents', most notably my father's, reaction. After all, he was part of the Downstate staff, and as he always had, he hated and had low regard for anything to do with that horrid "noise" I called music.

My parents made a special trip to the radio station in Philadelphia to deliver an ultimatum. "You have three choices," Daddy said with a steely fury. "One, you get your ass up to Brooklyn and into class, and I'll pay for the dorm." (I was to have gotten a student loan and paid for the schooling myself.) "Two, you get married and let your husband take care of you." (Now this was new. I was brought up to study, and barely go on a date, and now I was supposed to be instantly married.) "And three, you're on your own, kid; you'll never get another penny from me. I can wipe the last twenty years off of my slate, you know, like it was nothing." (You might find that statement a bit shocking, but I knew Daddy. He always made a big point of making his point.) My mother's only comment was to sniff, "Radio? The only way you'll get anywhere in that business is on your back." It took me a moment to understand what she was saying—that type of talk wasn't like her. Despite all their anger, I was shocked that my parents were actually treating me like an adult and leaving the choice up to me.

And so, I took Amtrak up to New York early one Saturday to discuss the matter. I would have to be back in Philly that night for my radio show. Feeling depressed, nauseated, miserable, guilty, and plagued with my usual chest pains, I dozed off unhappily on the IND subway and overshot my stop. Awakening with a start, I got out of the train several stops later, on Seventy-second Street and Central Park West, and emerged from the dark, dusty station to hot sunshine, directly across the street from the famous Dakota apartment building. I had seen it a few years earlier in a scary movie, *Rosemary's Baby,* and it certainly was an impressive fortress. Next to it was a tall, much newer white brick building, and immediately to my left, on my side of the street, was the entrance to another graceful old edifice, the Majestic. I entered the cool, dimly lit lobby, and marveled at the original marble work and art deco surroundings. If I ever moved back to New York, I thought, this might just be my neighborhood. Exiting the Majestic, I crossed Central Park West, entered the park, and numbly meandered toward the Great Lawn.

Which is where the fortune-teller in full hippie garb approached me with his deck of cards. As he turned them over one by one, I marveled at his accuracy, which I attributed to skilled trickery, or maybe some innate ability to read the brain waves of someone in close proximity. "You are choosing between two career paths," he said, and paused. Really, how would he know that? It had to be my brain waves. "But I want to help people," I blurted, out of nowhere, thinking of the honorable medical profession. "You would be helping people in either one," he said, gazing at me steadily. I paused and mulled it over. "So . . . which one do I choose?" I asked, returning the stare. "Oh, you've already made your choice," he said, "and you will help people by making them happy." All of this sounded too preposterous to be true, and it was, wasn't it? After all, this was some flakey weirdo with a deck of picture cards. Then his expression changed, becoming dark and disturbed, as he turned over a final card, which featured a morbid-looking specter. "What does it say, what's going to happen to me?" I asked, suddenly aware of my own premonitions about my family's unnamed fatal illness. "Does it say I'm going to die young?"

Unwilling to answer my question directly, the card reader haltingly responded, "Well, whatever you're going to do . . . you should do it before you're forty." With that, he packed up his cards and left.

I found my incredibly logical self adding this ridiculous information into my decision-making process. Things suddenly felt settled, or perhaps rationalized: I won't even be around long enough to be a doctor.

And so, I chose door number three, and went off on my own.

15

And so, in that late summer of 1972, still conflicted by doubt, and overwhelmed by guilt at having sorely disappointed my parents, I returned to Philadelphia to follow my new career path as the music director of WMMR-FM Philadelphia, also working as weekend "air personality," and "musicologist."

My mental catalog of every rock record ever recorded was helpful, but I lacked the smooth expertise in deflecting the groping hands of the self-proclaimed young musical rebels who visited the station, and the middle-aged three-martini Mad Men, whose era was lumbering to a close. Even in corporate structures like Metromedia, there were no guidelines for conduct, EEO regulations, or for that matter, any other easily exploited standards purporting to protect female employees from animals in the workplace. "Hey, where'd ya find her, Fourth and Race?" Kal R, industry reporter, had quipped laughingly at a promotional dinner back in December '71, referring to a popular spot for streetwalkers. "No, Carol's my new weekend DJ," smirked Jerry Stevens.

I had to give Jerry credit. He knew his progressive rock music, even though his roots were in AM Top 40, which I had heard was where the payola was. He was a product of his times, but he allowed his young air talent the freedom to present what they thought would please their contemporaries, and he had hired a college girl to be the first female rock DJ in Philadelphia. And for that, he deserves my thanks.

Although I was somewhat proud to have earned my new status, I didn't see what the big deal was, no reason for the newspaper and music magazine interviews I got. People seemed shocked that a girl could do this job; I was a curiosity, like a monkey using a typewriter. The difficulty and importance of being a DJ was nothing compared with what I was supposed to be doing—studying to become a doctor—and I had no way of knowing then that I would never lose my secret feeling of embarrassment and inferiority when in the company of such professionals. My parents, of course, with the best intentions, made sure to constantly remind me, and anyone else within earshot, that I was "wasting my life."

No, the real challenge of the job was the men. "Now that we're working together, we can have a closer relationship," whispered Jerry, as he wiggled his hand up my left inner thigh. It was the start of my tenure as music director, and he had closed the door to his dimly lit office for our first departmental meeting. I was taken completely off guard. With no doubt the humorless expression of a startled deer, I blurted, "I never go out with people I work with . . . uh . . . for," and I removed the offending hand.

Today, such a meeting might not even be conducted behind a closed door, or, as was the practice of a major company for which I formerly worked, there would always be a second woman of managerial status present to prevent a one-on-one meeting between a male executive and female employee. But back in 1972, my rattled younger self could only protest politely, for fear of losing my job, and get out of the situation as soon as possible.

Of course, my declaration of business morality did not stop Jerry from his pursuit, and he continued to make attempts to get me innocently drugged or drunk. "Here, take these," he would often say to me, shoving a small stash of various pills into my hand and pointing me toward the water fountain. Jerry was rumored to be a speed freak (whatever that meant). His erratic behavior lent credence to this claim, although I did not recognize it for what it was at the time. Dutifully, I would report to the water fountain while Jerry watched, lean over for a gulp, and silently drop the pills behind the fountain. My experience with Lily Tomlin's vitamin had taught me well. Years later, when the radio offices were dismantled and relocated to a different floor, I heard that a small pile of unidentifiable pills had been found behind the water fountain. Truth or rumor. I never bothered to check.

Ultimately, Jerry became vindictive because I wasn't playing ball, and promised that he was going to make my life miserable, which he did, employing various annoying tactics, like summoning me to his office by yelling loudly out his door every few minutes to run one menial errand or another and later chastising me for not completing the work I was really supposed to be doing.

Actually, much of the music director's job was clerical, and not really to my liking. Lots of opening boxes, filing records, and sending lists of albums, which the station had added for airplay, to various trade publications. Since the format was free form, and the DJs could play whatever they wanted, my own opinions on the music meant nothing, except when I was on the air. And that's what kept me there, in a Philadelphia office building: the anticipation of my weekend air shifts. Certainly, it was fun to meet the artists and go to concerts and promotional parties. But most of all, I loved hanging out over the radio with all my new friends, who often called the studio request lines or wrote me letters. I wanted to be broadcasting in a studio, where I felt at home, every day. And ideally, the studio would be in my real home, New York, which I missed very badly.

16

I had been dragged, unhappily and protesting, into the brave new era of women's lib, which I secretly thought was a diabolically clever male plot to make us think that the sexual revolution was our idea. The term *dating* (connoting bobby socks, a pledge pin, and a senior prom) was now archaic, and the new rules of socializing maintained that if you were "seeing" a guy, you were obligated to sleep with him. How foreign and immoral this concept was to me and the way I grew up. Now, you were expected to sleep with a guy after he'd invited you out a certain number of times (such number was hotly debated). You just were, or he would be seeing someone else. Which is not to say that you wouldn't like the experience. As I understood it, you might like it a little too much, and in fact get a little too attached—oh, what am I talking about? way too attached!—for your own good. Before you knew it, Mr. Wonderful would decide to "move on down the road" and pursue a fresh flower child, and you'd be left feeling like a crock of shit. Never mind the potential for pregnancy, or that according to your upbringing, you weren't a nice girl anymore.

Better to "explore your sexuality" in your own mind. Guys were out exploring "experiences," and you were, no matter how hard you tried to think otherwise, looking for a "permanent relationship," i.e., a husband. Going out with anyone who wasn't "husband material" would be a waste of time, and your clock was ticking, young lady. (And now that they had the green light to sleep around, guys could waste plenty of our time, going after all the formerly forbidden fruit. In my case, as a Jew, it was like there was a sudden pandemic of shiksa fever.)

Had I only taken stock of my own observations, I would have saved myself some trouble later on. But I convinced myself that men really got attached to whomever they were sleeping with too. They had to, right? And at any given time, a single man was really looking for a permanent relationship like I was; seeking his soul mate, in the new vernacular, wasn't he? Of course! All the magazine love-advice columns said so, and we 1970s girls pored over every word. Somehow, though, men seemed to breeze through the break-up situations more easily (it was amazing how they could do that) and continue on in what I believed was their search for romantic stability. At least once, though, I actually went with my observations, and was all the better for it.

𝄢 𝄢 𝄢

The dashing young movie actor had called from New York that spring of 1973, and I couldn't believe it. Why, I had just seen his movie, and then seen it again with my friend Harriet, giggling over the glimpse of his naked rear end, in a brief flash of a scene, no doubt included in the film for artistic merit. Murray Head, British star of the blockbuster movie *Sunday Bloody Sunday,* and vocalist on the prestigious double album / rock opera *Jesus Christ Superstar,* had been escorted up to WMMR by his record company representative in order to promote a new album in early 1973. And for me, as music director, there was a mandatory lunch at a tacky Italian restaurant. The recent glimpse of the ravishingly handsome Mr. Head's naked rear end on the big screen, and then the sight of it (clothed, of course) across a small, crowded lunch table in Philadelphia, struck me as comically absurd, and it was all I could do to keep a straight face. When Murray asked if he could keep in touch and get my reaction to his album, I wrote my number on a small cocktail napkin. (Okay, so it was my home number, but like he was going to call anyone in Philadelphia anyway?) Imagine my surprise, then, when he actually called to invite me up to New York to see a concert. Fool that I was, I was certain it was no doubt to explore the potential for a permanent relationship.

The concert featured the jazz/fusion artist Mahavishnu John McLaughlin at the Felt Forum. Murray said we could head to an extravagant party at the Manhattan residence of manager/promoter Jerry Brandt afterward. He was introducing the Next Big Thing, America's answer to David Bowie: the outrageous gay/androgynous persona of Jobriath. (Jobriath's alabaster, semi-naked image had been plastered all over Times Square, on the sides of buses, and just about anywhere Brandt could squeeze it in. After selling only a dismal number of albums, Jobriath would become known—and soon forgotten—as one of the biggest flops in the music business.)

This Jobriath party was an important place to be for an up-and-comer in the music business like me. And to show up with Murray Head? Unbelievable. No doubt about it, then, this was going to be a real date with a real British gentleman, who obviously considered me interesting enough to take around and get to know. That he would think of calling all the way to Philadelphia! There was no mention over the phone of what would happen after the date, which I also thought was very nice and demonstrated Murray's honorable intentions for maybe a long-term relationship. Not like so many of the rock musicians I would meet, who boorishly blurted out propositions.

So it was a very giddy schoolgirl who gassed up the 1970 gold-colored used Buick Skylark with the black roof and the FM converter for the ninety-mile trip up the Jersey Turnpike. I had high hopes. Talk about a Candidate with a capital C! Okay, so Murray wasn't Jewish. Exceptions could be made for totally fab, gear, exotic Englishmen (the ultimate being Paul McCartney, who had incomprehensibly married a Jewish girl from New York).

Murray had told me to meet him where he was staying—the funky/posh Gramercy Park Hotel, adjoining the quaint private park of the same name. Upon my arrival, Murray immediately squired me to Sal Anthony's, an equally elegantly hip nearby Italian restaurant on Irving Place, for an early dinner. As we crossed East Twenty-first Street in the late-afternoon sunlight, I remember asking the Adonis-looking Murray, "How old are you?" "Twenty-seven," he replied. How sophisticated—an older man, but not really. Just right. "I'm twenty-two," I offered, trying to project cheerful confidence, while beginning to realize the possibility that I could get in way over my head too quickly with this storybook-perfect catch.

It didn't matter that the jazz-fusion guitar stuff at the concert wasn't exactly my cup of tea. It usually put me to sleep, but not this time. I was sitting next to the Most Handsome Man in the Universe, who even seemed to share my perhaps lack of musical taste (if you don't believe me about how handsome he was, go ahead and Google him, ladies: "Murray Head, *Sunday Bloody Sunday*, 1971"). The Jerry Brandt party was right out of a movie as well: a stunning Upper East Side duplex (or was it triplex?), black-and-white marble floors, lots of Glitterati, including Carly Simon, also apparently newly under Brandt's management, hors d'oeuvres on silver trays, and maybe even some feather boas floating around wealthy necks.

Murray couldn't have been nicer or more attentive. And now it was approaching 3 A.M.; still no mention of the next destination. But after the type of meticulous deliberation usually reserved for a NASA space flight, I had decided on at least one possible trajectory. Although I'd never before considered sleeping with anyone on a first date, if he asked, I would allow myself an exception: Murray just could be Mr. Right, and I wanted to at least try and leave an indelible mark upon his memory until our next time. Besides, I had just seen his naked butt in cinemascope. In fact, in the film's story line, his butt was so perfect that he had to escape from the multiple women (and men) who pursued it, so he hopped on a plane to New York. There was no way I was not going to see this now world-famous rear end for myself! And anyway, now there was a logistics problem. It was too late to drive back to Philly, so where else could I stay at 3 A.M., other than my parents' house, where my guilt over their disapproval was already too much to bear, and my intrusion at that late hour would surely frighten them. So then, in my mind, the matter was settled—all I needed was the actual invitation.

However, while we were walking to a cab, a question like a bolt of lightning flashed through my brain. "Are you married?" I asked Murray. "Yes," he said quietly and matter-of-factly, staring into the distance. Oh. Sharp breath, mind churning. "So, it wouldn't be a good idea if, say, I called you at home?" I asked, hoping there might be some impossible loophole here. "No," he continued, as we got into the taxi. So all of this lovely date and party was for naught, my dreams dashed. And whose fault was that? I didn't even have to finish the thought—it was mine, of course. I should have asked the pertinent question before embarking on the trip to Fantasyland. But it had never entered my mind. Lesson learned. But now what? I thought, as we rattled downtown toward Gramercy Park. I really didn't want to see the night end.

Without commenting about Murray's marital status, I accompanied him to his hotel room. I had my laugh over the famous tush. Several hours later, I awoke at dawn. Silently, I freshened up, dressed, and stood over the sleeping Murray's bedside, reassuring myself that it was best that I escape from his magnetic beauty.

"Hey, where are you going?" he awoke with a start.

"Time for me to leave," I said with forced joviality.

"But why?" he asked. "We're going to have a lovely brunch." Carefully, I recited the lines I had been rehearsing: "Because you're married in real life. It's like an epilogue to your movie: You've run away to New York, and then you meet me. But I have to leave you, instead, in your hotel room. It's only fair." Murray sat up, astounded. Thanking him for a wonderful time, I smiled, said good-bye, got in the elevator, walked as fast as possible to the garage where I had parked my Skylark, and headed south and west for the Jersey Turnpike back to Philadelphia.

Would Murray Head ever remember me? I didn't know; probably not. Most likely he did this kind of thing all the time, and he was very good at it. There was really nothing bad I could say; Murray had been the perfect gentleman. Had I done the "right thing" by leaving? Or staying there in the first place? I didn't know, but I was pretty sure that I had saved myself from some heartache while, at least in my mind, maintaining some dignity by leaving. To this day, at least I can say that there was a time in my department of romantic disentanglements where I didn't feel like a sap.

One thing was certain, though: the weekend with Murray reminded me how trapped I felt in my mostly clerical job in far-away Philadelphia, with its daily confrontations with an increasingly antagonistic boss. New York was always full of energy, excitement, humor, the unexpected at every turn. Yes, New York was indeed the Center of the Universe. Philadelphia was provincial in comparison. I was a New Yorker; and there was no place like it. Somehow, I would have to find a radio job there. Or one would have to find me.

17

The barrage of rapid-fire red light from the telephone hotline pierced the dark, pensive atmosphere of the late-afternoon air studio. Just about every radio station had this necessarily silent but ominous visual alert system, which enabled the program director, or anyone important enough to be privy to the insider number, to immediately contact the person on the air—usually for the purposes of barking a reprimand. I had been contemplating the nature of the universe according to Joni Mitchell.

"I wish I had a river / I could skate away on" Joni bleated, and went into a piano interlude. Things could definitely get heavy like that in a relationship, but Joni Mitchell sure knew how to handle today's delicately souled sleep-around Desperados. Actually, despite her beautifully crafted melodies and revealing lyrics, she irritated me. I wasn't sure if it was her pin-straight blond locks or her self-absorbed bourgeoisity: "And ice cream castles in the air." Yeah, it had to be the hair.

My nearly black, ethnic semi-frizz fest had started to go prematurely gray, like everyone else's on my father's side of the family, and I was already dyeing it once a month and additionally enlisting the services of Vince of Bala Cynwyd to chemically straighten it. The fact that some people could actually wake up and have their hair look "normal" was infuriating. How many hours and dollars a month would I be able to save not sitting with a bunch of goop on my head? But that exhausting schedule of hours in the beauty parlor would provide me with a life-time's worth of wonderful listening experiences and insight into the lives and concerns of women much older than myself, and would serve to remove me from the collectively narcissistic perspective of my own generation.

The unfamiliar voice on the other end of the hotline had nothing to do with castles in the air, or hair relaxer, and everything to do with a possible radio job for me in New York. It was program director Jim Lowell (not his real name), from the ABC-FM station in New York, which had recently undergone a change in call letters from WABC-FM to WPLJ. "I'm here in Philadelphia to give you a listen," said Lowell. "We may have something for you at WPLJ." I didn't believe this for a minute. Why would a honcho from New York come down the turnpike to listen to some girl music director who was only on the air on the weekends? And how did he get the WMMR hotline number? Nevertheless, I agreed to come over to his center city Philadelphia hotel to meet with him after my shift was over. When I got to the hotel, I asked the front desk to ring Mr. Lowell's room. The receptionist handed the phone over to me, and within a split second, Mr. Lowell had a request: "Hey, how about com-ing upstairs and giving me a back rub? I could really use one." "What?" I said, surprised (but not totally shocked). And I hung up the lobby phone and left.

Within several weeks, a remorseful Mr. Lowell called again on the hotline. He apologized for his uncouth behavior, and extended an invi-tation for me to come up for a proper lunch interview and then a tour of the ABC/WPLJ studios on the southeast corner of Fifty-fourth and Sixth in NYC. I gassed up the Skylark and headed north on 95. The ABC building was formidable and refreshing at the same time. From its signature black cube bearing the letters ABC on the entry steps, to the stark white ninth-floor lobby reception area boasting a wall display of the letters WPLJ surrounded by its trademark concentric rings, the es-tablishment screamed "professional" and "big time," a far cry from the down-home hippiedom of WMMR.

Before departing for our lunch at Thursday's, just up Sixth Avenue at Fifty-eighth Street, the bearded, diminutive Lowell took me down one flight of steps to the eighth floor, where literally everything happened. From the devil-red lobby to the quarry of studios for WABC, WPLJ, and ABC local news, to production offices situated around the perimeter, the atmosphere bustled with good-humored professionals having fun at, while sometimes making fun of, their jobs.

We entered the small WPLJ FM-1 room, where a middle-aged male engineer sporting a green visor sat at the control board, while the DJ, another graying middle-aged man, puffing away on a cigarette, sat opposite him on the other side of the board in front of a flat tabletop. A movable microphone had been swung over to the DJs side, and the DJ paged hastily through a large black loose-leaf binder of commercial copy to be read. On his left was a small metal file box of colored index cards. Lowell explained that each card represented a song in the rock library; the DJ was programming his show from only those allotted cards. And all the songs represented on the cards were the most popular of the new rock era; such a programming process would likely garner a larger, more consistent listening audience than relying solely upon the vagaries of the hosts' personal tastes. Then, in a whisper, Lowell told me that he planned on firing this particular DJ, and that I was just the fresh new blood that the newly minted station format would need to take it to the top.

How disconcerting—what kind of businessman gives a stranger inside information about someone's impending dismissal? Probably not a very stable place to work right now, I thought, as if much of the radio business had any smidgen of stability anyway.

A couple of weeks later, back in Philadelphia, I received a call from Lowell saying that the ABC management was not yet ready to hire a woman for WPLJ; maybe another time soon. I was both disappointed and relieved. As it turned out, I had already made my entrée contacts at WNEW-FM, WMMR's Metromedia "sister station" in New York, home of all the überpersonalities like Scott Muni, Alison Steele, and Jonathan Schwartz.

Dennis Elsas, the young music director corresponding to my position at WMMR, with whom I had weekly job-related phone calls, had invited me up to WNEW's 1972 Christmas benefit concert, held at Avery

Fisher Hall at Lincoln Center several months earlier. It was the first New York performance of a British group called Genesis, which had an eccentric lead singer, Peter Gabriel, who wore makeup and shaved his hairline into the shape of a V. The dramatic, theatrical presentation showcased some of the lengthy progressive cuts from their recently released album, *Foxtrot*.

After the show, I was introduced to some of the station's stars, and my Skylark and I were, strangely enough, enlisted to give Scott Muni, Dennis, and I think another DJ, Pete Fornatale, a ride over to the Rainbow Room at Rockefeller Center for the WNEW holiday party. "Hey, great parallel park!" commented the curious, deep-voiced Scott Muni, as I deftly maneuvered the Skylark into a tight space. Muni, the forty-something program director and mentor of WNEW, was in great spirits, and he seemed at the same time totally aware of yet oblivious to his surroundings, beginning conversations in midthought. He mentioned my parking job a couple of times, not quite what I wanted him to remember me for, but I'd take what I could get. I returned to Philadelphia encouraged by my trip.

Late in June 1973, Dennis Elsas called to say that there might be a slot open at WNEW-FM for a vacation relief DJ with a possible weekend shift, and Scott Muni had given him the okay to get hold of me to cover it, starting in a couple of weeks. My hours would be Sunday mornings, 8 A.M. to 12 noon, and fill-ins. I couldn't have been more shocked or thrilled. Who was I compared with the big names that inspired New York? Since Muni had never heard me on the radio, I assumed it was my stellar parking job that he remembered.

A week later, Ed Sciaky invited me to check out a new musician. "You've gotta come and see this guy!" he rhapsodized about the new singer-songwriter. "He's just incredible!" As music director, I had added the artist's first album to the WMMR library in January, when it was being promoted. I remembered seeing a literary publication from Ocean Grove Community College in New Jersey, where this new singer-songwriter had honed his rather wordy poetic craft. But I had yet to see him perform in person. And so, on July 5, 1973, I joined Ed Sciaky and his wife, Judy, for a ride back to the Main Point on Lancaster Avenue in Bryn Mawr.

The Main Point club was located in a smallish house with wooden floors and benches and hippie waitresses serving apple cider and brownies. We arrived early, as we were there to see the opener, not the headliner, a comedy act called Travis, Shook and the Club Wow. The club lights dimmed, and a thin, earnest, brown-curly-haired, bearded young man sporting jeans, a white undershirt, and large crucifix took the small stage, sat down at a piano, and launched into an emotional vocal performance, beginning with a song called "Does this Bus Stop at 82nd Street." He was then joined onstage by his band, and he switched instruments from piano to guitar. After the show, Ed introduced me to the artist, still earnest and a bit overheated: Bruce Springsteen. "You were really great! Congratulations on your album. Sorry I missed you in April," I said, referring to an earlier performance at the Main Point. I told Bruce I would still be working in Philly, but "I just got another weekend job starting next week up at WNEW-FM in New York, and I'll be happy to play your record."

"Oh, thanks, that would be great," said Bruce shyly, and he giggled almost nervously. I was unaware that *Greetings from Asbury Park* had initially been banned from airplay at WNEW because of a political disagreement between the radio station and Bruce's manager. And since no one had told me about it, I did indeed become the first person to play Springsteen's record in New York. After I'd played it, the ban became a moot point, and the other DJs followed suit.

18

"People can you feel it? Love is everywhere / People can you hear it? The song is in the air." No, I didn't feel it. Or hear it. Free-floating, often drug-fueled animosity and pervasive low-grade paranoia were what was really in the air. An all-encompassing conspiracy theory, accompanied by an amazing musical sound track. Allmans, Stones, Beatles, Who, Steely Dan, Jackson Browne, Carole King, James Taylor, Laura Nyro, Linda Ronstadt . . . music to impeach a president by!

I didn't really get that either. So some GOP minions bugged the DNC at the Watergate. Not exactly the best place to ferret out deeply held secrets. Why would Nixon have bothered with this low-level nonsense, and so what if he found out after the fact? What was so earth shattering? Anyway, it had been reported that Bobby Kennedy had bugged Martin Luther King Jr. And then there was the much-talked-about covert espionage in the Marilyn Monroe situation. If you wanted to look for the real whopper of a cover-up, you needn't go further than the Warren Commission's report and their preposterous lone gunman postulate.

No, this pin-the-tail-on-Nixon scenario was seemingly turning our whole generation into a mass of scurrying subterraneans on a mission to overthrow The Man . . . or so I mused (to myself) while on the air that afternoon in 1973, inconceivably filling in for the kingpin of counterculture WNEW-FM, Scott Muni, who, along with the rest of the staff, was hosting an outdoor concert event in Central Park. Scott, a barrel-chested former marine, had seemed momentarily aware of my insignificant presence. His one piece of advice concerned my on-air mention of personal favorite artists; he said it was best for the host to remain neutral about preferences, so as not to alienate listeners who might not share them. I thanked him for the advice, but offered that since I was just a kid like most of the audience, and not a revered authority, the fact that I might have an enthusiasm for Bruce Springsteen and Janis Joplin might seem more normal and at the same time less consequential than if he'd expressed it. Scott paused, as if he were unused to anyone offering a different opinion from his own. "Hmmm. Maybe you have something there," and he trailed off.

Although Scott understood that I wanted to be on the radio, it was as if, in a fatherly way, he thought it was no place for a young girl. While he liked to flirt with the ladies, his first social overture was to suggest that I might be a nice companion for his son Mason, to whom he introduced me one day in the studio. (However, Scott had not taken into account the fact that Mason, a really nice fellow, was still in high school, and I had already graduated from college.) On several occasions that year, Scott tried to protect me from the "dark underbelly" of the music business, once insisting that I leave a convention at the New York Hilton because there were hookers there, and escorting me out.

Based on Scott Muni's simple okay that I marginally join the WNEW-FM staff, I piled my belongings into the Skylark and a friend's VW van and moved up the Jersey Turnpike to a small walk-down studio apartment in a (white) brownstone on Manhattan's West Side, near Central Park, where I had fatefully met the tarot card reader. As I was also keeping my Philadelphia radio shifts at WMMR, this meant at least two round trips in a row each week. It also meant a budget whittled down to nothing: my weekly earnings averaged somewhere around a hundred dollars.

Sometimes I would pay for gas and drive, and sometimes I would commute back and forth by train if I was very tired. (I had tried the Greyhound bus one time, but was frighteningly groped by a different passenger every time I changed my seat, and couldn't risk getting off the bus at night in the middle of nowhere.) Once, at Philadelphia's Thirtieth Street Station, I spotted a newly relevant face, and hesitantly approached her. "Excuse me, aren't you Ms. Steinem?" She smiled at me and I introduced myself. "Thanks for what you're doing for us," I said. I was not actually sure what it was she was doing except that it involved plenty of strident feminist flag waving—but even if I didn't agree with everything about the women's movement, I knew she was doing important things for our gender.

I picked up my bag and prepared to walk away, when the beautiful, long-haired brunette asked, in a soft, tentative voice, where I was going. She asked if she might ride with me; she was just going as far as (I think) Princeton. "Maybe I could be on your radio show," Gloria Steinem, the Queen of NOW, volunteered. I probably should have followed up on her request, but I just assumed she was being polite and that she would have no need for some twenty-two-year-old girl DJ. During the short ride to Princeton, I marveled at what appeared to be a disconnect between Ms. Steinem's brash public persona and her somewhat demure, even vaguely nervous, private demeanor.

During the ensuing months of working, traveling, and shyly attending industry events and promotions, I would encounter other movers and shakers on the way up to their destinies, mostly in the entertainment business. A young, newly married couple, fresh out of Carnegie Mellon theater school, had the larger apartment adjacent to mine, and the husband helped me move furniture and such. In return, I would watch and feed their huge angry cats when Mr. and Mrs. Ted Danson were away visiting parents.

I would see Bruce Springsteen many times, when he stayed on the Sciakys' couch in Philadelphia, at WMMR picnics, or at his own increasing number of area performances. Once, when my cousin Stu and I sat in a close-up row at Madison Square Garden watching David Bowie's Diamond Dogs show, a paper airplane landed in my lap. A few rows back sat Bruce and a couple of his E Street Band buddies, playing hooky from their own postponed gig at Philadelphia's Main Point to take in the Bowie show. "You'll be playing here soon," I said to Bruce, laughing, as I introduced my cousin. "Yeah, right, I wish," said Springsteen, giggling, something he did a lot.

An up-and-coming singer from the West Side, Melissa Manchester, came up to my show for an interview and became a friendly acquaintance. At a small party, I met her friend Bette Midler, who, like me, frequented the Soap N Suds Laundromat on Columbus Avenue. Bette was becoming famous for her performances at the Continental Baths. Ed Sciaky also introduced me to Barry Manilow. And as was the case with Springsteen, I was very pleased to be able to premiere his initial recording of "Could It Be Magic" in New York on WNEW-FM.

Through my friendship with Natalie Halem, the wife of a promotional agent, I met a gregarious young woman, Linda Stein, and her husband, Seymour, who ran Sire Records. Linda had befriended an English singer already on the way up named Elton John, to whom she introduced me at a new club in the Village called the Bottom Line. As Elton stood with Linda near the side of the small stage, she began to introduce me as Carol. "Oh yes, Carol Miller," said Elton. Linda had coached Elton to learn the names of all the DJs at WNEW, and I was impressed that he'd remembered. (I would later become friendly with Linda again in a different setting, about fifteen years before her much-publicized, horrendous murder by her personal assistant.)

For WMMR, I conducted a rather convoluted telephone interview with Yoko Ono about her artwork and Attica State Prison, and was excited to receive a thank-you letter personally signed by both Ms. Ono and her husband, John Lennon. Soon after, they appeared on the *Mike Douglas* television show, where I met them in person. Then I received a phone call at my apartment shortly after I got off the air at WNEW-FM one Sunday in New York; it was Dennis Elsas telling me I just had to come back to the studio right away because John Lennon had dropped by. And wouldn't you know it, I had just begun giving myself a facial with boiling hot water and my face looked ridiculous so there was no way I could leave. I was infuriated about the timing, but was intent on maintaining my dignity.

Meanwhile, my lack of confidence in my unheard-of career choice (who could count on earning a livelihood as a girl radio DJ?) led me to a backup plan—one my parents would be proud of. I applied to enter law school in the fall of 1974, with the idea of maybe doing something in media law. Although I was hoping to attend one of the more prestigious (and convenient) Manhattan schools like Columbia or NYU, I had barely any background in subjects like economics or sociology, so I wasn't exactly at the top of the list of most qualified law school candidates. However, the associate dean of Long Island's Hofstra University School of Law, David Benjamin, took an interest in my application and recommended my admission. I now had two part-time radio jobs in two different cities, and soon, a full-time academic schedule. I started to prepare for the arduous year ahead. I applied for a student loan and audited an introductory course in law and another in mass media at New York University. But my barely-there NYU experience would unbelievably result in my undoing at WNEW-FM.

The big names at WNEW-FM hardly bothered with me, the lowliest part-timer; they were wrapped up in their busy careers as New York's FM gurus. They seemed nothing if not polite and vaguely amused (e.g., Jonathan Schwartz, who repeatedly invited me to come to Palm Springs with him, "Because you're a little flower child," didn't really take me seriously). But I began to sense something brewing among the other scurrying underlings on the all-male staff, as they jockeyed for air shifts. One in particular, already somewhat more established, was becoming annoyed with me because I flatly refused his repeated invitations to go out on a date with him, since he was married. His marriage was not working out, he would say. He finally stuffed a long handwritten love letter of explanation into my home apartment mailbox; I was shocked to find it there one afternoon when I came home from the radio station.

I had never heard a cross word from the glamorous Alison Steele, and I admired her talent and work ethic. But one day during the summer of 1974, Scott Muni called me into his office. He said that he had been asked by the station's general manager, Varner Paulsen, to fire me, because of a complaint lodged by Alison. I stood there, incredulous. I had barely ever spoken to the lady. What had I done?

Apparently, Alison believed she had been booed by some members of the audience while being introduced onstage at a WNEW-FM Town Hall concert, and having commented upon it, had been convinced by at least one member of the air staff that it was my doing. All of us had been introduced onstage that night, I of course last, and I hadn't heard any booing of anybody. Especially not from that crowd. Just well-heeled, en-thusiastic applause; the concert was for the benefit of the trustees of New York University, who were among the audience members. But the story relayed to Scott was that because I was a student at NYU (two hours a week in that population of thirty thousand), I had gone around ahead of time to determine who was going to be in the audience, and urged some of them to boo when Alison was presented in an effort to cast doubt upon her popularity.

Scott didn't believe this ridiculous tale, but the damage was done; the scurrying underlings and their ringleader had advanced their cause. However, Scott told me he would not take me off the air until such time as he was literally forced to do so, and he didn't know when that would be. He was just warning me about my impending demise.

I couldn't have been more upset. All this work for maybe nothing. My parents were right; I was a failure and a disappointment for following this dream. Taking a few days off before my next weekend's air shifts— not knowing if I'd even be working in New York anymore—seemed like a good idea, so I hopped on a cheap flight to London and took my friend the DJ Luke O'Reilly (with whom I had worked in Philadelphia before his return to his native England) up on his invitation to visit.

19

It was on the plane to London, that July of 1974, that I discovered the first huge lump. Someone on the previous flight had left a *Cosmopolitan* magazine on my seat, and while waiting for takeoff from Kennedy, I mindlessly skimmed through the pages. Chuckling, I thought of how my mother had described the racy women's periodical to me when I was a young child: "*Cosmopolitan* is a magazine that teaches secretaries how to become prostitutes." I had never paid that much attention to *Cosmopolitan*, except for the *Harvard Lampoon*'s satirical edition. This time, though, *Cosmo* started me on a journey that would ultimately save my life.

"How to Give Yourself a Breast Exam" was more or less the title of the article, which featured a black-and-white diagram of a woman performing a manual self-examination. I had never heard of this; back in 1974, such issues weren't usually discussed—because they weren't issues—especially for girls in their early twenties. What the hell, I thought, nobody's looking, and I placed my hand over my blouse in the first indicated position. And immediately recoiled in horror. Unlike the multitude of painful marbles that I was accustomed to feeling when I changed my clothes, this one was the size of a bird's egg. No, it can't be, I thought, suddenly short of breath, as the stewardess launched into the how-to-buckle-your-seat-belt demonstration. I waited until takeoff, and attempted the exam again. The egg hadn't moved. I felt as if I was going to faint, and bent over toward the floor. Regaining my sitting position, I attempted some additional surreptitious poking, and noticed that while the other marbles seemed to be somewhat attached to the rest of my chest, the egg seemed to be somehow floating but stationary.

And here I was, some thirty-nine thousand feet in the air, rocketing to a foreign country; there wasn't exactly anything I could do about it. "So, you got some kind of a big lump here," I said to myself in the comforting Yiddish inflection I'd heard all through my youth, "and it's big enough that you probably had it now for a while, but look, you're still alive. You don't feel sick from it; you didn't even know from it five minutes ago. So there's a good chance you'll be alive if you still have it a few days from now, right?" I took a deep breath. Having momentarily parked the problem in the back of my brain, and deciding not to lose my special discount fare by rushing back on the next flight, it was time to open the peanuts. But I didn't exactly feel great. And I didn't want to touch my chest. And of course, I would tell no one my secret.

My first night in London, Luke had arranged for me to stay at the family home of two of his friends and business associates. Miles Copeland had been managing and promoting rock acts such as the Climax Blues Band, Wishbone Ash, and Renaissance, and had recently formed a company, BTM, to handle his business. His younger brother Ian was booking various acts, and the youngest of the brothers, Stewart, whom I never met, was in a band called Curved Air. (Within a few years, Stewart would become the drummer for a group called the Police, who catapulted to fame under Miles's wing.) As I remember, the Copeland home was a solid and stately brick edifice, and their father was reported to be a very important CIA agent, making my overnight stay in an upstairs guest room all the more intriguing. Who else might have stayed there, and what international secrets had they carried?

The next day, I went up to Reddington Road, where Ian Copeland and Luke O'Reilly shared a flat. I strangely remember an "official ordinance" affixed to a bathroom door, regarding taxation based on the number of toilet flushes per month. The notice had been signed "R. Soles." While I immediately understood the signature joke, I wasn't so sure about the flushing. Maybe the British actually had to pay for a certain amount of water in the loo? Luke explained that the satirical sign was inspired by a real British tax on television. I was stunned. Who ever heard of paying for television? Americans would never in a million years put up with that!

Luke was managing a British folk musician named Al Stewart, and although he wasn't performing that day, the three of us traveled by car up to the Cambridge Folk Festival, a long-standing traditional outdoor event. The headliner was the American Arlo Guthrie, of "Alice's Restaurant" fame, whom we met up with there, along with singer Sandy Denny of Fairport Convention, and the group America. I had been introduced to Arlo at a recent Philadelphia Folk Festival, and he was very flattered that I had come all the way to England to see him. I assured him it was just a happy coincidence. I was excited to meet Sandy, especially because she was the female voice who sang with Robert Plant on Led Zeppelin's "Battle of Evermore." The guys from America were very down-to-earth; I took a couple of pictures with them on the lawn. Before heading back to London toward evening, Al reckoned he'd fancy meeting a date to take along, so he picked a spot in the vicinity of the ladies' room cabin to observe the line of girls as they entered and then exited. Within what seemed to be an eternal ten minutes, he had selected and acquired his giggly blond companion for the ride home and the upcoming weekend.

While I was glad to be in London, I was filled with anxiety over my various secret plights, and my constant "happy act" was becoming more difficult to maintain. I didn't trust my own swirling emotions, and had also begun to entertain the idea that my charming young overseas host just maybe might be a possible Candidate for a Permanent Relationship, but I didn't know how he felt, and the last thing I needed was a complicated affair. I decided it was best for me to leave, but I wasn't ready to go home and face the music. Saying there were some other friends to visit, I thanked Luke, packed up my bag, and asked him to drive me to a taxi stand. I caught his eye as my cab pulled away in the twilight; was he perhaps a tad wistful that I was leaving? Could he have sensed that I had a secret ailment? Wow, this is heavy melodrama, right out of some weepy European movie, I thought, momentarily stepping out of my character.

And jumping back into it, a 1930s book title came to mind, *After Leaving Mr. Mackenzie,* by Jean Rhys. Wasn't that the story of some heartbroken woman flopping from guy to guy and withering away with drink in Paris? The flopping and boozing didn't sound like such a good idea, but Paris did. And I already knew my way around pretty well. "Heathrow, please," I said to the cabbie.

It was close to 9 P.M. when my plane landed in the bustle at Orly. *Ding, ding, ding* rang the familiar ascending notes on the public address system. Now what? I didn't want to spend the money on another private taxi into central Paris, and besides, I had no reservations anywhere and thought it might be a bit difficult to begin hunting down an inexpensive hotel at that hour. Maybe there were other Americans or Britons who had just landed, maybe some students who might want to share a cab in, and maybe I could find out where they were going.

In two minutes I spotted a small English-speaking crowd near the missing-luggage counter. My taxi companions were a middle-aged couple on vacation and a strapping light-haired American graduate student who had come to visit his French cousin at a school dorm in Paris. As I had given no destination to the driver, he dropped the couple off first at their hotel right near the Champs-Élysées. Now I had to reveal to the graduate student that I would be looking for a hotel, because in fact I had just "popped over" to Paris at the last minute.

In a most gentlemanly fashion, he offered to help, suggesting we go to his dorm first, to drop off his suitcase and greet his cousin. Like other old French dorms I had stayed in previously for summer classes, the rooms had a musty smell and dirty curtains, and the WC down the hall had the most primitive of plumbing. Through the cousin's recommendation, we found a tiny hotel on the right bank, and my new friend offered to come back in the morning. Over some breakfast rolls and premium octane coffee, he volunteered that the reason for his trip to Paris was a sudden gut-wrenching breakup with his fiancée. All this drama! Since I didn't know the fellow, I let down my guard and spilled the beans on my own situations. At least I didn't have to pretend, which was a welcome relief from all the silent self-control I had imposed upon myself.

Strangely, for me, I don't remember my friend's name, and I never saw him again after that week, even though he became my convivial sightseeing companion. And nothing more. Not that he wasn't interested. I told him I just couldn't handle any new complications, and he understood.

Soon my plane ticket said it was time to fly. Maybe someone more free spirited (or irresponsible) would just have said the heck with it and bummed around Europe for a while. But not reliable old me. Upon my return to New York, I had dinner with my parents at the house. Even though they didn't approve of my life, they loved hearing details about overseas travel, so I was happy to oblige, and I could pretend things were like they used to be.

As we were finishing up, I innocently but hesitantly broached my little health concern: "Um, you know how your chest is filled with all these little marbles?" I asked, in between bites of coffee cake. "Well, on my right side, one of them is a lot bigger than the rest." A look of terror, yet recognition, instantly crossed Mommy's face. My father dropped his fork.

"It's Mick Jagger," the intercom squawked. A few minutes later, another buzz: "Ron Wood." Then, in succession, "Eric Clapton," "Billy Preston," "Charlie Watts." The date was June 22, 1975, and the address was 52 West Eighth Street in Greenwich Village. The famous curved brick exterior marked the outside entrance of Electric Lady Recording Studios, where I waited downstairs in the circular, white-walled "satellite" lounge.

The Rolling Stones had just done a boisterous show at Madison Square Garden, replete with Jagger craning over the audience in a cherry picker, and Richards playing alongside a white blow-up of a long mushroom-shaped object. Since Eric Clapton was also on tour, a joint recording session had been arranged by his label, RSO Records, and I had been invited to witness history in the making by the company president, also a friend, Bill Oakes, who was married to RSO recording artist Yvonne Elliman. In those days, we free-form rock air personalities were considered important and influential, since in fact we selected everything that we played on the air, and so were invited to all sorts of promotional events, where we knew "everybody."

Since there were no other guests, and I was a lightweight compared with the sheer cultural gravity of the invited musicians, I felt a bit useless and self-conscious, waiting for nearly half an hour in the overly bright lounge area. But my head was spinning anyway; so much had happened within seven months. I had just finished my first year of law school. Scott Muni never did fire me from WNEW-FM; instead, I resigned from the uncomfortable, unresolved situation, after I had quickly sought out and secured a part-time on-air job at the new upstart WQIV. I was there on November 7, 1974, for its initial on-air sign-on and had been to preparatory meetings for several weeks beforehand. And in a preposterous silent comedy of errors, the "women's doctor" whom I had visited told me that I had a severe fibrocystic condition, and most likely a large fibroadenoma, a breast tumor that was almost always benign. I felt relieved. Whatever the doctor says goes, I thought, having been brought up to revere any medical opinion that was bestowed upon me.

The physician had left me in the examining room with a warning about "keeping an eye on the situation," saying that he was going out to talk to my waiting parents. But as I learned years later, he never did. And in an era where nobody talked about "the big C," we never discussed it either. Instead, as we got into Daddy's car to go home, my mother breathed a sigh of relief, "So, you're okay!" And that was it. I was momentarily relieved too. But . . . not really. What did "keeping an eye on the situation" mean? I assumed it meant poking myself in the chest from time to time to feel if there had been any change in the fibroadenoma. Okay, I thought, I can handle that.

Finally, down the entrance hall and inside stairway they came. Mick Jagger chattered and giggled to his companions, discussing something about fish as he rounded the corner and nearly bumped into me. I was introduced as a New York radio DJ to Ron Wood, who had just joined the Stones. Unbelievably, he immediately scrounged around in his pocket and produced a small, crumpled bit of paper with my name and phone number on it: "Carol Miller 212 EN 2-0133."

"Where'd you get that?" I asked.

"Oh, Steve M gave it to me. My, uh, dealer in Philly. He said I should give you a call when we got to New York."

"That's funny. . . . Uh, nice to meet you," I said to Ron Wood, not really wanting to know whether he actually intended to call me or not.

I wasn't sure which was more shocking, the peculiar coincidence that Ron Wood was carrying my phone number, or that one of my friends' husbands was a big-time coke dealer to the stars. This actually shouldn't have been that much of a surprise; while I had been at Steve's house a couple of years earlier, he and his wife had sat huddled with a group of hippiesque buddies over a small pile of white powder on the slate ledge of the fireplace. Someone had referred to it as "meth." Steve's wife had rolled up a ten-dollar bill and hunched over the powder. She then passed the bill to the next person. Everyone had long hair, which covered their faces as they bent forward and consumed the powder. I couldn't see exactly where the rolled-up bill was being inserted. In any event, what they were doing certainly wasn't sanitary, but no one seemed to be reacting poorly to the substance.

When it was my turn, I had put my finger around the tip of the rolled bill, to protect myself from germs, and put it in my mouth. That was the most likely place they were putting it, right? I had drawn in a small mouthful of the powder and swished it around my teeth, trying not to swallow most of it because it had a nasty bitter tang. Not knowing the function of this recreational medication, I then waited for "effects."

Soon, I realized I was grinding my teeth, shaking my foot, and feeling a bit "hurried." Time to invoke Captain's Orders and switch to Manual Override, just like Captain Kirk did when he wrested the ship's command from the computer. Dusting myself off, I left the snortfest, as quickly and quietly as possible, and as I recall, got on a train to New York.

Eric Clapton arrived at the bottom of the stairway next, accompanied by Pattie Boyd, George Harrison's beautiful model wife. She carried a Brownie camera and was clicking away at everyone. I was more excited to meet her than anyone else present. She had been my ultimate Swinging London dolly-girl mod fashion role model since 1964, along with fellow top model Jean Shrimpton. ("Slicker under! Slicker over!" Shrimpton had gushed from the TV ads, touting the yellowish tube of Yardley lip frosting.)

We entered the control room where the engineer, Ralph, sat; a heavy curved glass partition separated this room from a larger recording space. Large, trippy outer-space murals of aliens and hippie chicks covered the walls. Pattie Boyd was sporting a peasant look, as mod was not happening in '75. At first, I was surprised, but then concluded there would be no way she could possibly present herself as anything other than up-to-the-minute. She looked a bit older than the schoolgirl she had portrayed in *A Hard Day's Night,* but then again eleven years had gone by.

Pattie sat down next to me on a bench in the control room. "I always wanted to copy whatever you were wearing," I confided, and so began a very pleasant conversation with the woman who had just been musically glorified for the ages as "Layla." The soft-spoken and seemingly shy Pattie told me that she had once been attacked by some jealous Beatle fan when she was buying a skirt in Bonwit Teller on Fifty-seventh Street. How terrible, I thought. "Hey, where'd you get your shoes," I inquired, about her stylish espadrilles, then laughed as I realized, "See. I'm still trying to wear everything you do!" Pattie told me she'd gotten her shoes at the Off-Broadway, a boutique on the north side of West Seventy-second Street between Columbus and Amsterdam. Right near me! Oh, the irony, or the karma, or whatever.

Between the engineer at the control board, about fifteen feet from where I was sitting with Pattie, and the large adjoining performance room, a recording session was taking place. Mick Jagger was relentless in his quest for perfection as the musicians hammered away at repeated takes of a song called "Come to the Carnival." To the best of my knowledge, nothing public ever became of this effort. I especially remember watching Clapton and Billy Preston on their instruments and an animated Jagger addressing the engineer through the talk-back, "All right, let's do it again!"

At least a half hour went by, and the control room door opened—a new arrival and her apparent chauffeur/bodyguard. It was Bianca Jagger. She was dressed, as I recall, in something very crisp and black, perhaps a pantsuit jacketed over a white shirt. She looked all business and hard as nails as she whipped out a deck of cards and began an intense game with her beefy companion. If she glanced up at her already iconic husband singing on the other side of the glass, I didn't notice it.

The recording session plodded on; it was getting very late—or very early, on Monday morning. I certainly did not want to appear sycophantic enough to sit through the whole thing, and I had to be at work in several hours. Work was a summer legal clerkship at a downtown law firm. Bill Oakes gave me a ride in his limousine back to my dingy walk-down studio apartment on West Seventy-fifth Street. Without sleeping, I freshened up, changed into more sedate attire (bell-bottom jeans would not be proper), dragged off in the already oppressive summer heat to the IND, and took the CC to transfer to the IRT at Fifty-ninth and Columbus Circle.

Standing room only. The number 1 train was packed, sweltering, and there was no air as it rattled its way south. Unannounced, *mettle-schmerz,* my middle-of-the-month sharp pain, stabbed internally on my left side, and I began to feel very lightheaded. I clutched harder at the floor to ceiling metal pole, attempting to maintain consciousness. Within several minutes, we arrived at Fulton Street, and I was spared. I exited with the crush of the crowd and headed up into the financial canyons of lower Manhattan, the stately turn-of-the-century office buildings dwarfed by the twin towers of the new World Trade Center. (I had actually gone to an opening party for the media there, at the Windows on the World restaurant, a year earlier.) A short walk to John Street, into the crowded elevator, and up a substantial number of floors to the legal offices where I was gaining invaluable experience research-ing and composing a product warranty for Luxman audio equipment. The elevator door opened to the unsettling sight I had become accus-tomed to seeing: a deeply etched swastika on the metal face of the out-going U.S. Mail chute. As I entered the large front door of Boal Mcquade & Fitzpatrick, it occurred to me again for the millionth time that a full-time radio career, if such a thing were actually possible for a girl, might be more fun than this.

21

"Do a little dance, make a little love, / Get down tonight." As performed by KC and the Sunshine Band in 1975, this was arguably not exactly a critically acclaimed musical work of historic importance. Nonetheless, the ditty came to represent, instantaneously, the most important turning point in my career: my KC and the Sunshine Band Moment of Clarity.

The evening New York to L.A. flight landed around 10:30 P.M. that August 25, and I had rushed off to find the nearest pay phone in the American terminal. Marcus Xenakis, the chief engineer of WQIV, had answered my call on the hotline. "We've been sold," he said. "It's over."

Oh. That sharp pique of disappointment, but this time rather expected. Contentious from the get-go, WQIV had weathered a ten-month run on 104.3, under the ownership of Starr Broadcasting. That frequency had previously been known as WNCN, New York City's only wall-to-wall FM classical music station, when that format was dumped in favor of a novelty: free-form "alternative" rock, transmitted with a quadraphonic signal.

Never mind that only a handful of people were buying into "quad" as the wave of the future; when heard over a normal mono or stereo radio, a song broadcast in quad seemed to be missing half its sound. Maybe you wouldn't hear any singing, or say, any guitars. And if you were in the studio, listening to one of the few specially processed quadraphonic vinyl recordings, you became dizzy or nauseated by the continuously swirling sound.

But this was not the cause of public dissent; rather, it was the loss of New York's sole twenty-four-hour classical music station that had the citizenry petitioning the FCC. The city didn't need another rock option—and I secretly agreed, but needed the job. Other than working with the legendary Rosko, and establishing the first all-night Grateful Dead bootleg tape show, my experience at the "Quadfather" could best be described as harrowing. Led by a rootin'-tootin', sadly self-destructive, sex-and-drug-crazed hippie, Thom O'Hair, who had brought his anything-goes San Francisco vibe to the Big Apple, QIV was the devil's lair for any young woman on the premises. There was constant pressure for sex; drugs and booze were around all the time. I witnessed a couple of drug busts (during one of which once I personally watched the cops take the cash and run, leaving the pot and a warning).

So at that moment, starting a week's summer vacation after clerking at the law firm and working my two radio jobs, standing at a pay phone at LAX, I wasn't really too sorry to hear the news that the GAF corporation had bought WQIV and immediately restored it to its upright position as classical music's WNCN. But now, once again, I needed a rock radio job in New York. And because of my WNEW snafu, there was really only one place to try, the now formatted (as opposed to free-form progressive) WPLJ, which was rapidly ascending in the ratings, having just overtaken WNEW-FM's position as New York's most-listened-to rock outlet.

I had already twice visited WPLJ, the second time over a year earlier, when I had been point-blank offered a position there under what seemed like shaky circumstances: to replace a woman who'd been tried out for an air shift but had allegedly succumbed to excessive partying. Now, I was nervously telephoning the current program director, Larry Berger, at 6 A.M. (9 A.M. New York time) from my first day of vacation at my girlfriend Natalie Halem's home in Sherman Oaks. Had I not contracted a horrible virus, which was later diagnosed as a relative of polio, from eating a seafood crepe at the Magic Pan on Fifty-seventh Street the night before my trip, I would have been well enough to jump right back on a plane to New York for the job interview. (And as if things weren't bad enough, that afternoon I experienced my first earthquake, at the home of our friend Irving Azoff, now one of the most powerful men in the entertainment business.) Instead, I interviewed a couple of weeks later, and I was greeted on that same expansive ninth floor at the ABC building, this time by Mr. Berger, whom I would soon come to consider my mentor. Larry was a well-ordered redheaded man in his midthirties, about my height, with an air of exactitude and an engineering degree. He shared some of the more obsessive Jewish characteristics from my mother's side of the family. Aside from projecting confidence in his programming formatics, Larry seemed devoid of the oppressive, substance-fueled, "radio maverick," macho egotism that defined my former directors. Larry was there to run a business. It would certainly be a relief to work here, I thought, instead of the minefields from which I had come.

Larry explained his format in detail, how the music library of rock songs was subdivided into categories based on various criteria of popularity, time of release, and/or potential for popularity, and then further delineated by sonic characteristics such as tempo, and "hardness." The DJs would put together their shows by selecting music that fit these parameters according to a pattern sequence, which would vary for different times of the day. The goal was to present the widest variety of audience-pleasing music, to encourage people to keep listening. The focus now was on catering to and reflecting the listeners' tastes, and supplementing that with information and companionship, as opposed to the somewhat self-aggrandizing I'm-the-radio-personality-creating-my-art-and-you'll-appreciate-the-musical-education-I'm-meting-out-to-you attitude prevalent on the free-form progressive stations. Larry had based his format on some of the methods used in programming Top 40 stations but had modified and expanded upon them. Of course, the WPLJ format could not have been constructed without the sheer number of rock albums now available on the scene in the early to mid-seventies. Larry's type of format became known as AOR, for "album-oriented rock," and it worked.

But did the emphasis on established favorites mean that the audience would no longer be exposed to new music? Not at all. Several new selections were presented on air each week, during which time they would receive a significant but not overbearing amount of airplay, coupled with a live introduction and explanation by the DJ. This method of exposure would both give the audience a comfortable way to become familiar with the new material and encourage interest and record sales for the artists in a de facto fashion. The popularity and frequency of play of older recordings would be determined by several means, not the least of which would be reports on the number of copies actually sold. And unlike the rather counterintuitive philosophy behind the music presentation at more progressive rock regimes, where music was downplayed or dumped in an elitist inverse proportion to its popularity, on WPLJ, the music more people liked . . . would be played more.

At my first interview, Larry expressed concern that as a "free-form" host, I would find his format too confining. He asked me to listen to WPLJ, see if I could decipher some of his musical categories and patterns, and think things over. I thanked him, and began my listening assignment on my daily drives back and forth to my second year at Hofstra Law. But my decision had already made itself; during all my free-form shows, I had imposed a much looser but similar format, in the hopes of making a palatable presentation. (And I had been rewarded by *Philadelphia* magazine, which had named me "Best DJ" in 1973.) So I was thrilled when Larry offered me an evening weekend show a few weeks later. Now there was only one musical/philosophical hurdle to overcome. And in the grand scheme of life, it wasn't that difficult.

Larry Berger had aimed the programming of WPLJ to include both the more progressive album rock of WNEW-FM and some of the more Top 40ish pop music found on another FM competitor, WXLO (99X), in an effort to drive his station musically right through the gap in the middle and pick off the competition's listeners. That meant that in addition to playing my long-championed Bruce Springsteen, Beatles, and other artists who had "credibility" and "relevance" to the now-established countercultural FM audience, I would now have to present acts that were more familiar to the mass audience, such as the funky but respected Earth, Wind & Fire, the just plain bordering on sappy

John Denver, and the catchy but impossibly platform-shoed light-weights KC and the Sunshine Band. Yeesh—KC! What would "my" type of listener, who would no doubt soon discover or hear about me at a new location on the New York FM dial, think? Was I no longer into the progressive scene?

And so, when the big moment came (with Mr. Berger in the small room dutifully supervising my first show), I signaled the technical engineer to open my microphone (ABC had union-affiliated engineers, so the DJs were not allowed to control the equipment) and mustered up the nervous enthusiasm to begin: "It's ninety-five point five, WPLJ, New York's Best Rock, with KC and the Sunshine Band!"

The first runny synthesizer notes of "Get Down Tonight" doodled through my headphones. Taking a breath, I signaled for the engineer to cut the mike, whereupon the sound blared through the in-studio speakers. Momentarily, I glanced over at the large black listener-request-line telephone to my right, with its huge bank of lines coming into the studio. Suddenly, all of them lit up and blinked. The phones were, as they say, on fire. I hesitantly picked up a line. "Hey, Carol, how ya doin'? You on PLJ now? Glad you're back!" bellowed a youthful male voice, echoed by a chorus of cheery buddies in the background, obviously having a good time at whatever they were doing. No mention of my musical transgression.

A rapid tumble of internal questions ripped through my brain: Wasn't that why I was there, on the radio, to help people have a good time through the music, and to join in, as a friend? What was all the snobby posturing about? Why couldn't someone like the Kinks *and* KC, recognizing the musical legacy and social commentary of the former group and finding the latter to be just plain fun? Why did some of my peers wear their obscure musical tastes as a badge of purported intellectual achievement, when in fact there were surely others, such as myself, who were working on their doctorates and didn't hear things that way, who just thought the Bee Gees were fun and seemed like good musicians to boot?

No, now I was sure I wanted to play whatever more people would enjoy in the popular music world, while still lending my support to and imparting information about the "core" rock album artists. "Get down tonight! Get down tonight!" repeated KC. Okay, I thought, why not?

Larry Berger offered me another evening show the following Sunday, and said he would like to call me with news of a position when that opening could be arranged. This would be just great, I thought, school during the week and radio shows on the weekend, one still in Philly at WMMR, and now back on in New York at WPLJ—a lot of work and travel, but just my thing. I waited on pins and needles for my news, each day after school rewinding the small reel-to-reel tape on my two-year-old state-of-the-art phone answering machine. And Larry's call soon came, but it was not what I had expected.

"I'd like to offer you a full-time shift," he said, "Monday through Saturday, ten P.M. to two A.M. . . . it goes a little later on Saturday." Stunned wasn't the right word. Thrilled wasn't quite it either. How could I go to law school all day and work on the radio every night? How could I turn this down?

I didn't.

22

"Paul McCartney wants to meet you!" blurted fellow DJ Jim Kerr over the WPLJ studio hotline. What a patently absurd statement. Although I had never made a fool of myself at Beatles concerts, or in front of his house in London, since the age of thirteen I had secretly harbored the conviction that Paul McCartney was the World's Most Amazing Man. (Of course, people like Albert Einstein and Daddy could arguably hold that title, but they would be in a different category of World's Most Amazing Man.) And now, Paul McCartney wanted to meet me? Why? Impossible!

It was late in the evening on May 24, 1976, and McCartney and Wings were onstage at Madison Square Garden on their first U.S. tour. Before the show, McCartney had held court for the media, and one press pass had been doled out to each radio station / media outlet for interviews. In the case of WPLJ, this coveted entrée had most deservedly gone to Jim Kerr, the very talented and hugely popular "morning man," who, curiously, at the age of twenty-three, had the flaxen long-haired boyish appearance of a midwestern Little Lord Fauntleroy and the deep voice of an American James Bond, which made speaking with him in person a bit jarring.

But here he was, on the phone, describing his surprise when, upon his introduction to Paul and Linda McCartney in the press room, with tape rolling for Kerr's next program, Paul had exclaimed, "WPLJ?

Where's Carol Miller?" "Yes, we always listen to Carol," Linda had added. Jim explained that I really wanted to meet them but hadn't been given a pass. With that, he said, Paul apparently fired off some directives to his representatives that I be given a ticket and backstage credentials for a personal introduction the next evening, at the second of Wings' Garden concerts. "No! I can't believe this!" I screamed into the receiver.

Much of what I had experienced in the short eight months I had been with WPLJ seemed unbelievable. Larry Berger had given me a generous yearly contract of thirty thousand dollars; the station's general manager had pointed out that it had to be less than what was offered to the men, because they had families to support, but it was almost as good. This seemed reasonable at the time (1975), and I was thrilled at the prospect of saving almost every penny. The contract, however, did not guarantee employment for the entire term; rather, it contained standard AFTRA union thirteen-week guaranteed cycles, during which time, if one were terminated, the severance pay would be commensurate only with the remainder of the current cycle. Still, it was something.

And with my new paycheck, I was able to move into a much nicer studio apartment on a high floor in a safe doorman building in my then rough and tumble West Side neighborhood; my new window stared directly over the roof and into the windows of the famed Dakota apartment building. The rent was a bit steep—$360/month. "Three hundred and sixty dollars," my father had said, "that's a tough nut to crack! Think you can do it?" But safety was worth it; I had been terrorized in the brownstone by attempted burglaries while I hid in the bathroom. I was able to park my trusty Skylark in the new building's parking lot for the monthly fee of $50, which made driving to law school in the morning much easier.

I treated myself to two "fancy" items: a Pierre D'Alby (whoever that was) pantsuit with vest, which had caught my eye in a Fifth Avenue / Rockefeller Center store window, and a Louis Vuitton bag. I opened a passbook savings account at the Golden Savings Bank on Seventy-second Street just west of Columbus, and with no problem would have enough money (about four hundred dollars including airfare) for a one-week package trip to the south of France for a summer vacation.

Musically, at the time, so many things were happening: Albums were being delivered to WPLJ (now the nation's most-listened-to rock station), sometimes surreptitiously, often to be premiered on my show—of course after a sanction from Larry Berger. *Frampton Comes Alive,* the Rolling Stones' *Black and Blue, Presence* from Led Zeppelin. . . . I had begun doing personal appearances and "rock nights" for the station, and became part of a powerhouse team of DJs, guys with great voices who also had unique personalities, among them Jim Kerr, Pat St. John, Tony Pigg, and the former TV horror-show host, Zacherle. Working nightly at WPLJ felt strangely like the high school social experience I had never had. Ironically, my program was always at the end of an exhausting day of real-life law school classes, and I felt completely at home bringing my books and a cup of coffee into the studio, and "relaxing" through the radio with my favorite music and all my new invisible friends, most of whom had just spent the day in high school or college.

And now, I was going to meet Paul McCartney!

$$\text{\textsf{ʆ ʆ ʆ}}$$

Great seat at the Garden, and there he was, visible to the human eye, even without binoculars! Paul McCartney! Those other people around him looked unfamiliar, save for his cruelly much maligned wife, Linda, who simply looked out of place.

"Hey Jude." "The Long and Winding Road." So many of the Beatles' McCartney solos and the new Wings stuff too. And didn't he sound wonderful! But still . . . if only the Beatles could just be friends and play together again. What could be so impossibly difficult about that? Not the type of question Paul McCartney would want to answer, I thought, as I made my way to the backstage entrance after the last song. Displaying my all-access pass to the security guard, I was ushered past the velvet rope and directed to the elevator that would take me up to the fifth-floor dressing rooms. All of a sudden, there they were, McCartney and crew . . . mere feet away as they descended from the rear of the stage, before their mandatory encore!

Instinctively, I waved hello, and Paul smiled and returned my wave, with what seemed to be an (impossible) glint of recognition in his eye. Perhaps my hair and wardrobe had done the trick; I had tried my best to mimic the appearance of Paul's former fiancée, actress Jane Asher, whom I had deduced to be about my height and weight. My then-colored reddish brown hair with the long bangs and the new mod black Pierre D'Alby pantsuit worn with black boots must have momentarily rung McCartney's bell of familiarity, I thought humorously, and decided I was off to a good start.

In the elevator, I felt a pang of sadness for my doppelgänger, the young British actress who had allegedly broken up with Paul over some cheating incident at his London home, reportedly involving a girl named Francine Schwartz from New York. Surprising that he had been with a Jewish girl, and then even more curious that he had married one of us; the zaftig (sturdily built) Linda did not exactly epitomize the slim swinging birds of Britain look, which I perpetually dieted and straightened my hair to maintain. Yes, I definitely related to Jane Asher, and would most certainly not flirt with Paul McCartney, now a devoted family man. My appearance would just have to remind the ex-Beatle of what he had given up, I told myself, as the elevator doors opened.

Down the corridor leading to McCartney's dressing room was a line of media people. I took my place at the end, behind rock journalist and author Danny Fields. It didn't matter that other late scurriers cut ahead; being last might logically render my visit more memorable, or at least faintly recollectable at a future date, to the most revered man in music. Now, what else to do before meeting a Beatle? I popped a Certs in my mouth. "Certs is a breath mint, Certs is a candy mint; it's two, two, two mints in one!" I intoned silently, and freshly inhaled . . . exhaled. . . . Finally, it was time for my audience with Paul.

I entered the stark, cement-walled dressing room with Danny Fields, who made a beeline over to Paul, who (I think) was in a dark sports jacket, sitting on a metal folding chair near a tub of sodas on the left side of the room. Apparently they knew each other. So as not to be rude on two fronts, I immediately introduced myself to Linda, who was on the right side of the room. She wore jeans and a sweater, and she instantly struck me as more broad beamed in person than in photos. She couldn't have been nicer, and now I found my sympathies turning from the wronged fab, gear London bird Jane Asher to this nice *haimish* (down home), although wealthy, lady from Westchester, New York, who had to put up with half the women in the universe trying to steal her husband.

The press had repeatedly accused Linda of putting on a phony British accent, but I only noticed the type of natural melding of American and British (and a little Yiddish) that one might acquire from constant exposure to a different dialect. As she spoke with me, a fellow Jewish New Yorker, I began to notice a little bit less of the British, and a speech pattern closer to mine. After the pleasantries and the compliments on her performance, I asked if she was seeing her family here, which of course she said she was, but she missed her farm, and something about the horses. "You must come visit us at the farm," Linda said warmly. "You'd love it." I thanked her, but thought she must have just been being polite; what well-to-do celebrity would really invite me, a little working girl nobody, to the much-publicized McCartney farm in Scotland?

A couple of years later, I would interview Linda on the air, over the phone from the McCartneys' Concert for Kampuchea in London, and again she couldn't have been nicer, and genuinely seemed to remember me. A couple of decades after that, I would send her a letter of a sad, but hopeful nature. But now, on May 24, 1976, a mere fourteen years since I first saw him on the *Jack Paar Show*, Paul McCartney was saying hello.

"Oh Paul, this is Carol Miller," said Linda casually, as we walked over to one of the icons of the twentieth century. "You're Carol Miller?" said Paul. "I didn't think you'd look like this." "What didja think," I said, laughing, "I'd be older and maybe three hundred pounds?" Paul grinned. "Yeah, I mean I just didn't expect . . . here, sit down, let me get you a 7UP so you don't have to schlep," as he reached into the tub. Paul McCartney speaks Yiddish! So Linda's speech must have been rubbing off on him. I was floored.

"You know, it was very nice what you said about us on the air the other night," and Paul proceeded to mimic my voice, recounting listeners' enthusiastic reports about the level of musicianship displayed by his new group, Wings, in their performance at the Nassau Coliseum in nearby Uniondale, Long Island. I was momentarily embarrassed by his impersonation. "It meant a lot to hear that." So, that was it, then. Paul and Linda had been listening to WPLJ, and apparently I had given the first report they'd heard on Wings' performance that mentioned anyone other than Paul. He said they also listened to me when visiting with Linda's family here, in particular with a nephew. This was very smart, media-savvy PR on their part, I thought, keeping in touch and reinforcing their image with the people who actually played their records on the radio, and thereby sold them to consumers.

After thanking him for all the music (it seemed a whole lifetime then, but it had only been twelve years), I commented, "Boy, wish I would've had seats like this at Shea Stadium," referring to the stratospheric perch from which I had descended to the fence area behind home plate at the Beatles' last concert. "You were at Shea Stadium?" quizzed Paul. "You're not old enough. How old are you?" "I'm twenty-five." At which point Paul mused over his disorientation with his advancing age, which was thirty-four. "New York radio's changed a lot since the last time we played here," Paul offered, and I was then able to ask him if he and his fellow Beatles were in fact "putting on" or mocking some of the Top 40 AM DJs who had seriously interviewed them during the heyday of Beatlemania. Even as a thirteen-year-old, I was sure I had detected the Beatles' conspiratorial scorn, and now was pleased to hear that was indeed the case.

As I recall, some last-minute young stragglers who had won a meet-and-greet contest from McDonalds arrived with cameras, and I said my good-byes. I had thought it rude to bring a camera for a photo; I had been an invited guest. The McCartneys warmly said they'd be listening and we'd meet again. "Come see us at the farm," said Linda again. Oh sure. "The farm." I would encounter Paul McCartney several times in the years ahead, once at one of his recording sessions in London, but never at the farm.

Floating out of Madison Square Garden on a cloud of disbelief, I stopped at a pay phone to call my parents. After all the years of putting up with my Beatles obsession, surely they, especially my father, would have something humorous to say upon hearing of my encounter. True to form, Daddy quipped sarcastically, "So that's it, you met your idol. Now what's left for the rest of your life?" Hah. We should have only known.

23

And so, in 1977, I was on a roundabout trajectory toward my real life: I had a job, an apartment, and a salary. But according to my background, life did not begin until I was married (and in my parents' view, on my way in either the honorable professions of medicine or secondarily law). And this real life, I instinctively knew, was still on a collision course with a meteor of illness meant to end it. The tarot card reader's illogical prediction about life being over at forty resonated with my increasingly severe internal and chest pains. Then there were the accompanying splitting headaches, and the slightly increasing size of the egg that I carried in my right breast. The only painkillers that were prescribed for me that seemed to work for these conditions, Percodan and Fioricet, put me to sleep, so they were of no use to me during the workday.

The parental pressure to marry was still sort of new, but had been building over the past couple of years. As a teen, I wasn't supposed to go on dates, but now, as I was in my twenties, it was becoming a *shandeh* (embarrassment) that I wasn't automatically married. From what I could determine, twenty-five was the acceptable cutoff date. And pushing twenty-seven, I was already an *alta moyd* (old maid). "You better hurry up before the bloom is off the rose," my father would say, with the best of intentions.

It wasn't just the parental push. "Love is all around you" was the mantra—and if you weren't finding it immediately, and the perfect quiche for Sunday brunch, you'd failed. Ali MacGraw, Diane Keaton / Annie Hall, Marsha Mason—all the Goodbye Girls were saying hello to Mr. Right, and the Lonely Hearts Clubbers were doomed to endless, desperate rendezvous with Mr. Goodbar—or worse, just sitting in their apartments or taking evening "personal improvement" courses at the New School. Those perky career gals Mary and Rhoda, who were perpetually dating Mr. Husband Material himself, Casper Milquetoast—they were a figment of collective wishful thinking, which made them even more popular. Single girls, the thinking went, couldn't really be that happy. And Erica Jong's Isadora Wing? She was a desperate slut. The Big Relationship still equaled big happiness. We forged ahead, always prepared, legs always shaved. We could accidentally bump into Mr. Right at any time, right around the corner. And of course, he was actually trying to bump into us. He just didn't know it.

It was with this perspective on relationships that I walked up the narrow stairs of the tiny, crowded pit of a club on Eighth Street, behind a tall, handsome young man with long dark curls to whom I had just been introduced. He looked kind of familiar, almost in a familial way. It was so noisy I couldn't catch his name, but the club owner had attempted to introduce him and his equally tall friend to me, or the other way around, because we were all in the "music business."

My nightly hours on the radio and weekday school schedule made it impossible for me to go out anywhere in the evening, but often on Saturday nights, when my shift at WPLJ ended at 3:30 A.M., I would take a break from the weekly grind with one of the union engineers or newspersons. Sometimes I would have coffee with Rick James, a balding, almost middle-aged, chain-smoking ABC newsman with a somewhat defeated demeanor but of course a fantastic voice, as all radio guys were required to have in those days. We might stop in at Ruskay's, the newly hip, formerly regular luncheonette with the mirrored art deco motif on Seventy-fifth and Columbus, because it was right in my neighborhood, on the corner of my old block. Ruskay's had begun hosting the weekly *Saturday Night Live* television show after-party. A very rowdy over-the-moon John Belushi had more than once groped me there, and probably whoever else was next to him; the place was getting too crowded.

On this particular April middle of the night, I had hopped a cab down to the Village with Laurie Richman, a sweet, tragically fated engineer just my age, who already showed signs of the fatal Huntington's disease she had inherited from her mother. I spent extra time with Laurie because of this sad, haunting diagnosis, which resonated with me.

"So then, you work for Kiss, did I hear right?" I said to the young man, referring to the phenomenally popular cartoon-charactered, makeup-wearing rock group. "Sorry, what's your name? It was too loud in there," I continued.

"Paul," he replied.

"Oh really, what do you do for Kiss?" I asked.

"I'm in the band." He paused. He seemed so friendly; again, so familiar, maybe in a cultural sort of way.

"So which one are you?'

"I've got the star on my face," he answered, in a way that would certainly make no sense to anyone who wasn't acquainted with the personas of "those demons of rock."

"Oh yeah, Paul Stanley. Hey, how about that. We play you guys all the time on the radio. Nice to meet you." I smiled, thinking of the barrage of calls I would get nightly on the request lines from the "Kiss Army" fan clubbers.

"Yeah, Carol Miller," said Paul. "You have that kind of a name, people know it, like Patti Smith. Easy to remember. Wanna get something to eat?"

It took roughly ten seconds for me to surmise that I was talking to a fellow Jew from Queens, whose last name probably wasn't Stanley (maybe it was his middle name?), and within a few more seconds, Paul had me intrigued. Not because of his Corvette or his rock group, but because of his natural choice of late-night eatery: Sarge's Deli on Third Avenue between Thirty-sixth and Thirty-seventh, a long-time bastion of *ungeshtupt* (overstuffed), mainly Eastern European Jewish cuisine. Now here was a guy who felt comfortable with his background, and I leaped happily to that conclusion: definitely not like some of my former college classmates who rejected their own kind—of girls. Paul told me that although he was originally from Washington Heights in upper

Manhattan, he had actually grown up not far from Lefferts House, and I could hardly believe the coincidence.

When we got to Sarge's, still brightly lit after 4 A.M., Paul's bandmate Gene, the guy whose character, when wearing his makeup, stuck out his tongue and breathed fire, was already seated in a rear booth with a friend named Stephanie, who looked like another nice *haimish* Jewish girl from the neighborhood. The menus were out, and everyone was having the Souper Soup, which was a stupendous bowl of chicken soup with noodles and matzo balls and kreplach (wonton-like dumplings), so I joined in. Over a discussion about gefilte fish, Paul said that in preparation for cooking the High Holiday meals and making the gefilte fish, his grandmother would have the live carp swimming in her bathtub. Wow, that was dedication; my grandmother hadn't gone that far!

Pardon the pun, but Paul was already looking like a good catch. Sitting at the deli table with these nice boys from the neighborhood, I felt so comfortable, as if I'd known them forever. Why, they even had the same salty sense of humor that was a trademark of my father's side of the family, or maybe it was just something common to the natives of a few square miles of Brooklyn and Queens: that anything to be insulted or rejected should be (pardon me here) shoved up your ass: "You know what you can do with that [report card, broken screwdriver, fill in the blank], don't you? You can shove it right up your ass!" Positively heartwarming. Here these fellas were, also in the music business, just like me. At this point, though, if Paul would have said the garment business, it wouldn't have mattered. I felt like I was with a potentially great boyfriend. When Paul asked, "Hey, ya wanna go for a ride on the Staten Island Ferry?" the invitation sounded better to me than a voyage on the QE II. I felt like I was Cinderella getting the glass slipper.

And that was how I began a relationship with a handsome, artistic, commendably frugal, hardworking, and exceedingly neat and tidy young Jewish man of his own independent means, who just happened to wear cartoon-type makeup and spandex while singing, playing guitar, and jumping around in monster platform shoes on stages around the world for his job, which sold millions of records, concert seats, and other paraphernalia. So what about that? A job's a job, right?

I saw no evidence of any of this flamboyancy or costuming. He had phone calls, managerial meetings, recording studio sessions, and social events involving his business associates—the typical work-related sidebars. Paul's tastefully decorated East Side apartment boasted a real Tiffany lamp, and a dual identity posted on his front door above the bell: Stanley/Eisen. "Eisen's my roommate," Paul first joked, then pointed out the obvious: he was answering to two last names, when in fact Stanley was actually his first name, not Paul. Additionally, Paul pointed out, his friend Gene's name was really Hy, just like my father's. "Those demons of rock," Paul joked, referring to the Kiss moniker. "They should really call us those yeshiva *bokhers* (yeshiva students) of rock!"

My new date seemed very attentive; he visited or called just about every day, especially on the hotline while I was on the air: "Hey DJ, how ya doin'?" Among other places, Paul took me to Sammy's Roumanian on the Lower East Side, a longtime famous hodgepodge of a Jewish restaurant where you could make your own chocolate egg creams at the table. I couldn't have felt more at home. Then there was a drive out to Jones Beach one chilly afternoon where we just walked around; Paul dropped his car keys in the sand, so we spent some time retracing our steps and actually found them. At Kiss guitarist Ace Frehley's birthday party at the Bowlmor Lanes on University Place, Paul took off his gold Kiss chain and gave it to me. That meant something, right? Was it valuable? Were there a lot of these necklaces? I didn't care. It was better than Liz Taylor's diamonds. Then we went to a few rock shows; that my companion was himself a rock star, whose band had just recently been voted the number one group in America by an official Gallup Poll, could not have been detected from his behavior—"Too much smoke," Paul grimaced and waved his hand in front of his face when Rush let off their mandatory smoke display from the stage. A normal reaction from a regular patron, but not exactly what one might expect from the front man of a band whose extreme use of on-stage pyrotechnics was world renowned. But I'd all but forgotten that was his job.

Everything was going according to plan. I had a prospect here! And then one day Paul just disappeared. No calls, no visits. Kiss was about to go out on a major national tour, but I was pretty sure they hadn't left yet. After a few days of hearing nothing, I got up the nerve to dial the phone. When Paul answered, he seemed distant, and said something odd to me about "not wanting the responsibility," and then—silence. So that was it, then; it was over? Just like that, no other explanation. To say that I was crushed would have been an understatement. It was more like devastated; no, worse than that, annihilated! Numbly, I did the usual: I went on the air for my nightly New York radio show acting happy for a couple million listeners, while beginning a period of depression, intro-spection, and intense self-analysis. What had I done wrong?

Maybe Paul was angry that my friend, the ailing engineer Laurie, had shown up uninvited and unannounced while we were having dinner at Thursday's on East Fifty-eighth Street. Maybe it was my front teeth, they needed caps. Could it have been that my hair, then brown, was just too dark? Or maybe it was my apartment; I could tell Paul had not been impressed by my inexpensive decor. (Although he should have known that a smart Jewish girl was supposed to wait until she was married to invest in furniture.) I silently agonized over the smallest details of my behavior and appearance, and again ultimately concluded that I was just too ethnic, familiar, and unexciting to today's modern Jewish young man, who wanted a more exotic (meaning blond, Christian) rela-tionship experience. Yes, I was just some boring borscht, while my WASPy Christian counterpart would be a prohibited pork chop.

Out of total ignorance, I did not even consider the glaringly obvious additional point that a twenty-five-year-old world-famous makeup-wearing rock star who was constantly on tour might have another side to his personality, and just might not be interested in settling down to a life of domestic bliss while he was reportedly being constantly pur-sued by a limitless stream of groupies in every city. No, that never en-tered my mind. In defense of my stupidity, though, I had never actually seen Paul up close at a Kiss concert in his full studded-spandex regalia; in fact, I had never really thought of him other than in the ordinary way I knew him.

The shocking experience of seeing that masked, costumed, monster-sized cartoon character would come in December 1977, backstage at Madison Square Garden. I was at a loss for words as he approached.

This was my friend who liked cabbage soup and Elton John, and who had the same textured wallpaper in his living room as my mother had? No, I couldn't begin to imagine what personality transformation Paul might undergo while he performed as his alter ego.

And so, I forced myself to move on; I was already behind schedule on what I had begun to call the Agenda—the search for the husband I was supposed to already have. I would sadly have to start all over again, and time was a-wastin'. When Paul called the next year, I was already going out with someone else, whom I knew deep down inside I wasn't going to marry. The truth was, I was afraid to see Paul and get upset again, thinking his disappearing act would have an encore presentation. I never gave him another chance and didn't really know if he wanted one. As it turned out, I would see him many times over the next few years, and when I finally did get married, Paul would sometimes accompany my husband and me to places like Ratner's Deli on Delancey Street. I never let on that it still hurt. Later in time, Paul kindly sent me flowers when I was hospitalized. By then he had moved to California. And my husband, reportedly, had moved in with a nineteen-year-old.

24

"Be forewarned," newsman Rick James admonished at about 1:55 A.M. from his newsroom phone to my perch in the FM-1 WPLJ air studio on the opposite side of the eighth floor. "You have a friend who's walking around here looking for you, and he's wearing some kind of tights and scarves and has makeup running down his face."

This could only be bad. I had not given a second thought to Steven Tyler calling me again. I mean, it was great to meet him and hear some of the new stuff. He certainly was a talented singer. But he had nearly gotten me into serious trouble when he refused to wake up after downing nearly an entire bottle of red pills. And how had he gotten past the security guard in the lobby of the ABC building, into an elevator, up to the eighth floor, through the locked doors, and into the studio area? No time to inquire about that. Within minutes, Steven's face appeared through the glass cut-out window in the heavy soundproof door, which he opened. "I'm here for my interview," he announced emphatically, looking a little buzzed.

"But my show's just finished; I'm off," I pointed out, hugely relieved that I would not have to deal with refusing to put one of the world's major rock stars on the air live, because (a) I hadn't gotten clearance, and wasn't about to make calls to management at 2 A.M., and (b) every other word he said was *motherfucker.*

"Well, go back on the air, then," he said.

"It doesn't work that way. It's someone else's show now, and they'll be here in a minute."

"Okay, we can go for a ride." Steven's attention was immediately diverted. Of course, his ever-present black limo was waiting downstairs.

Why not, I thought. He seemed upbeat, fun, and likable, when he was awake—an earlier, less focused version of the same endearing personality he now shares with millions as a judge on *American Idol*. What else was I going to do? Go home and sit in my studio apartment? Besides my poor health and Paul's departure, the summer of '77 had been a particularly gloomy one for me. A schizophrenic radio listener had begun to stalk me. I had not gotten over the death of my beloved dog, Hunter, and my parents were more disgusted than ever about my choice of radio career. (If, in their opinion, one could even call radio a "career.") They had attended my graduation from Hofstra Law School, where Assistant Dean Benjamin had greeted my family and me on the campus lawn with, "It's over! Springsteen settled the lawsuit with Appel! They can go ahead with the record now!" referring to the managerial dispute that had delayed the release of *Darkness on the Edge of Town*. Not what my parents were expecting to hear on the day they figured I would come to my senses and forget this whole radio nonsense. But inside the radio, so to speak, nightly in my WPLJ studio, talking to my listener-friends was really the only place I felt comfortable, so I had decided to keep doing what I loved.

Aerosmith had been recording the *Draw the Line* album up at the Cenacle, an estate compound that had been used as a nunnery near Armonk, New York, about an hour's drive north of the city. They had recently completed a short European tour, and had embarked on a lengthy twenty-six-date U.S. jaunt. The single, "Draw the Line," had been released on October 6, 1977, but the album wasn't ready yet, reportedly due to all sorts of "distractions" at the Cenacle, and now in October, the group, in particular Steven and Joe Perry, were working at the Record Plant recording studio on West Forty-fourth Street with producer Jack Douglas, to get it finished.

They were again staying at the Hotel Navarro on Central Park South, where Steven's favorite activity was tormenting Mr. Russell, the staid,

With Joe, Fort Bragg, North Carolina, 1952.

Mommy and Daddy,
Hotel Regal, Catskill
Mountains, New York, 1941.

I dressed baby sister Jane;
Florida road trip, 1955.

Kew Gardens, Queens, New York, 1957.

With Ed Sciaky, a promotional representative, and Colin Blunstone of the Zombies, the Main Point, suburban Philadelphia, 1972.

Modeling shot,
New York City, 1966.

With Luke O'Reilly,
London, 1974.

WPLJ promotional
postcard.

With Jim Kerr and Al Stewart, WPLJ, 1977.

With Warren
Zevon at the
Bottom Line,
New York City,
1978.

With Peter Frampton,
New York City, 1977.

Some of my
ticket stubs.

With Ringo,
New York City,
1978.

With Meat Loaf,
New York City, 1978.

In the WPLJ studio, 1978.

With Jimmy Iovine, 1979.

With Stevie Nicks, Tony Pigg, and
Danny Busch, WPLJ, 1980.

WPLJ T-shirt ad, 1981.

With Jim Kerr,
WPLJ, 1982.

With Billy Idol, Tower
Records, New York City, 1982.

With Patty Smyth,
Meadowlands
Arena, New Jersey,
1983.

With Hall and Oates,
Tower Records,
New York City, 1983.

With Mark Goodman,
Stevie Ray Vaughn,
and Matt Dillon,
New York City, 1983.

With the late
Clarence Clemons,
New York City, 1985.

With Geddy Lee of
Rush at WNEW-FM,
New York City, 1985.

With Micky Dolenz of the Monkees and
Abbey Konowitch, New York City, 1986.

With Robin Zander
of Cheap Trick at the
Hard Rock Café,
New York City, 1987.

With Scott Muni, Paul McCartney, and Pat St. John, WNEW-FM, New York City, 1990.

With Robert Plant, WNEW-FM, New York City, 1993.

With Pete Townsend, WNEW-FM, New York City, 1993.

With Paul Logus,
Bob Seeger, and
Pat St. John,
New York City,
circa 1995.

With my husband,
Paul Logus, 1996.

Cooling off Scott Muni
with my portable fan, Rolling
Stones Press Conference, Bronx,
New York, 2002.

With Pamela Anderson,
New York City, 2003.

With Bruce Springsteen,
Randall's Island,
New York, 2004.

With Paul Stanley
of Kiss, Q104.3,
2005.

With Daddy, 2005.

With my sister,
"Dr. Jane" Miller, M.D.,
2005.

Family photo, 2006.

With Elaine Kaufman at Elaine's, New York City, 2008.

With Adam Lambert, the iHeart Radio Theater Presented by PC Richard & Son, New York City, 2010.

With Jon Bon Jovi at Premiere Radio Networks, for FMQB, New York City, 2010.

With David Coverdale of Whitesnake at the Q104.3 studio, 2011.

With Ryan Seacrest, New York City, 2011.

With Rob Caggiano of Anthrax and my nephew Robbie Vizcaya Miller, in Robbie's room, New Jersey, 2011.

With Steven Van
Zandt and Donovan
at United Stations
Radio Network
for *Get the Led Out,*
2012.

In the Q104.3 studio, 2012.

elderly hotel manager, as if he were a dotty old school principal. Dancing through the lobby with his boom box, setting the room curtains on fire, and, along with Joe, dumping over heavy sand-filled ashtrays in the hallways were some of Steven's extracurricular activities. Of course, all this really was funny, but as a "normal" person, I was embarrassed, and always tried to avoid eye contact with Mr. Russell.

One afternoon, I found Steven in the unlit bathroom in his suite, on his knees bent over the filled tub, methodically swirling the water in a circular fashion. "I'm doing my laundry," he explained, and sure enough, he had dumped a heap of clothing, including some reddish corduroy-looking pants, into the cold water. Another time, he showed up in typical flamboyant Tyler garb, hat and feathers, at the UJA (United Jewish Appeal) charity telethon where I was to make an appearance and then help answer the telephones on camera, along with other local "celebrities."

"There's someone to see you," said the event cocoordinator, opening the door to the large studio.

"I'm here to go on the air with you," volunteered Steven, completely innocently and earnestly, yet totally "on the planet Mongo," as he liked to say, referencing "Flash Gordon." Something about his costume and his flair for language made me think this might be a very bad idea. But who was I to insult him? It wasn't that I felt superior or anything. And a yarmulke wasn't required. It was just . . . well, this was the wrong planet. And what did Steven know about the UJA?

"Oh, but I'm really sorry, you can't come on camera with me," I said. And of course his reply: "Why not?"

"Well," I reached for an answer, "they don't have the plaque with your name already made up to put in front of you where we answer the telephones." This seemed to make sense to Steven. "Okay," he said amiably. "I'll just wait in the hall," whereupon he plunked himself down on the floor, against the wall near the studio door, until I was finished.

Although I was involved with Steven, I knew he wasn't exactly a marriage prospect for me. And of course, the Agenda demanded that I find one. Like some of the other rock musicians I had come across through interviews, etc., he seemed unusually childlike and in need of supervision. Did he, say, know how to use one of those new bank machines to get cash? Would he get lost in the subway? It didn't matter; those situations would never come up. He was taken care of by the Leber-Krebs management team; there was always an itinerary and chaperone ready, courtesy of their publicist and girl Friday Laura Kaufman, with whom I became friendly. And what about all the drugs? I saw tons of white powder around, which was offered to me, but Steven didn't seem to mind that I wasn't interested in what I was pretty sure was heroin. I did not have any real understanding of how or if it affected him—he was always "on the planet Mongo." But he was always very nice, and sincere. Yes. Nice. He reminded me of a fun friend one might have in eighth grade, who liked to snuggle and loved getting letters from his grandmother. "*Abbondanza*!" Steven would say when getting a letter from his grandma Tallarico, imitating the Mama Celeste's frozen pizza TV commercial.

Steven said he admired what he perceived to be my independent nature, and must have liked being with me because he began flying me out to his concerts on my weekend day off from my six-day radio schedule. Sometimes on a commercial airliner, once on his tiny personal plane, and a couple of trips back on Aerosmith's private jet, with the group. I went to Providence, Rhode Island; Evansville, Indiana; Omaha, Nebraska; Denver, Colorado (where the group collectively cut a hole through a hotel wall); Boston, and once to Steven's house, and I might be forgetting some of the other places I would never have seen otherwise. Of course, it was just plain exciting to be the guest of the lead singer, who always put his all into his performance, and watch the show from the side of the stage.

But something was troubling Steven. While I was with him, he would get repeated phone calls from a woman who said she'd just had his baby in July. Sometimes he'd hang up the phone on her, saying afterward, "No way it's mine. No way I'm takin' a paternity test. It's probably Roger Glover's." (Glover was in the band Deep Purple.) Sometimes at the Navarro Steven would just let the phone ring, saying it had to be her and he didn't feel like dealing with it.

I'd heard of Bebe Buell, a beautiful former *Playboy* model who reportedly had romantic relationships with a number of rock stars, like Todd Rundgren, Elvis Costello, and Jimmy Page. She was a friend of publicist

Liz Derrenger. Was Bebe a groupie? I didn't know. She wasn't an "official" groupie like the self-titled Miss Pamela or those gross Plaster Caster girls, or whoever Sweet Connie was. I had just gone out with a couple of musicians I'd met through my job, was well treated as a girlfriend, and had never seen any of the alleged debauchery (save for some hotel destruction) that people talked about. No, I'd seen airplanes, restaurants, and, most interestingly, the huge professional recording studios. (And I had studiously avoided interviewing the one group whose music I liked best, but who were surrounded by the most lurid and frightening stories about their behavior: Led Zeppelin.) Bebe Buell's reputation struck me as being more one of a prized muse to famous musicians. A woman whose feminine wiles must be staggering and inspirational, and certainly beyond mine.

So it was with complete surprise that I felt a sharp kick to my calves and a most painful slam to my ribs coming from behind. It was Bebe Buell attacking me as I entered the club Trax, having just come down the steep stairway with Steven Tyler. Stunned, but mainly embarrassed to be involved in some sort of brawl, I said something to Steven along the lines of "Hey, you can have her, I'm out of here!" as I walked quickly into the main dining room area.

And who should be sitting at a table with some friends, apparently back in town after tour dates, but Paul Stanley, whom I joined. "We're working on some stuff at Electric Lady," he said, "and there's a song you should hear. Wanna come down?"

"Sure," I said, a bit shaken, hoping he hadn't seen me enter the club with Steven and be beaten by Bebe. Grabbing a cab on down to Eighth Street and the studio, Paul played the tape of Kiss's version of "Any Way You Want It" by the Dave Clark Five, a song that I had once said might suit Kiss as a cover tune. I thought they'd done a great job on it. Paul said Kiss was going back out on the road, and dropped me off in a cab at home. I pretended to be cool about everything but ended up feeling both confused and sad, alone in my apartment.

My beating from Bebe didn't deter Steven from calling. As history tells it, years would pass before he realized Bebe's child was indeed his daughter and that he was the father of the now famous actress Liv Tyler.

And in the years since the incident, I've gotten along very well with Bebe, when I've seen her. By December 1977, the *Draw the Line* album was way behind schedule, and had to be completed. At the Record Plant studio, Steven sat down on a piano bench and asked me to join him, to his right. He started playing one of the new songs, "Kings and Queens," and morphed it into "Dream On." How simple the chords seemed, as he plunked away, and how familiar. Jack Douglas, Aerosmith's producer, seemed really burned out from all the work; plus he was going through some "heavy personal stuff." Also working in another studio at the Record Plant was David Johansen of the New York Dolls, who was accompanied by his wife, Cyrinda Foxe. As David turned around, a "little something" appeared to be going on between Steven and Cyrinda, seemingly right under David's nose. Steven and Cyrinda seemed to know each other. I felt momentarily bad for David; was his wife interested in Tyler because he was the bigger star? All this drama, in just a couple of rooms.

The *Draw the Line* album was released on December 1, 1977, to mixed reviews. My relationship with Steven had been going on for about six months. The backstage groupies even seemed to know about me, as they would whisper when I passed by. I was expecting to go on another Aerosmith "concert weekend," when the hotline rang as I was on the air at WPLJ. It was Steven.

"Listen, you know I'm no good on my own and I need someone to travel with me and be here all the time. You're independent, you have your career; that can't be you. So I'm going to give it a try with Cyrinda. So take a deep breath, and always remember I do love ya." I thought this was extremely gentlemanly. I did take a deep breath. Strangely of relief . . . even though I would really miss Steven. He would appear over the years for interviews and events, always asking if I wanted to go for a ride, and greeting me like an old friend who was giving it another try.

Around 1987, Steven and Joe were up to my radio show for an interview before their concert at the Brendan Byrne Arena in New Jersey. Steven was frightened that he was imminently going to be served with divorce papers from Cyrinda. The next evening, I broadcast my show from a press catwalk area dizzyingly high up near the arena rafters; we did these "concert coverage" shows for all the major area concerts, and the Byrne's accommodations were particularly difficult, if not just plain scary, to access. Prior to Aerosmith taking the stage, I was shocked to look up from my notepad and microphone to see Steven standing there alone with a panicky look in his eyes. "They just served me," he said; the legal process server had apparently gotten to him. "I've failed. I've failed before God," Steven said with completely sad but frantic sincerity. "What am I going to do?"

"Well, you're gonna go on and do your show and be great, like you always are" was the best I could offer, but I meant it.

By then, I thought I'd learned my lesson, all about not being in relationships where I just didn't fit in, or where there was no room for me.

I thought wrong.

25

Ba—ba—ba went the descending synthesizer notes of the 1975 instrumental track "My Sweetheart" from the album *Mother Focus,* as played by keyboardist Thijs van Leer of the Dutch group Focus. The beginning of "My Sweetheart" became our theme music at WPLJ, played near the top of every hour, over which the DJ would proclaim our station identification. Between the brilliantly highly compressed audio signal (an offense to self-appointed snotty music purists), specifically designed by Larry Berger to sear through car radios and boom boxes, and the sheer pervasiveness of station listenership (WPLJ often had an unheard-of Arbitron rating of a 25 share of teens), it was difficult to navigate even a couple of blocks in the New York City area without hearing this musical missile ricocheting from building to building.

From across the production board, I handed NABET engineer Henley Welch the top-of-the-hour Focus music tape in its plastic cartridge housing. The engineers' schedule had them moving between the various ABC studios on the hour or half hour. Henny, as we called him, slipped quickly into his chair after his methodical routine survey of the equipment and surroundings: he would slowly nod and appear to assess it all, as if entering the room for the first time. *Ba—ba—ba* went Focus. "Ninety-five-point-five WPLJ, New York's Best Rock," I declared proudly, as if reciting the Pledge of Allegiance, "with a Bee Gees–free weekend!" This meant that you, the beleaguered listener, could freely leave the radio on without the round-the-dial incessant assault of the group whose number one album, the sound track to the movie *Saturday Night Fever,* had coincidentally but nonetheless officially ushered in the disco era.

At WPLJ, we had already been playing the Bee Gees' 1975 and 1976 dance offerings "Jive Talkin'," "Nights on Broadway," and "You Should be Dancing," from their albums *Main Course* and *Children of the World,* but apparently a rock versus disco schism was brewing. This dance music was no longer being perceived as rock, and true to our slogan, "New York's Best Rock," program director Larry Berger began to prune Earth, Wind & Fire, Eddie Kendricks, and artists of that ilk from our library. Radio consultants, and in our case the very bright and affable Jeff Pollack, were rising on the horizon. From whatever source or directive, also leaving the library were the introspective, softer balladeers, such as Joni Mitchell (whom I had grown to like) with her impressive albums *Hejira, The Hissing of Summer Lawns,* and *Court and Spark.* Bye-bye to James Taylor, Carly Simon, and Linda Ronstadt.

Personally, I was very sorry to see them go. I liked it all, and still do. But it was hats off to Larry, as we also bid farewell to one of our soundly defeated two main competitors, WXLO (99X). Our Top 40 nemesis was forced to change format. Now WPLJ was free to turn its tanks toward its archrival, my former employer, the free-form WNEW-FM. Although they too would soon move from free form to a specific rock format, it seemed as though WNEW was cultivating a special, almost personal vengeance toward WPLJ.

WNEW balloons might sail over Wollman Rink in Central Park when I or one of the other WPLJ DJs hosted one of the Dr. Pepper (formerly Schaefer Beer) summer concerts such as Heart, or the Cars, and I was once physically picked up and removed from Radio City Music Hall by a burly security guard when I went backstage to say hello to Southside Johnny, who was performing at a WNEW-FM–sponsored concert.

It should have been "business is business"—after all, the DJs and station folk from the other city stations got along just fine—but suffice it to say that because of my successful run at WPLJ, when I returned to WNEW in late 1983, through to when I left in 1999 (due to a total format change), my tenure there would be fraught with tension, resentment, and insults along with the good times. After all, at WPLJ I had stepped off the pedestal and stooped to the pedestrian level of playing KC and the Sunshine Band.

While I wasn't playing James Taylor or Carly Simon on the radio anymore, however, I could still catch and promote them in concert, and one in particular was for a political cause. Shortly after the Three Mile Island nuclear accident, an activist group called MUSE (Musicians United for Safe Energy) was founded by Jackson Browne, Graham Nash, Bonnie Raitt, and John Hall to oppose the increasingly common use of nuclear energy. A series of concerts and events they organized in September 1979 included a huge rally on the north end of the Battery Park landfill in lower Manhattan. Among the performers at the series of five MUSE concerts held at Madison Square Garden were Crosby Stills and Nash, Bruce Springsteen and the E Street Band, James Taylor, Carly Simon, Chaka Khan, the Doobie Brothers, Jesse Colin Young, Tom Petty, and Poco.

I watched part of the Garden concerts from the stage, scurrying back and forth to the sound truck recording the event parked outside the Garden on Thirty-third Street. I had the privilege of proximity to the action and an all-access pass because of Jimmy Iovine, the twenty-six-year-old engineer on the recent Springsteen albums, and now the producer of Patti Smith's *Easter* album. He had also just produced Tom Petty's *Damn the Torpedoes* LP, which was about to be released on October 19. (Jimmy became one of the most powerful and wealthy executives in the music business, and you may now recognize him as the bespectacled baseball-cap–wearing musical Svengali from *American Idol*.) With Springsteen and Petty on the bill for the MUSE concerts, Jimmy had to be there.

Tom Petty preceded Springsteen on the bill, and while Springsteen was a local favorite (whom I had tirelessly supported on the radio and had recently interviewed) renowned for his theatrical, energy-filled performances with his E Street Band, Petty was hardly a household name around the New York area, with only two songs, "Breakdown" and "Listen to Her Heart," receiving moderate airplay from his then library of only two albums. One night in particular, from my vantage point on the left side of the stage, I could see that Tom Petty did not look happy. In fact, I thought he looked just plain petrified. The New York / New Jersey crowd began their now world-famous Springsteen chant, the elongated "Bru-u-u-u-u-ce!" I sensed that Petty thought they were yelling, "Bo-o-o-o-o-o-o!" and looked even more frightened during his performance of "Breakdown," which seemed almost appropriate. Within weeks, the Iovine-produced *Damn the Torpedoes* album (much of the recording of which I was fortunate to watch in various Los Angeles–based studios) would result in a commercial breakthrough for Petty, but he reportedly harbored a lingering dislike for performing in New York. Who could blame him?

Springsteen's performance was another matter. September 23, 1979, was to be his thirtieth birthday, and I experienced the full impact of the histrionics up close from stage right. It was with humorous missionary zeal that Bruce faked a heart attack, falling to the floor because of his "advanced" age. The audience roared with approval. Bruce and the band's performances were second to none. Then, Bruce apparently spotted Lynn Goldsmith, chief photography coordinator for MUSE, in the audience. I had already noticed Lynn, a fixture on the rock scene, who was a girlfriend whose relationship with Bruce had reportedly ended. She stood about twelve or thirteen rows back from the stage, and seemed to be talking to someone. Suddenly, Bruce announced, "Here's my ex-girlfriend!" walked down into the audience, grabbed Lynn's arm, hoisted her onstage, then moved her to the back in a single motion. A security guard then physically whisked Lynn offstage. I immediately ran backstage to check on the obviously distraught photographer, and found MUSE film producer/director and industry honcho Danny Goldberg and Elliot Roberts, Tom Petty's manager, literally trying to tug her away from the security guard. Lynn understandably seemed to be in shock, and kept repeating, "I want to go home. I want to go home." She then paused, regained her composure, and walked down the hall toward the exit. Over the years, I've attended press and gallery functions for Goldsmith, but have never pressed her for the details of the bizarre incident. Obviously it was traumatic, none of my business, and it's old news. That footage never made it into the MUSE film, which was shown in theaters.

A day or two prior to the start of the MUSE concert series, Springsteen and Steven Van Zandt (E Street Band member, producer, now *Sopranos* TV star and radio host) came over to Jimmy Iovine's apartment overlooking Central Park South. I had actually helped Jimmy find the apartment; he loved Central Park South and had coincidentally stayed for several months right down the street at the Navarro Hotel, where Steven Tyler and Joe Perry had tormented the hapless manager, Mr. Russell. When I visited Jimmy at the Navarro, I'd constantly feared that Mr. Russell would recognize me and conclude I was a "working girl." But now, in Jimmy's glass-fronted apartment with its sweeping views of Central Park, Iovine, Springsteen, and Van Zandt loosely huddled together near the front door. It was late afternoon, and the three were going to get a bite to eat at the Saloon restaurant on Broadway and discuss the upcoming shows. Springsteen had just joined the bill at the last moment and was hearing about the details. I had been invited along, and watched the three close friends, all genuinely sweet guys, laugh and joke around with accents and mannerisms reflecting their spirited Italian-American backgrounds. "Hey, why are they callin' it 'No Nukes,' anyway?" one of them said. "Ya know they ain't talking about the missiles," as more giggling ensued.

What was I doing at Jimmy's? He was a great friend, obviously brilliant, with musical potential, with whom I wound up having a relationship over a couple of years that never should have happened. The relationship part. Why? Because of my background. Jimmy had a wonderful, ever-present, closely knit Italian Catholic family from Brooklyn and Staten Island who could not have been nicer to me. It was I, the Jewish girl from Queens, who always silently felt out of place. No matter how I tried, I always felt like an uncomfortable outsider. Not the fault of the lovely family, in whose lives Jimmy was a daily participant. Had I been "just a friend," that wouldn't have mattered, but here there were expectations of potential marriage and inclusion in the family. Along the way, I would again observe the extremely intertwined relationships in some other Italian families. Jimmy knew that my father disapproved of the relationship on religious grounds, and in their one meeting, my father was not very nice to Jimmy, which made me feel terrible. But from my perspective, it wasn't the religion per se, it was the all-embracing cultural aspect. It would take me years, and indeed a failed marriage to a fellow Jew who even found me "too unassimilated" to his notion of American culture, for me to realize just how pervasive my Yiddish culture truly was, and how much a part of me it still is.

But it was with Jimmy and some of his great friends, like Danny Goldberg, that I had some of the best times; among them searching for fresh-squeezed orange juice at 2 A.M. in Los Angeles, because that's what Stevie Nicks wanted after a session of dumping her entire wardrobe on her bed to select an outfit. We had been to her place in Santa Monica, where she had the first huge rear-projection TV I had ever seen, and also a penchant for placing her scarves over lamps. I couldn't stop myself from pointing out the potential fire hazard.

I spent a weekend driving Jimmy, Tom Petty, and his wife, Jane, around San Francisco in a rental car—we were all there to see Bruce at the Warfield, and I also attended Bruce's famous Agora show in Cleveland. I had the privilege of watching Jimmy put together the Dire Straits *Making Movies* album, and sat across from Mark Knopfler at Jimmy's apartment while he composed one of the album's tunes—"Romeo and Juliet"—on guitar. "What do you think of this," Knopfler said, as he picked out the entire song, minus a few words. Knopfler, a former teacher who came across as quiet and intelligent, told me a bit about his family and his sister, Ruth. He would marry a woman, Lourdes, who booked the recording sessions for the *Making Movies* project at the Power Station studio.

Jimmy also played me his mixes of Springsteen's *Darkness on the Edge of Town* album, which he had recorded, and expected to mix. (That job, however, went to Chuck Plotkin, a Californian with a more laid-back approach, and understandably Jimmy was very upset. I thought Jimmy's mixes were much more powerful and energetic, and I liked them much better.) Jimmy was with me my first time at New York's renowned

Elaine's restaurant; I was there for a party revolving around a national radio special I had narrated for syndicator Bob Meyrowitz. Patti Smith was also at the event, and developed an instant dislike for me. "I don't like you coming here with my producer!" she yelled out from her table. "I don't like you!" That was the only time I ever met the now celebrated artist and author. Maybe she was just having a bad day, but the experience made me hesitate to return to the famed eatery. About twenty-five years later, the late Elaine Kaufman would become one of my dearest friends, and I miss her terribly.

❧ ❧ ❧

Jimmy was producing Graham Parker's *The Up Escalator* album along with his trusted engineer Shelly Yakus, and had Springsteen in for a session at the Record Plant in New York to record duet vocals for the song "Endless Night." I asked Bruce for his permission to petition the New Jersey State government to make "Born to Run" the official New Jersey State song; an article in the *New York Times* had reported that one was being sought. Bruce's name was becoming synonymous with the Garden State, and I thought it would be a really great way to honor him, and a fun radio campaign. Bruce giggled and seemed embarrassed, if not a little surprised by the request. But he agreed, and it was all in fun anyway. I asked for listeners' signatures on WPLJ, and we got at least a million; there were just boxes and boxes, which a small team of us, including one of Jimmy's cousins, drove down to Trenton for a public hearing at the House of Representatives on May 19, 1980. As it was an election year, this rock and roll proposition was regarded as a bit too controversial, and the House merely designated "Born to Run" as the Official Rock Theme of New Jersey (whatever that means). Not being a nut, I didn't push the issue and take it to the Senate. However, the attempt made it into the history books, and the campaign went much further than I'd thought it would.

In the fall of 1980, Jimmy began spending a lot more time working with Stevie Nicks out in California, and he eventually moved there. Although it was very difficult for me because he was such a dear friend, I knew our breakup after the two-year relationship was imminent, but would be amicable. A long time after that, Jimmy helped me with an important project, and I would still consider him a friend today.

Around the time of the breakup, there was something else weighing heavily on my mind. On May 1, 1980, just before the trip to Trenton, a series of events had been set in motion that would radically change the course of my life. And it was anything but fun.

26

It was very unusual for my mother to venture into Manhattan to meet me. I was hard-pressed to remember if she had ever accompanied me on any jaunt that didn't include the whole family. But she had insisted, with great urgency, that she come with me on that sunny Tuesday, May 6, to my appointment with Dr. Rogers, a breast surgeon whose plush office was at Park Avenue and Ninety-second Street. Frankly, I didn't understand Mommy's new concern. I had always taken myself alone everywhere, to any appointment of any nature, except for that strange visit to the Nassau County "women's doctor" in 1974, when both of my parents had escorted me, sat in the waiting room, and driven me home, all of us confident that everything was okay because the doctor had never spoken to them.

But it wasn't my imagination anymore. The lump was getting larger, and the nagging lifelong inkling that I would somehow join my mother's side of the family in dying young was still there too. And always in the back of my mind was the Central Park tarot reader whose turn of the cards foretold some sort of possible life-ending calamity before I turned forty. I decided to err on the side of caution and at least have the lump checked. But by whom? I don't recall ever having gone to a "women's doctor" after the 1974 incident. When Daddy had told me back when I was in college, "What? You don't go to a gynecologist until you're married!" was this for practical money-saving purposes or for what I suspected was Daddy's assumption that no activities in that department would ever occur before a wedding? "No *hoopie*, no *schtuppie*!" (no wedding canopy, no shoving it in) was the ever-popular Yiddish expression.

After nosing around, I had come up with the name of a Dr. Crawford on East Seventy-ninth Street, who had examined me on Thursday, May 1, with more than a little look of alarm. He had ordered a mammogram to be taken the next day, Friday, by a Dr. Zuckerman, whose bustling East Eighty-seventh Street office was packed to the gills with nervous middle-aged women, each of whom must have waited the nearly four hours, as I did, for her appointment with the balding radiologist wearing eyeglasses with extremely thick lenses. I was then instructed to call the surgeon, Dr. Rogers, on Monday, and he thought it important enough that I be seen right away, on Tuesday. My trusty red Daily Reminder appointment diary saved from 1980 tells me that I also made a "personal appearance," as we called it, for a WPLJ Rock Night at a place called JJ's Ballroom on the intervening Saturday night. I have no recollection of this no doubt suburban event. But the mandatory cheer and calm of my job were therapeutic and helped to temporarily banish any foreboding thoughts.

After my physical examination with the gray-haired, distinguished Dr. Rogers, he then greeted my mother and me in his wood-paneled office for a chat. "Did anyone in your family ever have breast cancer?" he asked. I was just about to say, "Not that I know of," when my mother, nearly shaking, blurted out, "Yes! Everybody! My mother, my aunts, and some of them with the other stuff, too," pointing in the general direction of the lower regions. I sat, speechless. How could no one have ever told me? Well, of course I would never have been told, I quickly realized. Our family had long had its own Don't Ask, Don't Tell policy firmly in effect. Was this what I had sensed all along?

"How old were they when they were diagnosed, would you know?" asked the doctor. "Late thirties, early forties, I think," said Mommy in an understandably shaky voice. "Nobody made it out of their forties. I'm the oldest one, and I don't know what I'm doing here." I knew she was telling the truth. Shortly after her fiftieth birthday, my mother had taken to calling me on the studio hotline while I was on the air, telling me that this was going to be her "last Passover." Her calls had become so disturbing that I asked for our hotline phone number to be changed, and I then told her, seriously but lightly, that she was not getting the new number because she "hadn't learned to use the phone responsibly."

Dr. Rogers then addressed me. "You have an extremely fibrocystic condition, and a fibroadenoma that has to come out as soon as possible." The fibrocystic condition, he explained, was evidenced by all those painful little marbles in my chest, which I'd assumed everyone had. The fibroadenoma was the large lump, a tumor that was usually found to be benign, at least at the beginning. Both diagnoses pointed to an unhappy path. So that was it, then.

My mother walked out of the office first, and I turned back and addressed the surgeon. "So, Doctor, would you say I'm a marked man, so to speak, for this cancer?"

"Well, he said hesitantly, "I'd say no doubt you're a candidate, but let's at least get this fibroadenoma out and take it from there." I was twenty-nine, and would barely tell a soul about the situation. Those things just weren't spoken about, even to your friends. But I had to tell Larry Berger in order to get the time off from work, and asked that he keep my secret.

Mommy and I left Dr. Rogers, with instructions for me to call his assistant to schedule the surgery. I was frightened for my mother when we took the nearly silent cab ride down to Penn Station so she could take the Long Island Railroad home. It was difficult to watch her disappear down the steps with the crowd of commuters. Mommy shouldn't be traveling alone, I thought, after such news, but my radio show would be starting in a couple of hours.

Before reporting to the ABC building, I took a walk, just to clear my head. I haphazardly asked the cabdriver to drop me off on Madison Avenue, somewhere in the mid-Sixties, just to look at all the fancy items in the store windows—furniture, antiques, clothes, glassworks. I wandered into a small store selling women's clothing on the east side of the street. A cheery reddish-pink short-sleeved shirt with a small blue embroidered bird beckoned, so I bought it to commemorate. . . . to commemorate what? I decided to name it my "lucky bird shirt." Freud would have enjoyed analyzing the nature of my other purchase, a new bra. Who knew if I was going to be able to wear it? Later, I would precede each of many surgeries with a purchase I would call my "garment of optimism"—something like a tank top or other item that couldn't be worn unless I was put back together. At the time of this writing, I recently purchased another such garment, a pair of black stretch leggings with fashionable side zippers.

Realizing that there were some important dates coming up, the "Born to Run" campaign trip to Trenton on the nineteenth, and then a talk I had promised to give on the twenty-second to a class at my former high school, Herricks, I scheduled the surgery for Tuesday, May 27, even though the doctor had suggested an earlier date. There was no way I could blow off my high school, as they had additionally given me the honor of being the upcoming commencement speaker for the graduating class of 1980 at the end of June. Nowadays, a surgery such as a biopsy or removal of a tumor would be just that, but back then, you had to sign a consent form beforehand for a full mastectomy if the surgeon felt it to be necessary while he was doing the operation. So I didn't know what they were going to find, or how long it would take to heal up, and didn't want to run the risk of missing those events. Also, back in the "old days," you would (brace yourself for this) check into the hospital the day before your surgery, as if you were checking into a hotel, and get treated like a person. And the bills? You had your major medical coverage, and everything worked just fine, or fine enough. Don't get me started!

I checked myself into Roosevelt Hospital on Manhattan's West Side on Daddy's birthday, Monday, May 26, to a continued chorus of nurses and techs clucking, "Oh, too bad, you're so young." The food was passable, mainly because I ordered the fruit salad, but that evening's episode of *Dallas* had Miss Ellie being diagnosed with breast cancer.

The next morning, I was sedated in my private room and wheeled into surgery. I awoke with my chest completely bandaged and flattened, and had no idea what was underneath. My parents were there, along with my father's sister, Aunt Mildred, and her husband, Uncle Saul, and

I awoke to the sounds of a loud Yiddish conversation. Two-year-old Marc, Mildred and Saul's grandson, made his presence known by immediately throwing his bottle under my bed and then crawling through and around the medical equipment to retrieve it. Mommy told me I did not have a mastectomy, but frankly, I didn't believe her until the bandages were removed days later. What did a mastectomy look or feel like anyway?

Dr. Rogers was happy to tell me that the fibroadenoma was benign, but things looked "a little messy" in there. He and Dr. Crawford would in effect check me four times a year, and I would have a mammogram every eighteen months. There was to be no coffee or chocolate, and the Pritiken diet was recommended. The Sword of Damocles was now officially over my head. But still, you didn't talk about those things.

27

It was because of one of my money-saving binges that I saw the assassin. Growing up with Depression-era parents, the penny-saved-is-a-penny-earned concept was never lost on me. Actually, they never exactly said it that way. In Yiddish, the term for being frugal is *shporadic* (as opposed to being a *shnorer*, which means "cheapskate"). For me, being *shporadic* translated into weeks in which I would forgo the convenience of five-minute taxicab rides in favor of circuitous thirty-minute MTA bus rides to the same destination, just to save a few dollars.

On that partly sunny Friday afternoon of December 5, 1980, I disembarked from the M10 just above the northeast corner of Central Park West and West Seventy-second Street, having avoided an unnecessarily expensive taxi zip home through Central Park. Looking west while waiting for the traffic light to change, I took in a familiar sight: an NYPD police car double-parked in front of the Dakota restaurant, an overly large coffee shop / luncheonette so named because it was almost directly across the street from the famed nineteenth-century fortress of an apartment building of the same name. The Dakota was home to a number of celebrities, at the time, most notably Lauren Bacall and John Lennon (with, of course, Yoko Ono).

My window stared directly down at the roof and western wall of the Dakota. Just the idea of having a Beatle move in "right next door" was exciting. Lennon would often be seen around the neighborhood, say, at the Green Cleaners across Columbus Avenue, or the Ve za Ve haircutters further down the south side of West Seventy-second Street, between Broadway and West End Avenue. Paul and Judy ran the shop, but my hair-cutter and colorist (I was in there all the time covering those premature grays) was Bob. Bob also became Lennon's haircutter, and he called me one day to let me know that my color appointment coincided with Lennon's trim. Not wanting to chat with the world-renowned musician while covered with a glob of brown dye on my head, I changed the appointment.

Sometimes Bob would be dispatched to the Dakota for an in-house cut for Lennon, and a couple of times had taken a note from me, telling John, an avid radio listener, that I would be playing his new record on WPLJ that night. Bob noted that Lennon had commented on the lax security at the Dakota; despite the manned outside guard box and the formidable gate to the inner courtyard, he'd called the security situa-tion there "a joke." The fact that Lennon had taken notice was encour-aging. Frankly, I thought he had been looking a little thin and zombielike, as if he were on some kind of sedative, and appeared at times oblivious to his surroundings as he floated down the street, especially when he was with Yoko. He did not look particularly happy.

Crossing Central Park West and approaching the Dakota guard box, I noticed another familiar scene, someone loitering in the entrance to the driveway, right under the guard's nose. What's wrong with this place? I often thought. There were some celebrities in my building too, but front-door hangers-on would be discouraged and repeatedly dismissed by our crackerjack team of doormen. It seemed like there was always at least one person hovering in front of the Dakota driveway gates, waiting for a brush with greatness or posing for a picture. Today's loiterer was par-ticularly peculiar. He was a young man of average height, with brown hair and heavy glasses, who was clutching a John Lennon album and rocking back and forth, side to side, as he waited directly next to the guard's quarters.

At this point, the policemen across the street seemed to be sharing a joke as they exited the Dakota restaurant, clutching what looked like a couple of cardboard cups of coffee and maybe a doughnut. For a split second I thought to call them over and ask them to usher away the nut job, but what for? He'd only be back, and the Dakota security would again do nothing about it, I figured. As I brushed by the strange young man, the security guard, who stood slightly elevated above ground level in his box, momentarily caught my eye as he looked up from the comic book in which he was heavily engrossed. "Hi, honey," the uniformed guard said, chomping on a wad of gum and nodding and immediately returning to his reading. Apparently the agitated loiterer with the John Lennon album was of no concern to him that day. Or the next. Whether or not it was the same guard working on Saturday, I have no idea, but there he was again—the guy with the glasses and the John Lennon album, rocking side to side, side to side.

I had gone for a ride to New Jersey on Sunday, my day off, but of course was back for work on Monday, December 8. The entry for that day in my appointment book reads "Call Janine during show," and lists the phone number and address of a friend on East Sixty-first Street. Leaving work that night at ten (my air shift had been changed to an earlier slot, 6 to 10 P.M., in 1979), I sprang for a cab from the ABC building over to the Isle of Capri restaurant on Third Avenue, which was on the corner of the street where Janine lived. After a quick snack, we went up to her apartment, where I would say a brief hello to her husband, Jon.

When we came in, he reported he'd just heard about something to do with John Lennon. Saying good night, I made my way into the elevator and down the street west to Lexington Avenue, and caught another cab (my money-saving bus rule didn't apply at night), which made its way around into the north drive of Central Park en route to home. The cabbie was listening to a police band radio, which is not an uncommon entertainment in New York. "Man down on Seventy-second," it squawked; then the words "John Lennon" and a garble of other sounds and sirens. It's him! I immediately thought. My stomach began to knot, and as the cab approached West Seventy-second Street, the wooden police barricades already blocking the exit came into view. "We'll have to go around again to another exit," said the cabbie, to whom I replied, "No, just let me off here, in the park."

Jumping out of the cab, I ran frantically toward the barricades, where a large group was already gathering. "They just took him away. He's dead," whipped through the crowd. I immediately felt faint, over-whelmed, nauseated, and tearful, and said to no one in particular, "I know who the guy is. I'm tellin' you, he's crazy. I saw him. I saw him! He's been hanging around!" A reporter for *Time* magazine, already on the scene, overheard me, asked for a description, and then my name. Not thinking of any consequences, I told him who I was and what I did, never imagining my comments would end up in print. But they did, as the closing words of *Time*'s report on the tragedy. My description of the now identified assassin as "looking crazy" did not go unnoticed by his lawyers, and they began calling the ABC legal department in order to use me as a witness for their planned insanity defense. Of course, I wanted no part of this, and was greatly relieved, if such an emotion could be attached to this horror, that the confirmed assassin decided to enter a guilty plea.

The next morning, Tuesday, December 9, the world had changed. Everyone was calling everyone from his or her childhood on up to commiserate. We had a planned eleven thirty music meeting at WPLJ, which I, along with several others, numbly attended. "How could this have happened? How could this have happened?" was the constant refrain. And what a terrible *shandeh* for our neighborhood. The pundits waxed philosophical about fame, society, and violence, and certainly noted that the transportation of the murder weapon, the gun, into the city was a huge factor. Perhaps the assassin's aberrant behavior might have been noticed at another location, and he might have been frisked and the gun discovered. Even if he had not been subject to a search, had he not been able to stake out and remain at one location waiting for his victim, his crime might have been more difficult to commit. So if you ask me "How could this have happened?" I always reply, "Bad building security." I told this to Yoko Ono a couple of years later during a conversation with her and her companion Sam Hadtavoy, after a national live interview show I had just done with her for Westwood One syndicators. Perhaps she had something else on her mind, but strangely, Yoko did not seem that concerned. Or perhaps she already knew.

28

The reddish rented town car cruised the streets of Fort Lee, New Jersey, in search of a tacky little bar called the Loft. MTV had picked that location for its launch party because it was near the technical facility that would broadcast the brand-new cable service to a few thousand local residents. Brenda, Mark, and I got out of the car in the bar's rear parking lot and made our way into the small, dimly lit entrance for the festivities. Brenda Cooper was my British friend and we looked very much alike. Actually, the person Brenda most resembled was her identical twin sister, Sandy, whose boyfriend Phil was one of the guys who ran Trax, which is where I had met the twins. "Triplets!" people would often say after a quick passing glance at the three of us together on the street. I had thought it would be fun to have Brenda come along to the party, plus it might bolster Mark's ego to appear with two look-alike dates. Not that his ego needed any bolstering, but this was a special occasion. It wasn't every day that MTV would begin its first broadcast, which would commence at exactly 12:01 A.M. EDT on August 1, 1981, and Mark Goodman was to be the first on-screen VJ, or video jockey. Within a year, he would be my first husband.

I had met Mark in 1980, at WPLJ, where he briefly followed me on the air as a DJ before leaving for this new brewing video venture. It was shortly after my breast surgery; I was still wearing a bandage, feeling more unsettled than ever about my prospects for a date with cancer, and now especially, in light of the health development, any date with marriage. But Mark seemed to fit the bill: I instantly fell for his tall, curly-haired good looks; we had similar interests, such as skiing, music, and broadcasting, and coincidentally some of the same friends; plus, he was Jewish. Of course, I would have to reveal my health issues, hoping that he too would keep my secret, which still only a couple of people knew about. Mark said he didn't care if I faced more breast surgery in the future, adding that he "wouldn't care if I had them both cut off." That sealed the deal for me. A dreamy, successful Jewish guy with compassion! Now here was my Candidate! I let the scenario play out without pressuring him, and after two years, we were married. We had a lovely wedding ceremony at Tavern on the Green in Central Park, officiated over by a rabbi recommended by my father, and we accepted my parents' gift of plane tickets and a hotel for our honeymoon in Paris. It was hard for me to believe that I had finally accomplished the marital goal. My studio apartment was really tight for two people, but we were saving up for a bigger place in our now expensive co-op building. Most of our free time was spent socializing outside of the apartment anyway.

Entering the launch party, Mark was of course greeted by his new fellow VJs, directors, and executives. You probably know the story, that MTV was basically the creation of a brilliant young programming executive, the charismatic Bob Pittman, whose business trajectory has continued upward like the rocket on the first MTV logo. Pittman is now the CEO of Clear Channel Media and Entertainment. Everyone in the radio and acting businesses auditioned for the VJ jobs, and even though I would never have quit radio even if forced to do so for MTV, I auditioned, but didn't make the cut. Of course, I sniffed around and inquired as to why, and the scuttlebutt was that certain appearance types had been cast, and I fit neither of the two female molds: the childlike, perky, clean-cut, brunette girl next door (which went to Martha Quinn) and the slightly decadent rocker chick with the blond shag haircut (which went to Nina Blackwood). "Too New York and Jewish," was what I heard about me. I was slightly miffed that my mental compendium of musical knowledge based on my then already nearly ten years of being a major-market radio DJ didn't matter. But working at America's most-listened-to rock station was my priority anyway.

I couldn't see this video service actually eclipsing radio, because it seemed to me to be a different animal, more of a complement. You had to watch it, and who could do that while driving a car? Who could have cable TV in a car anyway? However, many radio programmers reacted heavily to the new medium as it grew, and I contemporaneously wrote several "scholarly" pieces about how playing only the one new hit song represented by a video from any rock album was killing our AOR (album-oriented rock) format and skewing our library toward albums from the pre-MTV era, where several songs from each LP had become familiar to the mass audience. This was the de facto beginning of the Classic Rock genre.

Not that the radio programmers did not have reason to feel threatened; MTV aggressively positioned itself as the wave of the future, which would surely leave fuddy-duddy old FM rock radio in a cloud of dust along with the Lone Ranger and his faithful companion, Tonto. After all, the first video to be broadcast on MTV was called "Video Killed the Radio Star," by the Buggles, and was presented by Mark Goodman. I couldn't help taking this personally. And it was my impression that all the principal presenters soon began to develop rather grand opinions of themselves and their importance, except for the late J. J. Jackson. My opinion of at least one of the future celebrities was formed within seconds of meeting her at the launch party; she was wearing a loosely crocheted vest, and there appeared to be nothing under it.

Perhaps in reaction to all this, but perhaps not, and just for fun, I accepted a couple of offers to actually appear in music videos. One was for MTV's production of George Thorogood's "Rock and Roll Christmas." I wanted to see how these videos were made. My best "acting" job can be seen in the 1983 video for "All of the Good Ones are Taken," by Ian Hunter. If you find it on YouTube, I'm the girl with the side ponytail who rolls her eyes in a riveting display of mock boredom. My appearance is confined to the first part of the video, however, because there was no way I was going to stay up two nights in a row with no sleep after my radio show for seventy-five dollars. I also played the role of the introductory newscaster for "Sentimental Street," by Night Ranger a couple of years later, because in real life I had a stint as a bit music reporter from New York on *Entertainment Tonight*.

It was for *ET* that I got to cover the Live Aid concert in Philadelphia in 1985, conducting on-camera interviews in the 102-degree heat, first with Robert Plant, surrounded by roadies and of course the video crew. Plant said he had just spoken by phone to his teenage daughter back in England who thought Dad's performance was less than stellar. I also interviewed a very sweaty, bare-chested, chubby Ozzy Osbourne, from whom I tried to keep my distance because of his flying perspiration. Then there were Chrissy Hynde, Cher, and several others. Some of my fellow radio comrades were annoyed because the national television crews were given preference over radio for first crack at the interviews. Their feelings were understandable, but it wasn't my fault; I was working for TV that day.

For me, the highlight of these first MTV years was their annual star-studded New Year's Eve bash, held at various slightly decaying but hip ballrooms around New York. As the wife of one of the VJs, I was allowed a special all-access pass and could bring a friend; my husband would be working and have little time for me. My sister, Jane, already a physician, was there one year, and became engrossed in a conversation with Cyndi Lauper about how Cyndi's new CD was great to play in the operating room during surgeries. But my usual companion was Joann Brancale (now Moorhead), an ABC technical engineer, who was always up for joining me in a few drinks and mischief. Sometimes her husband, Cliff, would show up as well. I would finish my radio show and be met downstairs by a fancy black limousine, which would take me uptown to the apartment, where I would change as quickly as possible into the party clothes I had set out on the bed. Extra makeup would be slapped on, and then I'd go pick up Joann in the limo. We clutched our passes tightly, and our purses, ready to fight the crowds milling about in the freezing winter temperature, hoping to gain entrance.

One thing was certain every year; even though I was the wife of one of the hosts, I would be shoved around like a second-class citizen if I tried to get anywhere near him. Especially for the Happy New Year's countdown toasts, which were held for each time zone. Who would care if I accidentally got in range of the camera along with all the other lunatics? Would my head block the view of one of the Georgia Satellites? By the end of the evening, each year, I would be hoppin' mad, my anger no doubt fueled by a couple of glasses of chardonnay and champagne.

At the end of this particular bash (I think it was 1986), when it was time to leave and proceed on to who knew where, after first running around in the street to attempt to identify our limo among the fifty or so others that were waiting, I was dispatched to get our coats. No problem for me; I had hidden mine under a sofa and periodically checked on it. But when I went upstairs to the open VJ room, Mark's coat was nowhere to be seen. I was livid; these were expensive coats, and Mark had paid for his through our jointly run little entertainment corporation because he could wear his coat on camera.

Now I began a blazing, if not methodical, sweep of every floor of the premises. Downstairs, near the ballroom floor, sat a scrawny group of rockers I didn't quite recognize; I think they were the Church, but I'm not exactly sure. Obviously drunk, they began mocking and baiting me in their Australian accents, saying things like "Aw, didja loose your head, sweetheart? I'll help ya find it—it's probably up your ass." I continued to check under the various chairs, and the lead little scrawn continued to blabber his insults at me. Finally, I could take no more. "Listen, you douche bag!" I roared at him. "While my husband was busy introducing you and your no-talent piece-of-crap group, someone was stealing his coat, and I'm lookin' for it!"

Elated, and suddenly transfixed, the scrawny little perpetrator said, "Douche bag? Did you call me a douche bag? Wow. How cool. I love you! Can I come with you wherever you're going?" Huh? I shook my head in disbelief, and disgusted, returned upstairs, found Mark, and reported that his coat was still missing. Tagging along right behind me was my new douche-bag friend, who indeed managed to squeeze, uninvited, into our limo and on to a party at a place with strange white and green wallpaper. Mark never did find the coat, but reported that he thought he'd seen someone wearing it in the street.

As for the strange phenomenon of guys who enjoy being insulted, this was not the only time I would experience it. In a very similar situation at an MTV New Year's Ball, where I'd had just about enough of being pushed around, Ian Astbury, lead singer of the Cult, grabbed a cigarette out of Mark's mouth. When Astbury then immediately crossed over to my pedestrian side of the adjacent red velvet rope, I grabbed the cigarette back, hit him with my purse, and grabbed his long hair. "Whaddya know, it's not a wig!" I said. Barely a couple of days later, Ian Astbury was scheduled at the last minute to come up to my radio show for an interview. When he entered the studio, he recognized me immediately and gave me a huge grin. "Hey," he said, "aren't you the girl that hit me with the purse? That was pretty good! I didn't see it comin'!" The interview went off without a hitch.

29

But the eighties were not without plenty of other hitches. My endless rounds of cancer-seeking examinations, probes, and mammograms (which I secretly called "death watch") had begun, plus, of course, my now legitimatized-by-marriage visits to the gynecologist. There was a link for cancer between the two areas, so that was another thing to watch. Actually, I didn't use the word *cancer*, and it still makes me very uncomfortable even to write it. In person, I still call it "you know," and then, if explanation is needed, "the Big C." I always had a few days' pause, a mental deep breath of relief, after "passing" a Big C exam, and then the date of the next appointment loomed closer on my calendar. I grew accustomed to the feeling of living from exam to exam, and subconsciously developed a habit of purchasing only the minimum number of personal necessities—rolls of subway and bridge tokens and the like—because who knew if I would ever get to use any extras?

I had a friendly acquaintance named Susan Buchbinder, who was a friend of Laurie Richman, the technical engineer at ABC who I thought was already displaying early symptoms of her mother's fatal Huntington's disease. The three of us would sometimes get together for lunch at a place on lower Seventh Avenue called the Buffalo Roadhouse. At the time of my initial surgery in 1980, Laurie told me that Susan had gone in for a similar operation, but the Big C had appeared. Since no one spoke of it, I was instructed never to reveal to Susan that I knew of her operation, and I assumed Laurie had told the same thing to Susan about mine, so the three of us would just sit there and pretend to be jolly. When it came about that Susan had returned to the hospital out on Long Island for further surgery (during which time her father had suddenly died), Laurie told me it was now okay to call her there to wish her well. "I'd like to visit; I have a present for you, a special book I'd like to bring out," I said, never revealing my own situation. "Thank you, but keep your presents, don't bother," said Susan. Within a few days she was dead. Within a few years, Laurie too was dead, of Huntington's. My rounds of "death watch" continued, and I dutifully never missed an appointment.

In the spring of 1983, Mark and I went to an Arista Records party at the invitation of Mark's lifelong friend Abbey Konowitch, a promotional executive for that company, and as usual, Abbey was accompanied by his friendly and adorable wife, Candace. The event was held at some new darkly lit country-and-western-themed restaurant downtown, and among the other amusements was a fortune-telling Gypsy with a head scarf. Ha ha, what the heck, as I sat down across from her in the wooden chair and presented my right palm for the reading. Within seconds, a look of consternation crossed her face. Of course, I had seen the same expression on the face of my Central Park tarot card reader. "What?" I said. "Whatever you do, do it before you're forty," she admonished. There was no time for me to question the Gypsy about this coincidence; the next party reveler was in line for his chance with the savant. I dismissed the prediction, thinking that this must be something all fortune-tellers did, a gimmick, but if you hear the same thing twice, well, it's got to stick somewhere in the back of your head, right?

Bearing no relation to the Gypsy's forecast, however, a major change in my career was about to happen. Mark and I had just returned from our early summer vacation, a week in Cannes, France. Traveling was a much more affordable and easy journey in those days, even flying business class, or whatever class it was where you could walk around, go up and down a staircase in the plane, and, if I remember correctly, get a drink at a bar. We had stayed at the Hotel Majestic, toward the western end of the beachfront La Croisette, and I had begun a humorous count of the number of days since I had heard a Led Zeppelin record. I actually missed them; the mighty Zeppelin were still my blast-out-of-your-mind favorites. "It's five days now," I would laugh. "You play more Led Zeppelin than anyone," Abbey Konowitch had recently joked, and I calculated it must be true, because WPLJ had "dayparted out" some of the heavier guitar-riffed songs and designated them for evening play, which was predominantly on my shift. Abbey had subsequently presented me with a soft-covered Led Zeppelin songbook as a birthday present. Along with Mark and Candace, we'd had a funny car ride one day where we attempted to sing "Stairway to Heaven" from the songbook. We were up to nine days when Mark and I returned from our trip.

We landed back in New York on Monday, July Fourth, so I could participate in the yearly WPLJ boat ride around Manhattan, where the DJs would mix and mingle with contest winners as we took in the Macy's fireworks display. The boat was to depart from the West Side, at. . . . where? Which pier was it again? We had stopped at Little Italy's S.P.Q.R. Restaurant on Mulberry Street for a bite to eat en route to the event, and I went downstairs to make a pay-phone call to the WPLJ studio hotline, to double-check the departure address.

Pat St. John picked up the phone, and as was the custom when the DJ was just about to speak on the air, simply placed the phone down on the side of the desk near the microphone. I could hear Pat speaking rapidly over the introduction of a pop Rod Stewart song—it was either "Young Turks" or the newly released single "Baby Jane." Throughout our competition-fighting evolution at WPLJ, the DJs had been instructed either to speak over the introductions (talk-ups) or, in a more laid-back fashion, simply to introduce the song cold, without speaking over the music. When I had left on vacation the week before, we hadn't been doing rapid talk-ups, and we definitely weren't playing that Rod Stewart song.

"Hey, Pat, it's Carol. Just got back from vacation," I said. "Is there, uh—something I should know about?"

"You might say so," said Pat, in a dry tone.

I returned upstairs feeling like I'd just been punched in the stomach, and apparently had a shaken look on my face. "You're not gonna believe this," I said to Mark. "WPLJ just changed format!" Indeed, there had been a meeting on June 30, when I was away, announcing that the station was abandoning the rock format for a CHR (contemporary hit radio) configuration, more or less a new euphemism for Top 40. But why?

Of course, there were many corporate reasons, to which I would not be privy, but basically WPLJ's great ratings were based mostly on teens, the twelve- to seventeen-year-old audience, and the station wanted to "up the demos" to the eighteen- to thirty-four-year-old populace, who would have more money to spend, and hence the commercial sales department could bring in more lucrative commercials than Oxy 5 pimple cream ("Hate pimples? Oxecute 'em!"). Also, there were new fault lines developing in musical tastes; the new-wave Elvis Costello / B-52's enthusiasts were losing interest in the lengthy dirges by Neil Young and Yes. And, of course, there was the MTV factor. As I had suspected, many of the rock programmers were jumping solely on the song from a new album that was released as a video; such a song would be immediately co-opted and played more frequently by a CHR / Top 40 station in a particular market. And rumors were swirling of the impending arrival of such a CHR station in the New York market: Z100. I was never sure whether or not beating this potential competitor to the formatic punch was a factor in WPLJ's June format change, but WPLJ had recently started adding some uncharacteristic, "out of context" selections to the library, including—the most shocking—Irene Cara's "Flashdance—What a Feeling," which left many listeners scratching their heads. (I had heard a report of one guy driving off the road.)

To the more silent majority of WPLJ's listenership, the now-official-as-of-June-30 gradual morph from the AOR to the CHR arena was not noteworthy, and many of them, especially young women, left their dials on 95.5. However, when we began playing Sergio Mendes's "Never Gonna Let You Go," and "True," by Spandau Ballet, I started getting violent reactions, even bomb threats, on the request lines. "Just don't answer the phones," said Larry Berger.

Why did the format have to be so drastically changed? Why couldn't it just be carefully updated a bit? WPLJ had a huge listenership and dedicated following; why couldn't some of the longer Neil Young dirges like "Cowgirl in the Sand" be retired, and mostly up-tempo MTV pop hits be mixed in with our usual fare of Pat Benetar and Van Halen? After all, Eddie Van Halen was proudly playing guitar on Michael Jackson's "Beat It." I didn't recall a huge video for "Never Gonna Give You Up" by Sergio Mendes, for example, so why did we have to play that?

I expressed my opinion to Larry. Maybe I shouldn't have, but it wouldn't have mattered anyway. I fully intended to stay on with the new format even though the change left me very surprised; indeed, I relied upon the work to support myself and, most importantly, now needed the AFTRA union benefits for my cancer scans. WPLJ had been my home for eight years, and New York radio positions were extremely hard to come by. I wasn't going to leave this great job over having to play a couple of different recording artists. But one by one, some of our small staff of DJs were fired, and of course I was nervous. As the early evening mainstay, I couldn't imagine whom Larry would be considering at this exact point in time to take my place. I found out on Columbus Day, Monday, October 10, 1983, which was coincidentally the day before Mark's birthday.

Larry Berger had called me in to a meeting that day, an odd time, since the ABC business offices were empty. The 4 P.M. sun filtered from the west through the blinds and made me squint as I sat in the chair facing his desk. I was already a bit tense. Actually, any personal meeting with Larry would cause a stomach ache, because such meetings would always include the playing of a "skimmer tape," a tape from a cassette machine that was triggered to record only when the radio microphone was on and to contain only what I'd said on my show from a random night—without the music. Then Larry would offer his criticism, correction, and guidance. I found it very difficult to listen to my own voice under these circumstances.

But this time, I didn't see a cassette box. Not a good sign. Larry seemed tense as well, as he began the comments he had prepared. Unknowingly, Larry agreed with Abbey Konowitch: From the audience's point of view, he said, I was the most highly associated of his staff with Led Zeppelin and the rockers of that ilk. I had aligned myself with them and gotten into the persona of being the champion of their music and lifestyle. Well I had, hadn't I? And I loved the music. According to Larry, the audience would not "believe" my earnest presentation of an Irene Cara. While I acknowledged that this might be true for some listeners, I figured the rest of them just knew my voice and expected to hear me on WPLJ, where just a few years earlier we had presented Earth, Wind & Fire and Barry Manilow. Another paramount issue to Larry was that I had not come from a Top 40 background. So what? I thought. I could do the talk-ups, and the listeners didn't know or care what format background the DJs came from. But Larry had made his decision. There would be no place for me at the new WPLJ.

In tears, I entered the adjacent "jock lounge" office, gathered my belongings from my locker, stuffed them into a paper shopping bag, and walked into the air studio to say good-bye to Pat St. John. But Pat already knew of my dismissal. It seemed that the new on-air schedule had already been posted on the studio bulletin board, with the name Peter Bush in the 6 to 10 P.M. slot. Who was he, did Pat know? Apparently someone from a smaller-town Top 40 station in Connecticut. In the end, Larry would keep only morning man Jim Kerr and afternoon host Pat St. John, the two guys with the great voices who had started their careers as Top 40 DJs in Michigan.

My mascara was beginning to run and burn my eyes from the tears as I clutched my white paper shopping bag and made my way downstairs to Sixth Avenue, where I hailed a cab home. Within two blocks, the cab got into an accident, hitting another car. Despite the protest of the cabdriver, I immediately jumped out and ran before the police came; no way was I going to deal with this hassle while my professional life was falling to pieces. Arriving home in a different cab, I dropped my paper shopping bag on the floor and turned on the radio to hear Peter Bush. He sounded pleasant, but I didn't think he was doing anything I couldn't do. Taking the high road, so to speak, I called him on the studio hotline to wish him well, and he was very gracious. After all, my termination wasn't his fault. (But for whatever reason, Peter Bush would only last about a year at WPLJ.) Mark came home, I told him of my plight, and we went downtown for his birthday dinner with a group of friends he had invited. I was supposed to have joined them after getting off the air as usual at 10 P.M. Suffice it to say, it was very hard for me to pretend to be in the mood for a birthday party. And my eyes were puffy from crying.

The next day, I got on the horn to several radio stations to look for a new job. This type of call would be difficult for anybody, but for me, with my lifelong phonophobia, it was gut-wrenching torture. The most likely station for me to work at because of the rock association would be the more eclectic but now formatted WNEW-FM, where I had previously worked before becoming one of their archenemies from WPLJ. Mark put in the call to Scott Muni, saying, "Hey Scott, someone wants to talk to you," and passing the phone to me. That way I wouldn't have to set off a firestorm of gossip by announcing myself through the phone secretary at the main desk. After then talking to the program director, Charlie Kendall, who told me there were no positions available at the time but we'd have lunch (which we did) and he'd "keep me in mind," I called the rather new on the scene (and ultimately short-lived) WAPP, where I was assured that they'd squeeze me into the schedule somewhere. We'd stay in touch, and I would call on an appointed date within a couple of weeks.

I made the customary cassette copies of recordings from my on-air performances, called "air checks," which were used for job seeking, and sent them around. Somewhat ironically, I received a full-time offer for a midday slot from Frankie Crocker, the late program director of rhythm, blues, and dance-oriented WBLS. Apparently Frankie did not know of my "inappropriate" rock background as he reviewed the Top 40 CHR WPLJ sample I had sent him.

During these several weeks of unemployment, I considered getting out of the radio business and possibly finally going into law but wondered who would want to hire me, as I was now in my early thirties and had not yet practiced. I also wondered how I would be able to keep up my heavy schedule of "death watch" doctors' appointments while working an all-day job with normal business hours. I sorely missed sitting there every night with my music and my radio friends.

When Mark received an assignment from MTV to interview Paul McCartney at the AIR recording studios in London, where he was recording the music for his *Give my Regards to Broad Street* film, I jumped at the chance to go. McCartney remembered me as the WPLJ DJ from my previous encounter with him, and it was really exciting to see him working alone in the studio with George Martin as he produced incidental music to match the film footage. "Hey, that looks just like you," I said jokingly of McCartney's image on film, as I stood right next to him. "Yeah, well, it's not me, you know. Remember, I'm dead," he said dryly, referring to the ridiculous rumor that had floated around in the late sixties. I had several amusing conversations with him in the studio canteen, and then asked for a restaurant recommendation for dinner. He mentioned one of his favorites (I forget the name) but then quickly added, "But it's a little expensive."

"Expensive for who? For you?" I instantly mouthed off in my best Jewish New York accent. McCartney recanted and said he'd have reservations made for us, and that if we told the maître d' that we were his friends, the sommelier would bring us a free bottle of wine. I thanked him but said with a half smile, "Oh, sure, like the maître d' is going to believe us." We were very surprised to be treated especially nicely at the restaurant and indeed received a free bottle of wine.

Upon our return to New York, I received a phone call from Mike Kakoyiannis, the general manager of WNEW-FM, saying there was "no way" he was going to let me go over to WAPP, where I had been told I could start that weekend. "Everybody knows you," he said, which I thought was very kind. He told me to meet him downstairs at a bar/restaurant near the UN, which was not far from the WNEW studios at 655 Third Avenue. Although there wasn't an immediate full-time opening, Mike said there would be one very soon, and I should start by doing some weekend shifts. It was now December. We shook hands on an agreement, and I reported to the late-night show to learn how to engineer the equipment. The DJs at WNEW "ran their own boards" (as had the DJs at WPLJ for a year or so, since those engineering union positions had been "bought out" by ABC).

The WNEW air studio, with its somewhat tattered carpet and walls jammed with albums, was funky and felt like home. It was good to be back surrounded by my rock music. I sat down at the side table to the right of the DJ on the air, manning the board at one of the microphones used for interviewing guests. "We have someone special here tonight. I think you know her," the host said as he switched on and potted up my mike. The first words that popped into my head were meant humorously, but they were truthful. "I thought I'd never see another Led Zeppelin album again!" We had stopped playing them at WPLJ. I laughed out loud, having concluded that my long-standing favorites were the most representative group of rock-formatted radio.

After working a couple of weekends and filling in for other DJs during the week, especially during the evening, I was given a secret tip-off by the program director, Charlie Kendall, as to the start date of my full-time job, but I was not to be told the hours. "See my desk blotter," he said of the flat board covered by a large calendar. "Now watch my pencil," as he let it fall on Monday, January 9. I reported that day for a meeting in his office at 3 P.M. "Congratulations." He grinned. "You've got the evening show, five to nine P.M." Unbelievable. I'd gotten my job back.

The pressure was on and the welcome was predictably frosty when I rejoined the WNEW-FM staff for my full-time evening shift after those few weekends and fill-ins. Two DJs had been fired in order that I be hired, never a morale-booster for the rest of the team. Besides program director Charlie Kendall and general manager Mike Kakoyiannis, the only person who overtly understood the reason for my hiring was the station's founder and guru, Scott Muni, whose relationship with me was perpetually misinterpreted by the rest of the staff.

I had kept in touch with Scott over the decade since I had worked there and was always grateful for the opportunity he had given me, his semi-fatherly protection, plus the tip-off about my impending dismissal back in '74, even though it never happened. Scott was a smart cookie, and was also clever about when to appear to appease the staff. Business was business; he knew that, albeit he often had his own interpretations of that principle. "I don't know what they taught you in that shit hole," Scott would say, referring to ABC, where he had also worked in the sixties, as a Top 40 DJ, "but they sure taught you something," he would continue in his familiar grunt. "You know what you're doing." Over the years, he would sometimes calm the rest of the air staff by concurring with them that I didn't.

WNEW's management expected immediately higher evening audience ratings when I came on board, similar to the ones I'd had at WPLJ, and they paid for a TV commercial showing my face and trumpeting my arrival. Also not appreciated by my new co-workers. But there were a few key factors being overlooked here, perhaps the very least of which was that according to many dial-turning listeners to whom I'd spoken, they thought they were still listening to me on WPLJ when their car radios were on in the evening. After all, it had only been a couple of months since my switch, and I was on the air at virtually the same time. When some of the handwritten Arbitron audience diaries were filled in and sent off, they indicated WPLJ for some of my hours rather than WNEW-FM.

But the first real issue management didn't consider was that I was a music DJ, not an überpersonality like the rising Howard Stern. Although I strove to be your consistently dependable and informative friend on the radio, the star was the music itself, and should it not be to the audience's liking, well, just how many people were going to wait around to hear their old buddy in between records they didn't like? On my own time, I attempted to calculate and estimate this number by looking at the percentage of "exclusive" listeners to WPLJ during my hours (people who did not report changing their dial to another radio station), figuring they would be the most likely candidates to at least give me a trial listen at WNEW. But then, of course, there was the issue of the music itself.

WNEW-FM had kicked off its free-form progressive rock programming in 1967, which meant that the DJs' tastes ruled supreme, and they could play whatever they wanted, with no guidelines. I had enjoyed working there back in '73 and '74, and previously at Philadelphia's WMMR, as a "progressive jock," which is how I'd begun my career. Like every other DJ at that time, I thought my musical choices were absolutely the best. However, as the 1970s progressed, WNEW-FM's ratings had declined in comparison with those of their competitor, and my employer, WPLJ. A format was then imposed at WNEW, but at the time of my return in December '83, it was only loosely enforced. The on-air personalities basically picked only what they liked from the card file of permitted songs and ignored the ones they didn't. The air of station eclecticism still ruled: each personality had his own staunchly defended musical preferences, and artists he or she deemed unworthy of airplay.

Often, artists deemed in some way inferior, or "corporate," such as Journey, happened to be the most commercially popular at the time and were the ones most studiously avoided.

For my part, I constructed my shows from the allotted rock songs in the card file that matched those formerly played by WPLJ, and I tried to make it seem that I was doing the same show I'd done before, as if I'd just picked up from where we had left off, and we were all just hanging out as usual. After studying the most recent Arbitron radio ratings report, I clumsily estimated that if my exclusive WPLJ listeners actually came over to WNEW to check me out and then decided to stick around on a daily basis, WNEW-FM's ratings for a whole day would improve by a mere two-tenths of an audience share. Not much, but at least a rise. And that's exactly what happened after my first full "book" (seasonal report) in their Arbitron ratings.

A couple of special features made daily appearances on my new show: One was Live at Five, taken from a television feature of the same name, but here the emphasis was on live or recorded live performances from artists, and sometimes live interviews with the recording stars. One such celebrity who made several appearances over the years was Robert Plant, the lead singer of Led Zeppelin, who had embarked on a solo career in the eighties. At first, I was a bit frightened to have him on my show, even though I had always loved his music, because of Zeppelin's long-standing reputation for wanton craziness. But Plant proved to be interesting and charming, not threatening. Ever the ladies' man, he seemed to enjoy reducing every woman in his presence to a fit of silly giggles. I made sure to contain myself.

Plant's visits also complemented my other nightly feature, *Get the Led Out,* which is still running at the time of this writing, as a Denny Somach Productions, United Stations Radio Network syndicated show that airs on many rock stations round the country. I had started doing *Get the Led Out* as a nightly fifteen-or-so–minute run of Zeppelin songs at WNEW, under the auspices of then program director Mark Chernoff. Although this feature sprang up elsewhere around the country, I hadn't heard of one prior to the start of mine. Indeed, my gut feeling that Led Zeppelin were the definitive act of the rock format had started to spontaneously gain ground on its own. In its current form, I co-write and host five one-minute daily vignettes relating to the group's (often outrageous) activities on the particular date in history, and a weekly hourlong program that includes interviews and commentary based on a theme relating to the group, with, of course, plenty of their music.

At staff meetings throughout my tenure at WNEW, I continued to champion, in retrospect maybe a little too vociferously, commercially popular music (whether I personally liked it or not) for the purpose of garnering the highest ratings possible. This stance never won me friends among the air staff, who claimed to be just as concerned about the ratings but appeared to have more overriding concerns about the musical "legitimacy" of the artists. I could never decipher exactly what these musical parameters of credibility were, especially because they differed from person to person. Certainly, some long-term artists, such as a Bruce Springsteen, could be considered more serious musicians than, say, Loverboy. But whenever I would predictably suggest that Loverboy's song "Everybody's Workin' for the Weekend" would be good to play on a Friday afternoon or evening, I would be categorically dismissed as being frivolous.

In general, it's still my opinion that this smarter-than-thou attitude was a major factor in the ultimate destabilization and lack of focus of WNEW's legendary rock format, leading to a switch to a "hot talk" (meaning young men acting like jackasses and outrageously belittling women) format in 1999. But in contrast to the opinion of some of my fellow air-staff members that the station management found me stupid, in fact I was the last of the long-time regulars kept on board by the management, and received a kind and glowing letter from Scott Herman, the general manager, upon the station's demise into the world of hot and genuinely stupid talk. But all that would be sixteen years into the future. And a lot would happen, some of it unthinkable, before then.

31

"Here, quick! Get in the men's room!" said David Lee Roth as he grabbed my arm and pulled me next to Mark into the grungy white-tiled facility. We were in a nondescript, run-down building used as the secret, float-ing after-hours Club Zero somewhere around Hollywood. "It's a drug bust!" A loud Blue Thunder police helicopter with sweeping search-lights hovered outside the window, just like in the movie of the same name.

This was not what I had in mind when I headed out to L.A. in the summer of '85 to record a national radio special. I was doing many at the time, one even at London's Abbey Road Studios, a live call-in show with the Alan Parsons Project. How exciting to be in the very room where the Beatles had recorded! Other shows featured various concerts, and interviews with Elvis Costello, Lou Reed, Deep Purple, and a laun-dry list of other artists. This time I was recording for the Westwood One syndication company, run by astute and ahead-of-his-time Norm Pat-tiz. Hours earlier, Norm had impressed us by standing several yards from his luxury car in the Westwood parking lot, waving a small, thin black object with a red button, attached by a chain to his ignition key: "Look at this. I can unlock my door electronically from over here!"

Mark's popularity as an MTV VJ was soaring, the eighties were in full swing, and now here I was, at 4 A.M., in some dump of an L.A. building, waiting for it to all end, as a small squad of police barreled through the door. Mark had met Dave through MTV, and I'd already spent a weekend squiring them around the hot spots of New York in our Volvo a few months before. Dave had decided that we were "like his friends from Hebrew school." He lamented his treatment by the Van Halens, who he said at the time were anti-Semitic and often a little too inebriated. Now, after having finished my radio recording session, Mark and I were in L.A. on this particular evening with Dave and a couple of his friends; we'd gone to a kick-boxing match, a restaurant, and a small bar, practically empty but for a few older Asian people, one playing a small keyboard. Always the showman, Dave had jumped onto the club's tiny stage and belted out renditions of Simon and Garfunkel and Animals songs to an audience of nobody. He had also insisted on paying, which I thought was totally unnecessary. "Why do you feel you have to pay for everybody?" I had asked. "So they'll like me" was the strange response, more befitting a sixth grader. I got the feeling that when Dave was not "on," he was not happy.

"Hands up, everybody freeze! Out of the bathrooms, now! No talking!" I had already slipped out of the bathroom a few seconds earlier while the police clambered loudly up the stairs, having thought my presence in a men's room would automatically imply I was guilty of something. Dave stood behind me, and I tried to at least obstruct the police's view of his recognizable face, his hair piled under a baseball cap. A sweep of the room was conducted, and then, as I recall, the police, with guns at the ready, ordered everyone in the club down the stairs into the street, where we were directed into two lines and ordered to march off alternately to the right or left of the entrance near Highland Boulevard. The officers walked by each of us, staring intently into our faces. "Go, that way, don't talk, and keep walking." I marched in a northerly direction, as fast as I could without running, and figured I'd later locate Mark and Dave by wandering around the neighborhood, waiting to be spotted by them in their cars, which is what eventually happened. Me, I had luckily been just an anonymous face in a club-busted crowd, but reports of Dave's and Mark's appearance made it into the newspapers.

Had anyone been arrested? I didn't know and didn't care. That would be the last time I went to an illegal floating after-hours club.

Not that I hadn't frequented other unusual clubs in New York, including the outrageous fun house of the seventies, Studio 54, where there was always something bizarre to see, such as women dressed only in see-through mosquito netting, and men dancing in leather chaps with their naked rear ends hanging out. In the eighties, the Limelight (often referred to as the "Slimelight"), located in a former church on Sixth Avenue and Twenty-second Street, was a notorious hot spot. The church setting made the late-night club seem that much more debaucherous. I recall that Mark and I took Dave there, perhaps on the same night Teri Toye, allegedly a man who presented himself as a woman, sat nearby on the couch, looking very pretty. On one particular night, I got into an argument with a very drunken Joe Strummer of the Clash, who insisted that what people really wanted to hear on the radio were solely old blues records, and anything preferred by the homeless denizens of the then shady Times Square area where Joe apparently liked to hang out.

"What do you play on your station, Bruce Springsteen records?" he derisively demanded. "You're no DJ!"

"Yeah, well, if you could write a song half as good as Bruce, maybe we'd play more of your stuff!" I had shot back. Ornery little fellow, who unfortunately died of a heart attack in 2002.

I ran into Robert Plant at the Limelight too. Robert introduced me to his companion, a short, pleasant woman most likely of Indian descent, who was dressed in full Indian-style garb—a pinkish sari and a symbolic dot on her forehead. "This is Shirley," he said, his arm around her shoulder as if to protect her from the undignified, weirdo club goers of loose morals. Strange, I momentarily thought. Didn't I read that Plant's wife of Indian background, Maureen, had a sister named Shirley? Maybe he was showing Shirley around New York. Then again, maybe not. The Limelight was not exactly the Statue of Liberty.

Somehow, between nights like the one at Club Zero and my Big C appointments, I failed to notice that my marriage wasn't exactly working.

But then again, whose was perfect? Who cared? Where I came from, in my old-world world, the family was the family, and everyone just stuck together, despite plenty of yelling and hollering. There'd be a blowup, and then, poof, it was over. Time to eat, and where's the seltzer? Nobody worried about a "relationship." I never heard the word mentioned.

32

Of course it had started way before, and of course I was oblivious, but to me, the dire reality of the state of our marriage set in after Mark visited a psychic, one who "read" your jewelry, by holding, say, your watch or ring in her hands, which led her to your spirit guides, or something like that. Not that I was pooh-poohing the readings themselves, as I'd been accurately tipped off by psychics in the past, but frankly, I figured that anyone who was locating rifts in the fabric of the space-time continuum had to be using twenty-third-century technology, which the rest of us could only glimpse once a week during the voyages of Captain Picard, aboard the *Enterprise*.

Mark had visited a friend of Abbey and Candace Konowitch, a woman who was apparently so well respected in her field that she aided Long Island police departments in solving murders. She'd told Mark that he'd move to California, would thereafter have a daughter, and would ultimately want to move back to New York. Mark casually gave me this information while we were driving to the wedding of Tony Pigg, a former WPLJ DJ and friend of mine. Mark had shown a tiny picture of me to the psychic, who'd then said that I had a light emanating from my eyes which indicated that I too had psychic potential, and that she wanted to meet me. The only psychic experience I had upon hearing this news was the revelation that I wasn't going to have a great time at the wedding, and there was no way I was moving to California. For lots of reasons, not the least of which were my longtime career here in New York and my father's recent bout with kidney cancer. The psychic had said Mark would be moving but had not mentioned me. Why would Mark want to move to California anyway?

In a case of either prophesy initiating reality or the other way around, Mark took up acting lessons with the intention of leaving MTV, moving to California, and transitioning into an acting career. He also, reportedly, had a nineteen-year-old female partner from class, whom I would never meet, but who apparently resembled me. People casually began asking how I'd enjoyed such and so restaurant or club, and despite their claims, I would assure them that I'd never been there. I would soon find out that Mark had moved in with the mystery woman on Fifteenth Street, before moving to California but after "officially" leaving me on the night of March 19, 1987.

He'd gotten out of bed, plunked the car keys down on the kitchen table, and run out the door for an MTV promotion with a small suitcase he had already packed. In a scene straight out of a Lifetime channel Movie of the Week, while crying hysterically, I took the elevator down to the building's basement, which had a pay phone, thinking Mark would need to use it, at least to call for some transportation. I found him there speaking urgently into the receiver, and upon seeing me, he said, "Not now, not now, my wife is standing right here!" Mark went back up to the lobby, got into the cab he had ordered, and left. He soon moved to California. I would see him only twice within that year, regarding the separation and divorce papers, but never again by my own choosing. Mark wasn't a bad person, just a bit self-absorbed. He hadn't intentionally hurt me, but I was very hurt. Why revisit pain, and I'd had plenty. I didn't need "closure," the latest fiction of amateur psychobabble.

In 2005 I accidentally ran into him at the SiriusXM Satellite Radio studios in midtown Manhattan. Mark seemed incredulous that I "hadn't changed a bit," as he stood in the Sirius offices and touched my face. He should only have known what actual physical changes I'd been through in those ensuing years. And then, as if reading from a script, he said, "I was a fool. I didn't understand what we had." Mark then told me about his daughter, a talented singer, who had recently moved with her mother, a second ex-wife, from California back to the New York area. He'd moved back too. Talking to him seemed dangerously easy.

Although I had been emotionally devastated by the legal separation that had been foisted upon me, I tried my best to keep the weeping to myself and go about my on-air radio business. But my father found the situation extremely embarrassing, which made me feel like a failure and a disgrace to the family. When I drove out to visit my parents, I would stop at a pay phone in College Point, Queens, right off the Long Island Expressway, so Daddy could tell me if the next-door neighbors were sitting on their folding chairs in their driveway. I could then take a slightly different route that would allow me to approach the house from the opposite direction, and potentially avoid a neighborly inquisition as to the whereabouts of my husband.

Although his implication at first was that I'd done something that had caused Mark to leave, my father came up with a new theory, and piece of advice: "You know Mark, he's on the television, and there are all these girls—they're over here, they're over there, they're all over the place—and he thinks, well, you know, let's just say, it's hard to resist. . . ." Daddy trailed off. "Give him a year, and he'll get tired of it, all the running around, these guys always do. He'll wanna come home. Then, make him get an AIDS test, and just tell him you'll take him back. He's your husband."

I took Daddy's advice seriously, a couple of girls shouldn't matter, and after the year of legal separation was up, I met with Mark in an upscale midtown luncheonette. He seemed shocked by my offer, and said, "I hadn't considered coming back as an option." But he had other commitments to some other new girlfriend, apparently having already moved on from the reported nineteen-year-old. As I dropped him off in the Volvo at the MTV studios on West Fifty-seventh Street, where he was doing a special project, Mark's last words were "I know I'm an asshole."

Still, I tried to figure out what it was about me that had caused Mark to leave. The marriage counseling sessions we had attended in the months before the separation had not answered this question. It was easier to follow my father's advice.

As I tried to sort out our finances during the separation, I realized that for months Mark had been paying for flowers, phone calls to strange numbers around the country, and hotel room amenities, usually coordinated with MTV traveling promotions, out of our earnings, through our joint corporation. But the capper was the fifteen-hundred-dollar-a-month check noted for "acting lessons," which in fact was rent Mark was paying for the other woman's apartment down on Fifteenth Street. And here he had put our car keys on the kitchen table in March and absolved himself from paying our mortgage or any of our other expenses, all of which I was now carrying myself.

Why hadn't I seen all those bills as they came in? The answer was easy, and I learned my lesson. Mark had arranged, and I had agreed, to have all our bills sent to, and paid by, our accountants. And according to them, he had purported to be our representative, telling them that I had scant understanding of financial matters. No. What I had scant understanding of were twentieth-century marital relationships. And now I'd found that my earnings had been helping to fund his affairs.

I got the bills from our accountant in early May 1987, and on the same day I appeared as the cover girl on the New York *Daily News Sunday Magazine* for their story on "Radio Dames." In addition, that same evening I was to have an interview with David Coverdale, the lead singer of the group Whitesnake. He was promoting the group's newly released, self-titled album, which had the hits (featured in corresponding provocative MTV videos) "Here I Go Again" and "Is This Love." (Several years later, Coverdale would be touted as a singing rival of Robert Plant and indeed put out an album with Jimmy Page, to the apparent dismay of some Zeppelin fans.)

To say that I left for work that afternoon seething with anger, still confused, and weary with sadness would be an understatement. Here I was, perpetually nickel-and-diming it, contributing to the retirement plan for Mark and myself and saving up for our vacations during the few weeks guaranteed per year under my radio contract with WNEW, while my hard-earned money was secretly being spent on at least one someone else. The phone and credit card bills were burning a hole in my briefcase, which would remain nearly attached to my person through the entire evening. It was fortunate, I thought, that a guest would be showing up for an interview to take my mind off things. And when David Coverdale's manager and record company representative invited me to come out for dinner with them after my show, my briefcase and I gladly accepted. I didn't want to think about the bills or my separation or anything to do with Mark and the whole business that night, but I wasn't going to let go of "the evidence."

It was fun to be picked up and taken to a nice restaurant in one of those fancy black limousines. This one even had a telephone! I asked permission to use it, not just for the excitement of actually making a call from a moving vehicle, but it was ten o'clock, time for my appointed nightly phone call to my mother. To her credit, Mommy tuned in and attempted to listen to at least some of the "noise" I was presenting to the populace. Mostly, though, she just wanted to know that I'd made it to work safely.

"Who was that British guy on your show, the one with the speaking voice that sounded like God," she inquired. Indeed, if you have ever heard David Coverdale speak in his deep, resonating tone (he did the introduction to the Broadway show *Rock of Ages*) you might think he was addressing Parliament. "Well, it just so happens I'm going out to dinner with him and his representatives, and I'm even calling you right now from a telephone they have in their limousine!" I told Mommy. "Well, you have a good time," she said. "You deserve it." Mommy had taken to listening to psychologists' radio talk shows, like that of her favorite, Dr. Joy Browne, and had been giving me uncharacteristically strange (for her) advice. When my trouble with Mark was brewing, my mother said I should go out and get some sexy lingerie to wear around the house. "Not everybody's like us," she said, referring to our old-world family, "shlepping around the house in some old *shmates* (rags)."

"Look, if he doesn't like me already with the clothes off, what makes you think he's gonna like me any better with them on?" was my reply. But I took Mommy's advice and purchased some lacy stretch body stockings and the like. I felt like a desperate idiot parading around in costumes better suited for *Barbarella*. Besides, such garments did not meet my one requirement for apartment attire: that they render me presentable enough to go down the hall and dump the garbage down the shoot whenever I damn well wanted to without having to get dressed for the occasion.

Then there was also Mommy's strange encouragement for me to go out and "have an affair," also because I "deserved it." No doubt she got that one right off of Dr. Joy Browne. Exactly how would that help matters?

After the dinner with David Coverdale and his people, we headed to the Indian-themed Nirvana club, which had moved from its original location atop a hotel on Central Park South to a new haunt right in Times Square. Passing muster through numerous bouncers and elevators, our group arrived at the darkly lit, expansive top-floor perch, replete with huge Oriental patterned carpets and large plants. My briefcase and I were finally relaxing, having a couple of drinks, just hanging out, and for once not thinking about my personal and financial woes. This was good. Now if I could just stay here. No, I definitely didn't want to go home, because then I would start staring at the contents of my briefcase and get all upset again.

But of course the time to leave came, and in the limo when (you guessed it) David Coverdale asked me to come back to the hotel with him, I agreed. What was I getting myself into? I knew, or should have known the answer, but all I really wanted to do was keep hanging out and not open the briefcase. We were dropped off at the Intercontinental on East Fifty-second Street, and I entered the glass revolving door. Going around in the door directly across from me was Jeff Beck. Apparently he was hanging out in the hotel bar, which at that moment was really where I wanted to be. But that, of course, was not what David Coverdale had in mind, and I knew that when I accepted his invitation.

It's not that he wasn't extremely attractive, but I had considered myself a nice married woman for what seemed like ages, and before that had never run off with a musician I had just met, with the intention of having a one-night stand. My head was in a jumble. Entering David's suite, I saw that a pile of pink While You Were Out telephone message sheets had been slipped under the door, and there were more on the couch. Nearly all of them said Tawney Kitaen had called, and there were references to "picking up her mother at the airport." Tawney Kitaen was the well-endowed actress/model/sex object who played the part of Coverdale's steamy love interest in his Whitesnake videos, and to whom he was later married for a short time.

Great, I thought, another Steven and Bebe situation. Strange that those guys would want to be with me, I thought. Among other things, I didn't look anything like their obviously preferred voluptuous bomb-shells. "You have the body of a teenager," Coverdale had said to me while the microphone was off during the radio interview, and inquired about my age. He was surprised to hear I was a year older than him, until he admitted to knocking two years off, making him a year older than me.

And so I spent the night in David Coverdale's suite. I'm not going into the details. You already know what they are. Except to say that he thought it was odd, and he seemed just a tad offended, when I asked if Coverdale was his real last name. I mean, just about everyone in New York's real last name had been changed when their families had arrived as immigrants from other countries at Ellis Island. Obviously, this was not the case in England, where the Coverdales had some sort of semi-royal centuries-old legacy. The next day, Coverdale invited me to go to Boston with him for a major bash thrown by a radio station up there, but I declined. Always, there was work to go back to, and I was extremely grateful for it. He took me out for dinner after my show again, and then I simply went home.

I would have to open the briefcase and start dealing with the issues, and there were many more than I'd thought there could possibly be.

I hadn't realized it was going to cost so much money for my husband to leave me. And there was nothing I could do about it. The full financial impact would hit me in a few years, when I needed the money for something really urgent. Then I would pay a visit to famed divorce attorney Raoul Felder, who would tell me to just let the forty-three thousand dollars go; after I'd paid assorted thousands for other issues relating to the divorce—to keep my house, my pension, and my parrot—and to get well, it would cost me more than forty-three thousand dollars to legally dispute the issue.

Mark stipulated in the separation agreement, which was merged into the divorce decree, that I had to pay him forty-three thousand dollars to stay in our jointly owned co-op. Otherwise I would be forced out. This figure was determined by a professional appraiser to be half the amount of the profit that would be made had the co-op been sold at market value at the time Mark left. In 1987, New York State law did not recognize co-ops as marital residences; rather just as investment properties. This loophole was closed shortly thereafter as co-ops gained in popularity. Mark admitted to me in 2005 that it was wrong of him to have forced me to "pay to stay." For his part, Felder graciously charged me a cut rate for my visit.

While I was certainly hurt and embarrassed by my impending divorce, which went through at the end of 1988, the more appropriate emotion—anger—and the projected appearance of dignity became my focus. Not wanting to dismantle that for which I'd worked so hard, I bought Mark out of the little corporation and pension plan, which I still retain. I also kept our much-loved big red green-wing macaw, which Mark and I had gotten at the time of our wedding. Mark loved the parrot so much that word had earlier trickled down that he'd never leave me, because of the parrot. I am very happy to report that Br-Br (who ingeniously decided to rename himself after Mark left) is now thirty years old, and is as feisty as ever. I put up a large headshot photo of Mark behind Br-Br's cage for a while, although it was disheartening for me to see when arriving home at night, so that Br-Br wouldn't mourn his absence and get depressed. I also let Br-Br watch Mark on MTV, from his special perch in the bedroom. It's impossible for me to imagine being without Burbie (his nickname), and now his "sister" parrot, Babie Gracie, the multitalented African grey. Both of them talk and sing, but Gracie's vocabulary is outrageous; she would definitely take home the prize on *Are You Smarter Than a 5th Grader?*

Then I found myself at the psychic who had told Mark of his alternate Californian future.

The jewelry reader first stared deliberately into my eyes. Then she held my wedding ring. "You understand," she began, referring to my supposedly implicit psychic potential.

It was an unusual place for me to start, but I was trying to understand what had just happened to me over the last few years. "All information is good information," my mother used to say, although I don't always exactly agree with that assessment. So I continued to investigate various sources, even dubious, or should I say unconventional ones, in the hope of learning something and not making the same mistakes again. Time was a-tickin', and I wasn't getting any younger.

At Barnes & Noble, I stocked up on numerous current books from the psychology section purporting to analyze and give instructions pertaining to romantic relationships. The most memorable one was called *Jennifer Fever: Why Older Men Pursue Younger Women.* After all, I was an elderly thirty-six and had reportedly been left for a much younger nineteen-year-old. Besides the usual analysis of the male psyche, I learned that bitterness was not an attractive quality in a divorcée, so that emotion was purged from my repertoire. It hadn't been in the forefront anyway. "Don't get mad, get even" and "The best revenge is living well and/or looking good" were my mottos, and the "looking good" part I had already begun translating into "looking young," continuing my longtime daily practice of slathering on sunblock.

Continuing on for a few more sessions with the marriage counselor to pick up some pointers, it was then I learned that she had known all along about Mark's affair(s), which she had been discussing with him in their private sessions. The therapist had one unbelievably memorable suggestion, which I found so shocking it stopped me cold. I had told her that since I would now have no husband (and it was not yet an era when it was socially acceptable for single women to just go out and have a baby by any means), my prospects for becoming a mother were slipping away. She suggested that I agree to either move out of the apartment immediately or come up with Mark's forty-three thousand dollars right away, in return for . . . stand by for this now . . . his getting me pregnant so I could have a "legal" baby, as we were still not yet officially divorced. I would then raise the child as a divorcée.

Talk about self-respect and getting *shtupped*! This trade deal was her logical legal solution, offered with the best of intentions. Noting that Mark had not been interested in me for some time, this undignified pregnancy would most likely have to commence via a sample in a physician's office. And yes, I knew a wonderful doctor in that up-and-coming field of in vitro fertilization and the like—my own sister, Dr. Jane Miller. This thought made it even more ridiculous. Pay my own husband, who'd already left and found me too unattractive to touch, to clinically give me a baby in my own sister's office practice? Not on your life. I could never be that desperate. Not even sadly and ironically noting that I'd had one wretched abortion in my life—it was Mark's baby, we were not yet married, and I didn't want to disgrace my family. I thanked the counselor for her time, and never went back.

Tawdry bits of information now filtered back my way, since I was legally separated and the impending divorce decree loomed. Understandably, people don't want to get involved in their friends' relationships.

You can't blame them, although you usually would have profited from the often reliable scuttlebutt and made some different decisions. There were the predictable tales of MTV groupies around the country, and indeed elsewhere, surfacing and performing their sex acts for my husband, just like "Sweet sweet Connie" in the Grand Funk song. The kind of situations my father had imagined, of which he figured Mark would tire and just want to come home. The motto "What happens on the road stays on the road" had been the VJ's credo of allegiance while traveling. Nothing really shocking there.

But it was an allegation about one particular person, whom I'd heard about from several sources, that has stuck in my memory through the years. The purpose of my story here is not to spread nasty dirt about other people, but sometimes, well, someone just deserves it. You don't know this person, unless you traveled in the same circles, so it doesn't matter if I tell you: she knows who she is. And literally, in my book, she gets the lowlife-character piece-of-shit award. Of course, that is only if the allegations are true, but as they say, "Where there's smoke, there's fire."

She was a tall and beautiful friend of some of the male DJs at WPLJ. I never inquired into the nature of these friendships; there were always girls and friends around. On several occasions, she approached me on the steps of the ABC building, asking if I could get her in past the security guards; she was meeting someone upstairs. Okay, who cared? I had to go to, or was leaving from, work at the building and would let her in. After Mark left the marriage, I heard that she had been sleeping with Mark right before and up to our wedding day and had allegedly boasted to her friends that after our honeymoon trip, Mark had "come right back" to her. Now things may happen during the course of marriages, but that one takes the WTF! slut-bag cake, which I now sincerely hope is an "old bag" cake.

But back to the psychic: Like others in her field, she seemed particularly sensitive to other people's countenances and demeanor. Perhaps my original theory, which I had postulated back in Central Park, was true, and she could sense brain wave activity. Biofeedback was a topic being bandied about at the time. This Long Island lady had no doubt sensed Mark's uncertainty about his future plans, which is possibly what allowed her entry into his private thoughts. Or something like that. She still insisted he'd want to come back from California, but she didn't say when. And she wouldn't confirm whether or not his daughter would be mine. Maybe she didn't want to hurt my feelings. But at some point during my jewelry reading the psychic stopped. "Whatever you're going to do about it, you should do it before you're forty." There it was again.

In the ensuing months after Mark left, I developed a relationship with a very handsome record company executive who soon, coincidentally, moved to California. Of course, in retrospect, I was not ready to get involved with someone else. My brain was still befuddled, which is why these rebound things don't work. Plus, my father had advised me to give Mark a year of celebrity "fun" and had predicted he would come back, whereupon I should let bygones be bygones and get back to the business of being married. But at the same time, I was getting a lot of family pressure to get on with my life and find a new husband in case this one wasn't coming back. Contradictory, wouldn't you say? It was as if I'd lost my adult status and was now back to sharing a hotel room with my sister on a family ski trip and arguing over a hairbrush.

So the cross-country weekend-type relationship with my new friend fit the bill. "You can't always get what you want, but if you try sometimes . . . you get what you need" went the insightful Jagger-Richards lyrics. Besides hitting the hotspots of L.A. and mingling with recording artists like Cher and Guns N' Roses, my friend's hospitality extended to bicycle excursions on the beach in Santa Monica and drives in his new Porsche convertible. Since he is a private person who comes from a lovely family, I am respecting what I would imagine to be his wish of remaining anonymous in this book.

But the highlights of the next couple of years, during which I was gratefully broadcasting nightly, sorting my situation out, and additionally suffering from increasing chest and internal pains, were most certainly the eight or so elaborate European trips I would arrange for my friend and me during my allotted vacation weeks. And those trips took us to France, Holland, and all around Italy. From Taormina, Sicily, to Lake Maggiore and the Italian Alps, to Venice, Florence, Milan, the Italian Riviera, the Amalfi Coast, Sardinia, and Rome.

My friend and I had been to Rome several times over the few years and frequented a restaurant in the Trastevere area called Sabatini, where we were always remembered and given a warm welcome. Such a warm welcome that the owner, Salvatore, had an eight-by-ten photo taken with us and put it up on the wall of his "celebrity gallery." During a trip the following year, my friend arranged to meet up in Rome with an important man in his business whom he wanted to impress. We made dinner reservations for Sabatini, and after we were seated, I went to secretly check the celebrity wall, ostensibly while walking to the ladies' room. The photo was still there, prominently displayed! I gave my friend the thumbs-up, so he later escorted his business associate past the wall on the way to the men's room. To say that our photo on the wall of this five-star Roman restaurant so many thousands of miles from home made an impression on the older gentleman would be merely an understatement.

Ultimately my long-distance relationship didn't work out. My gut impression along the way was that my friend would never really want to commit to a marriage to me. Sometimes your gut impressions are accurate. Is he married now? I don't know. He had a terrible temper, which could be set off at any time, by anything, and he could say some really awful things to me. I didn't want to live like that, and in 1992 it was time to move on.

I was still involved in that cross-country relationship on the evening of May 31, 1990, when, after my radio show, I picked up the Volvo, which had been in for service and left for me on the lot of Martin's Manhattan Volvo, then at Fiftieth Street and Eleventh Avenue. My trusty friend and service representative, Trevor Scott, had completed the

maintenance check in time for me to take a cab ride over to the lot, open
the car with my duplicate key, and pick it up after work. I got into the
car and drove north on Eleventh Avenue, and moments later, as I made a
left turn from West End Avenue onto West Seventy-ninth Street, a reck-
lessly speeding car coming from north of Seventy-ninth Street smashed
into the front passenger side of my Volvo, sending me flying upward to
hit my head on the crank of the sunroof. (No, I wasn't wearing the seat
belt, which was not against the law at the time, but the police later told
me that if I had been wearing it, I would have broken my collarbone.)

The pain in my back, neck, and head was severe before I lost consciousness, then quickly regained it. I could also feel that the cup of
yogurt I had just purchased had exploded onto my hair and jacket. A
crowd gathered, an ambulance appeared. The police and medics removed me from the car and strapped me to a stretcher with a head and
neck brace. On the way into the ambulance, I asked to be wheeled
around to see the damage to my car. It was totaled, no doubt about it,
and it was at that point that I let out a scream. "My car! My car!" I could
not have cared less about myself, even though I was in a whole lot of
pain. The perpetrator of the accident, who remained on the scene in his
damaged vehicle, could not speak English, and was uninsured.

In the ambulance, locked into the uncomfortable gurney, I showed
the policeman my driver's license. "Hey, are you the DJ?" he asked. "I
listen to ya all the time. Say, you look really good for your age!" I was
thirty-nine. "Where are you towing my car?" I asked, and the cop
handed me a card with the address of an auto body shop in Queens. To
my recollection, I passed out again for a short while on the way to Roosevelt Hospital, the site of my breast surgery ten years earlier. My immediate concern was to call the radio station, and I asked to be wheeled
over to a phone in the emergency room. I spoke to Harris Allen in the
studio at WNEW and told him I anticipated not being able to work the
next day. That turned out to be the least of my problems.

The back and neck injury were treated with ultrasonic physiother-
apy, and I wore a neck brace for several weeks. Sometimes it still hurts.
But the head injury was more severe, and I was not able to sit up without
feeling extreme dizziness and nausea for a few days. I also could not

remember words, at first, like *television* and *fork*. This symptom abated somewhat, but my immediate short-term memory seemed to have disappeared. How could I talk on the radio, and be the voice-over host for ABC television's American Rock Awards show, which was coming up within a couple of weeks?

I decided to carry around a pad and pencil and write down everything I might forget. Things like the order of subjects I would be talking about on my show, like "first, song title, then into traffic report," and any names or phone numbers I would have to announce, such as the request lines. A talk break like "Genesis from their *Duke* album on WNEW-FM.... Hey, you're with Carol Miller, and don't forget, we've got those Van Morrison tickets for April eighth to give away next hour. Our WNEW forecast calls for overnight lows in the forties and partly cloudy with a high of fifty-seven for tomorrow.... Let's check in with Shadow Traffic and Valerie Segraves . . ." was impossible for me to put together and articulate without writing it all down in advance. I was told that off-air I asked people the same question several minutes after having gotten an answer. I remember once I sat on an examining table at the physical rehab center but forgot what I was there for and neglected to change into the robe that was given to me by the nurse.

At the Rock Awards show, which was held downtown at the Lexington Avenue armory, I was asked to go onstage before the telecast, present some instructions and information to the entertainers and audience, such as which side of the stage the winners should approach, and generally warm up the crowd. So there I was, with my neck brace and on painkillers, walking out and staring at the likes of Keith Richards and Eric Clapton, who were sitting at large dinner-type round tables right in front of me. I introduced myself and pointed to my neck brace. "This isn't a fashion statement, by the way," I deadpanned. "Some jackass ran into me on West Seventy-ninth Street." The audience momentarily seemed shocked, but then became amused. I hear I did a great stand-up act courtesy of the painkillers, but I can't remember most of what I said. Except for pointing out the stage directions for the potential winners. "See, you have to go over to the right side, which is my left. That means you too, Keith Richards."

It would take more than two years for my short-term memory to be restored, even though I practiced daily. At the beginning, my inability to even repeat a phone number that had just been given to me was frightening. My father considered sending me to some type of institute for help, but I didn't have the time, or the inclination. I would do it myself.

What I did have the inclination to do was to get a new Volvo when I was able to drive again. This business of taking the bus with the neck brace was a pain in the ass. Through the sales department at WNEW, I was introduced to some really nice people up at the Volvo North America headquarters, then located in suburban Rockleigh, New Jersey, who let me test-drive some of their newer models for a few weeks. But I knew what I wanted. The same boxy 240 model that had saved my life.

I asked my father to remove a couple of the exterior ornaments from my totaled 1984 model when he visited it in June in the body shop. It was the last week in August when I picked up my brand-new 1990 white Volvo 240 at Martin's Manhattan, and service director Trevor Scott affixed the two turbo logos from my wrecked car to the front and rear of the new one, where they still remain. I took pictures to commemorate the occasion.

35

"Did you see the mammograms?" I asked Dr. Rogers as I lay on the examining table in his office on Eighty-eighth and Park. The time was roughly 2:45 P.M., the date was Thursday, October 25, 1990. It was customary for my surgeon to review the recent films taken by the radiologist at one of my "death watch" sessions just a few days before a visit. "No, I was on vacation, but she says they're okay," replied the kindly Dr. Rogers, referring to my new radiologist, Dr. X. I had asked for a new radiologist after ten years of visiting the elderly doctor with the very thick glasses on Eighty-seventh Street. He just made me nervous. About a decade later he would be found negligent in the deaths of several of his patients, so my instincts hadn't been wrong.

I left Dr. Rogers's office with a weird feeling. Something wasn't right. He should have checked my mammograms. I didn't know this new radiologist lady from Adam, and she had been a bit flip with me in her office. "Your tissue is so dense you could be hiding a golf ball in there," she breezed, giving my mammograms a once-over. Of course, she would be giving them a more thorough review later.

I stopped for a Diet Coke and went on my way to do my nightly radio show. Over a week went by, and the unsettling feeling hadn't gone away. I was less than two months from my fortieth birthday, and as if in some sci-fi movie, the three psychics' identical warnings over the years came to the forefront of my mind: "Whatever you do, do it before you're forty."

That did it. I called my sister, the doctor, for counsel. "Sign them out," she said, referring to the mammograms. "Take them somewhere else for another review."

"Uh-oh, we've got problems," said Dr. Deluca, looking at my films. I had signed the mammograms out of Dr. X's office, shown them to my father on his own light box in our basement at home, and met my mother on Thursday, November 8, in the Westbury office of Dr. Deluca, the radiologist who had detected my mother's in situ (walled off) carcinoma in 1988. Mommy had been sixty-five at the time, and the small tumor had been removed with a lumpectomy, after which she'd had radiation. "I got off easy," my mother had said.

Dr. Deluca took a fresh set of mammograms for me, and while they were being developed, I waited by myself in his examining room. "You put your right foot, in, you put your right foot out, you put your right foot in and you shake it all about. You do the hokey pokey and you turn yourself around. That's what it's all about," I sang as I danced in a circle. "What are you doing?" said the doctor, as he reentered the examining room. "The hokey pokey," I replied. "I don't know why."

The doctor then summoned my mother and me into his office. "You see here"—he pointed to an identical cluster of small dots on my left mammograms, taken both by him and Dr. X. "This has to come out. Immediately." Dr. Deluca called his associate, my mother's surgeon, Dr. Grieco, at Glen Cove Hospital. No time or thought was given to going back to Dr. Rogers in the city. My biopsy was set for that coming Tuesday, November 13.

At Glen Cove Hospital, I stood beside a screen showing an enlarged version of my mammogram, and a wire was inserted into my chest at the location of the dots. This was painful, and the nurse/technician's commentary didn't help. "How long have you known Dr. Grieco?" the petite blonde inquired in a suspicious tone as she twisted the wire needle deeper into my left breast. Oh for goodness' sake, I thought, she's worried about her boyfriend, and all he's gonna do is cut me up in a few minutes. When the wire was suitably inserted, I was taken into the operating room and given the anesthesia that would knock me out for the surgery. In the early nineties the anesthesia took longer to wear off, and you would stay overnight for such an event.

"Which do you want first," said Dr. Grieco, standing at my bedside the next day. "The good news or the bad news?" "Bad news first" was my immediate response. "The bad news is you have invasive intraductal carcinoma, and you need a mastectomy, and I would highly recommend taking the right side off too," said Dr. Grieco. "What's the good news?" I sputtered. "Well, you can have reconstruction, and if you do what I say, you could be all right. If not . . . ," Dr. Grieco trailed off momentarily, "well, let's just say I'd still like to hear you on the radio in a couple of years." Oh . . . here it was: a bad-sounding kind of cancer. And what exactly was reconstruction? I didn't know.

I turned my head toward the window on the left and noticed a bird flying by in the cloudy gray daylight. "You know that book *First, You Cry*?" I was referring to the pioneering volume about breast cancer by Betty Rollin, which I had never read. "Well, in my case, it's *First, You Throw Up*," I said, overcome by a wave of nausea and a feverish feeling. Dr. Grieco grabbed a shallow yellow plastic dish and stuck it under my mouth, but nothing came out. Suddenly a strange feeling of—could it be?—some sort of relief took hold. "It's Showtime," I declared. This cancer thing had been hanging over my head for nearly twenty years, and I had been living from checkup to checkup, waiting for the inevitable. Now, at last, I had some kind of fighting chance. My cancer was right in line with the family schedule, but now it was a whole new ball game.

"Someone's got to tell my mother," I said to the doctor as I dialed my parents' number. "Would you please do that?" Mommy answered the phone. My father was already on his way to pick me up from the hospital. "Dr. Grieco wants to talk to you," I said, handing him the receiver. The news, and then the predictable high-pitched scream. "Lookit, I'll be okay, Ma," I said, taking back the phone. "Don't worry," which of course was a ridiculous statement given the circumstances. Except it wasn't ridiculous to me. Now I was on a mission. All of these emotions in what seemed like just a few minutes. I really didn't know anything about breast cancer; I had studiously avoided investigating the actual details over the years, and this was still the era when you didn't talk about it. No Breast Cancer Awareness Month, or Race for the Cure, or anything like that. "Listen," Dr. Grieco said, "you're in shock. You have cancer. It'll be your first thought when you wake up every morning. That's now. But in time, it won't be." He was right. For a while.

"Chop-chop, let's get out of here," said Daddy, clapping his hands together as he entered the hospital room from the door to my right. "What are you still doing in bed? Why aren't you dressed?" he demanded in his usual spirited fashion, meant to put a positive spin on the situation. "Oh, I guess you haven't heard the good news," I said dryly. "What good news?" he asked. "I have cancer" was my deadpan reply. My father sat down at the foot of my bed, and tears came to his eyes. "You know what you just did, don't you?" he said, shaking his head in disbelief. "You just saved your own life." Daddy began to rock back and forth. "We'll do what we have to do. We'll do what we have to do," he repeated as he davened. Here was my father, the doctor, praying over a situation set in motion by three fortune-tellers, without whom I wouldn't even have this chance to save my life. You couldn't get less scientific than that.

At this point you've probably heard more than enough about breast cancer. You can't escape the charity drives and pink ribbons, the endless articles in the women's magazines, and the results of new studies, often erroneously reported, in the newspapers and online. So I'll skip over that stuff. Except, twenty years ago, it wasn't like that. This was a whole new world for me, and I would have to navigate it alone, and try to keep it to myself, or at least from the radio audience. I didn't do such a good job of keeping the information from my co-workers; in fact, to some, I over-blabbed, after my first mastectomy. But I have never mentioned it on the air. Hopefully, if you have listened to my radio show over the decades, this will be the first you're hearing of it. Not on the radio, but in a book. A cancer patient is not a very attractive image to conjure up while listening to a rock radio show; it kind of takes the fun out of things, wouldn't you say?

After the required rounds of second opinions with different doctors, the date of my first mastectomy was set with Dr. Grieco for Tuesday, December 11, 1990. He'd done a skillful job with the biopsy, and I thought it would be easier for my parents to visit me at a hospital nearby on Long Island than in Manhattan. Also, I could bring Br-Br out to their house to stay with them.

Further tragedy struck the family in the intervening weeks between the biopsy and the mastectomy. One of my mother's younger, identical twin brothers, Seymour, died of lung cancer at the age of sixty. I had been visiting my uncle in the hospital, the last time imploring him to get better so he could visit me after my mastectomy. But he didn't make it. I had to leave Uncle Seymour's funeral by myself and drive over to Glen Cove Hospital for the required pre-surgical tests for my operation.

But before I left, I located the graves of my female relatives who had died at my age from breast and other related cancers. My grandmother Katya, whom I had never met. Her sisters, Rose and Mary (Miriam). Fanya, Hilda, and the others. Caught up in the sorrow of the day, I tearfully approached each grave. "Not this time!" I said out loud. "Not this time! I'm going to win this one for you." It was a dramatic gesture, but a sincere one. But should I not win, I needed a place to be buried, and I wanted to be here with my relatives. I didn't want to further upset my parents, so I inquired secretly about a plot for myself, which I finally purchased years later.

In retrospect, although Dr. Grieco did another fine surgery, selecting the hospital on Long Island was a mistake, not the least of which was the reconstructive surgeon who was recommended for my case. I would soon wind up at the nation's premier cancer hospital, Memorial Sloan-Kettering on York Avenue, where I fortunately still remain under their watchful care. Obviously, I would have to take time off from work, and the program director of WNEW at the time, Dave Logan, and the general manager, Ted Utz, couldn't have been nicer or more understanding. I promised not to miss more than a week off the air. This was preposterous to my doctors; they insisted that much more time would be needed for recovery, both physical and psychological. It was then that I decided to eliminate the mental element. Either I was an idiot or a genius, but I decided that delving into all sorts of emotional issues and social/sexual ramifications of my upcoming mastectomies just wasn't worth the bother. Yeah, all this chopping up probably wouldn't do wonders for my social life, and here I was, again unmarried, but so freakin' what? I'd had it with the fallout from the divorce. I was just going to have to toughen my ass right up.

⌇ ⌇ ⌇

I awoke from my first mastectomy feeling like the same person I'd been before, albeit in a lot more pain. Dazed from the anesthesia, I still realized I was being delivered into the wrong room, by a hospital aide named Victor. Victor tried to shove me from my gurney onto a bed next to another woman's, whose name was Rosa. But I had arranged for a private room.

"This is your room," he repeated forcefully.

"Oh yeah, then where are my clothes, and where are my parents?" I asked, no doubt in a garbled fashion. Victor was having none of it, and assumed I was just under the influence of the anesthetics. I remembered noticing when I was admitted that morning that a Cindy Miller was being admitted as well. "What do you think my name is?" I demanded.

"You're Cindy Miller," said Victor. "You're twenty-seven years old. There's a Carol Miller here, but she's an older woman with a mastectomy."

"I am Carol Miller, you jerk," I bellowed. "I am your older woman with the mastectomy!" Having the odd luxury of the anesthesia, I freely and loudly insulted Victor as he wheeled me, lying on the mobile bed, around the hall to my correctly assigned room. Turning a corner, I spotted my parents waiting in a doorway at the end of the corridor. "Would you believe this *putz*?" I shouted. "Here he is shlepping me all over the damn place. Trying to stick me in a room with Rosa. I don't know any Rosa. What a moron!" My parents, obviously overjoyed to see me animated after the ordeal of the mastectomy, appeared to be laughing and crying at the same time. I had arrived forty-five minutes later than they'd been told to expect me. "You think this is funny?" I said. "This is not funny! This guy's a jackass!" As I was deposited into my own bed, I promptly fell back asleep.

I stayed in the hospital for five days. My IV drip would repeatedly malfunction and stop dripping, the plastic tube drains releasing the bleeding and fluids from my chest would back up, and a sharp, unexplained pain stabbed through my back when I lay down. After three days, I discovered that it was one of the small pointed metal leads from the surgical monitors, which had been mistakenly left on.

The main question now was had the cancer spread to my lymph nodes, most of which had been removed, causing the bulk of the excruciating

pain. (Nowadays, only one sentinel node is initially removed.) I personally doubted that there had been any spreading into the nodes, as the
tumor was not near my left underarm, where the nodes were located.
"No nodes! No nodes!" I would sporadically chant for the first couple of
days. The results came in from the lab: no spreading into the nodes.
Much relief.

Toward the end of my stay, I asked Dr. Grieco if he could take off the
bandage and I could see what remained beneath. He hesitated at first,
perhaps afraid that I might faint at the sight. Then he walked me over
and stood behind me as I looked in the small hospital bathroom mirror, and he began to unravel the gauze until he had finally removed his
blood-soaked primary bandage. What I saw before me looked like some
sort of futuristic surgical marvel from a sci-fi film. The left side of my
chest was washboard flat, with a perfectly straight line of metal staples
running across it. No lumps, bulges, or crooked cuts. "Wow!" I stared at
Dr. Grieco's handiwork. "That's amazing! You did a great job! I bet
this'll come out great when I have the reconstruction surgery!" Dr.
Grieco looked completely shocked, almost as if he were going to faint.
Not the screaming and crying response to the mastectomy that he had
expected. Upon my discharge from the hospital, Dr. Grieco checked off
"sex" as a permitted activity. "Who the hell would want to have sex with
me?" I asked. "The only person who would find me exciting would be
the Swingline staple salesman."

The next mastectomy was scheduled for March 19, 1991. I picked
that date because it coincided with the date Mark had left me four years
earlier, and I wanted to blot out the bad anniversary with something
good, as my reconstructive surgery would commence at the same time
with a specialist in that field. I had already purchased a fake exterior left
breast prosthesis to wear in my clothes for the intervening months. Unfortunately, that reconstruction would turn out to be extremely problematic and painful, and over the years, I would have the surgery
repeated elsewhere ten times on each side. That's right, ten times, and
not for cosmetic reasons but for complications, including two ensuing
deadly hospital staph infections, which resulted in further hospital
stays and home care. But we finally got it right. I also had a sneaking

suspicion from the get-go that my right mastectomy had not been complete; I still felt there was breast tissue in there under my right arm. Everyone else throughout my endless round of checkups would disagree. Fifteen years later, I would discover another lump, which turned out to be another fibroadenoma, and so I had another "completion" mastectomy. I would develop a whopper of an infection after that surgery.

And so, after my first mastectomy, I left Glen Cove Hospital alive, just days before my fortieth birthday. You had to hand it to those psychics; they sure knew their business.

The day after I checked out, my father checked himself in to Booth Memorial Hospital in Queens, where he was on the staff. Daddy had suspected a problem but had waited for me to come home first. My father had scans and surgery and was diagnosed with lymphoma. My poor mother literally had a nervous breakdown, was barely able to speak, and was unable to write. I drove her around with my one good arm and took her to the hospital to see Daddy. Then I would take her to my apartment in Manhattan and lie her down on the floor with a pillow under her head until I finished my radio show at WNEW, whereupon I would go back to my apartment and drive her back to Long Island.

I stayed on a bit at the house after Daddy came home, and drove into the city for work. I had kept my word, and only missed a week of my radio show. I began driving Daddy to some of his chemotherapy treatments and scans, and bought him a handmade wig from the Edith Imre Foundation, which required a number of fittings, some humorously involving Saran Wrap. Ultimately, Daddy was too embarrassed to wear it, and suggested we donate it to the Smithsonian. We called ourselves the *Nuchshleppers* (those who drag behind).

37

"Excuse me, Miss Miller?" asked the young man toting a boxy briefcase as he rose from his seat near the potted plant in the WNEW-FM lobby. "I have some perfumes you might be interested in."

"Well, maybe another time; this is not a good day, thank you anyway." I asked the station receptionist to please not allow strange people without appointments to wait for me. And today, I certainly wasn't in the mood. It was my first day back from the first mastectomy, and I was in searing pain. The station had kindly arranged for one of my co-workers to run my equipment, as I was barely able to move my left arm and had never bothered with any of the prescribed recovery sessions or exercises because of my father's illness and mother's breakdown. Over the next few years, as further surgeries ensued, I would effectuate my own pay cut of twenty thousand dollars to pay for my co-workers' assistance, because the resulting pain and fatigue would leave me less than capable of running a "tight board." I owe a debt of gratitude and friendship to Ian O'Malley, Mark Francis, Eddie Trunk, and most of all, Earl Douglas Jr.

But I also learned that although many people jump at the chance to participate in hat- and bracelet-wearing charity runs, fund drives, and dinners, usually for the purposes of curing a serious illness or helping those afflicted, not all of these fund-raising participants care about the affected patients on an individual level, especially if the patient in question (like me) is pulling off a successful effort of seeming fine. Vomiting in the ladies' room and not in my seat at ten minutes to the start of my show? Unacceptable. Unable to drive forty miles to a promotion at an automobile showroom after doing a five-hour radio shift? Cause for calling the Human Resources director to a meeting regarding my unwillingness to comply.

The topper occurred on February 26, 1993, when I was at an appointment with my beloved oncologist, the now world-famous Dr. Larry Norton, in what was then a below-ground-level Sloan-Kettering facility on East Sixty-fourth Street and Third Avenue. No televisions in the waiting room; at that time no super-portable cell phones or other devices. When I got into my car, roughly an hour and a half before my show was to start, the streets—every one of them—were jam-packed with vehicles at a standstill. Turning on the radio, I learned that a terrorist's car bomb had exploded under the World Trade Center while I was underground, and the city might be under siege. My car was now on East Sixty-third Street and Second Avenue, heading south, only twenty-one blocks from the WNEW studios. The ride would usually have taken tops ten minutes, but traffic was going nowhere. And I was in the center lane! But I did have one of those amazing new analog car phones in my 1990 Volvo. A telephone to the rescue! I called the program director to let him know of my situation. "You should have known about the bombing. The hospital's no excuse!" he said angrily.

An hour later, approaching my show time but still gridlocked in traffic, I had an idea. I called Earl Douglas Jr., who was to run my radio controls, and proposed that I actually do my speaking breaks and announcing from my car phone, empathizing with the thousands of others who were similarly trapped in traffic, while Earl would run the commercials and music from the studio. I thought it worked out just fine, and even added a little good excitement to a very difficult day, but the program director didn't see it that way. I had now earned the reputation of "being late." And as everyone in business knows, once you get a reputation for something, it can take years to shake it, if you ever can. So much for charity from others. I began to develop my own spin on *charity* anyway: when applicable, doing your very best to take care of your own burdens and those of your family so that you don't constantly have your hand out begging others for help.

Amazingly, one person, whom I didn't even know well, contacted me several years ago with a most generous offer. It was Walt Sabo, a radio consultant who was affiliated with a National Association of Broadcasters group that gave financial aid to lifelong broadcasters who might be in dire straits. Hearing through the grapevine that my medical bills might be high (well, yeah; in fact, I had already spent about $190,000 of my own money during a period of years when my union insurance coverage wasn't so good), Walt offered me a monetary donation from the organization. I was floored, and very grateful, but I couldn't accept it. I was fortunate enough to be able to continue working, albeit now seven days a week, while surely there were others who could not.

But charities do need funding, and medical research charities need subjects. As I'm not exactly loaded with extra dough, I've been involved in cancer studies over the years, genetic, physiological, and otherwise, usually orchestrated by Dr. Norton or others at Sloan-Kettering. At one point, I had given nine vials of blood for testing, and a tug-of-war erupted when a Georgetown University study wanted them. Imagine, two institutions fighting over my lousy, defective DNA. I've done some charity work and fund-raisers for Dr. Norton and Evelyn Lauder's Breast Cancer Research Foundation, but I can no longer afford to chip in to attend their annual gala with Elton John. That's okay . . . those fantastically expensive seat prices all go to this amazing charity. In 2000, though, I did have the honor of introducing Sir Elton at the foundation's Cipriani dinner.

But back to 1990–91 and my return to work after that first surgery. Things were popping in the music world, and I couldn't fall behind. The grunge movement was picking up, which would ultimately have a major impact on the rock radio landscape, and not necessarily for the better. Guns N' Roses were smokin' hot, and Slash paid a visit to WNEW, whacked out of his mind. First, he'd dropped a bottle of whiskey in the stairway, and his limo driver was dispatched to find another. Then, he used the potted plant in the lobby as a men's room facility. Finally, he encouraged the DJ who followed me on the air to play "Get in the Ring," a Guns N' Roses song loaded with profanity. I stood behind Slash, shaking my head with a frantic no to my co-worker, but he went ahead and played the song anyway, which resulted in a week's worth of suspension for him. (Slash subsequently changed his ways and is a very nice fellow to whom I recently spoke. He remains extremely talented.)

I began doing a weekly radio show that ran in Japan, called the *New York Rock Exchange*, which was produced by Gary Chetkoff, a former corporate attorney who now owns radio station WDST in Woodstock, New York. And for a while, VH-1 hired me as an on-camera host for their *Countdown* show.

All of this was great, at the time, but I did have one particular score to settle, with that insolent radiologist who had misdiagnosed me. And the Big C was far from done with me.

"Hello," I said crisply over the phone to Dr. X, the radiologist. "This is Carol Miller. I have the blond hair, don't know if you remember? I saw you fairly recently for mammograms. You said I had the very dense tissue that could be hiding a golf ball?"

"Oh . . . yes," the doctor said. "What can I do for you?"

"I'd like a few minutes of your time to speak to you in person," I replied, in my best professional voice.

"Well, today is not really a good day," said Dr. X. "I have the decorators here in the office. We're dealing with some wallpaper now."

"Well, it's important," I insisted. "I'll be brief."

I had already nervously rehearsed at least some of my scenario, and was going to call it my "Joan Collins Moment," channeling some of her cold and calculating *Dynasty* demeanor. But for a good cause.

I arrived at Dr. X's office with her original mammograms in tow. "Nice decorating job," I began. "You must be doing very well for a young doctor." She appeared to be about forty. I paused, getting into character. "Can we speak alone in your examining room?" Dr. X showed me in and closed the door. "You see," I said, pausing dramatically, "I can ruin it all for you." She looked confused. "Would you mind taking a look at these mammograms again?" I asked.

The radiologist put the films up on her light box. "You need better lights," I pointed out. "These are a little dim. Now, what do you think this is?" I said, pointing directly at the small cluster of dots that had sealed my fate. The doctor hesitated. "I'll tell you what this is," I said coldly. "This is an invasive cancer tumor measuring just under point five centimeters. And you missed it. Even I can see it, and I'm not the doctor. If I hadn't signed your mammograms out of here and taken them somewhere else, I'd be dead."

At this point, the radiologist's nurse burst into the room, all aflutter. "Sorry to barge in, but I just realized you're Carol Miller, the DJ on WNEW," she flapped. "My husband loves you! He listens every night. Do you think you could just sign an autograph to him?"

"Sure," I said, smiling on cue. "What's his name?" I signed the white piece of notepad paper. "Please tell him thank you very much."

"Oh, and excuse me, doctor," the nurse said to Dr. X, "the Guttmans just called. They have some films." The Guttman Institute was well known and respected for mammogram analysis, and they obviously farmed out the radiological readings.

"Oh, you read for the Guttmans too," I said with forced cheerfulness to the doctor. Dr. X looked pale, and very much as if she was going to be sick. She hastily excused herself.

A few minutes later, she returned and asked her nurse for privacy. "I'm so sorry," she said, with tears rolling down her face.

"Well, so am I, and I'm going to be real busy this year with surgery and stuff, and I don't want to waste time bothering with you," I said, more or less just as I'd rehearsed. "I know what it's like to be a young doctor and have your own practice," I said, softening. "My sister has one, and it's tough. Anyone can make a mistake, like you did. But you have a bad attitude. You're too flip with your patients. What you said to me about how you couldn't tell if I was 'hiding a golf ball' in my chest, that wasn't funny."

"Oh," she cried again, "I am so sorry."

"So here's the deal," I told her. "You're lucky you made these mistakes with me, because you know what? I'm not going to try to sue you or anything. I know you'll never make these mistakes again. Not after this. I want you to go on and be the best damn radiologist in New York, and help people like me," I said, winding up for my finale. "I won't tell anyone your name, and you'll never see me again. But I guarantee, you'll never forget me." I thanked the doctor for her time, took my coat, and left the office. The decorators were busy rearranging a plant in the newly wallpapered waiting room.

"You're damn right she won't forget you," my father said that evening. "She's probably going to be up all night with her head in the toilet." For my part, I've kept my end of the bargain. I never told anyone her name. That's why I call her Dr. X. She's still practicing, but not in Manhattan; I just now Googled her. I hope she's one of the top radiologists in the country.

39

"If you see something you don't like about my driver's license, just say so and . . . uh . . . this won't go any further," I said. It was early spring 1992, on an evening right after my radio show at WNEW, and I was sitting in an Indian restaurant on West Forty-ninth Street with a very tall, handsome young man who had been assisting me with a music project relating to the station. I was not yet used to my endless schedule of cancer scans, and I was still in pain from my mastectomies and initial breast reconstruction. But I had decided to forge ahead with new things and was trying to get all this *meshugass* (craziness) off my mind.

I had met a pretty young singer-songwriter, Annie O'Shay, who was working as a phone intern up at the radio station, and I wanted to help her with her career. This would be something different. And I did know someone at a record company, my old compatriot Jimmy Iovine, who was running Interscope Records. He was kind enough to arrange a recording session for Annie at Unique Recording Studios on West Forty-seventh Street near Times Square. After contacting Unique, I was given the phone number of an engineer who would be running the session, Paul Logus, whom I was supposed to contact at his home in Brooklyn.

When I called at the appointed time, a woman whom I assumed to be his wife (until, strangely, she voluntarily told me otherwise) said that Paul had gone out to the store to buy milk, which was odd, because he was expecting my call. Later, he apologized, and told me his girlfriend had just made up the milk story for no reason, maybe because she didn't like another woman calling their house. I made arrangements to accompany Annie to Unique and meet Paul.

The first thing that struck me about him (well, probably the same thing anyone would notice first) was his height. He had to be about six feet six. He really seemed to know his way around the studio, and he was very amiable as well. There was a kindness about him. I spoke a bit with Paul during a break in the session. He was originally from Dayton, Ohio, and lived with his girlfriend, Denise. I surmised from his last name that he was Greek. Of course, he had to be younger than I, now forty-one, but really I had no idea how old he might be because he was so tall. After one of the short recording sessions, I was having some internal chest pressure and, stepping out of character a bit, mentioned my recent bout of surgeries to Paul. Something about him made me feel comfortable enough to talk about it. He seemed appropriately concerned, but not put off.

Later in the session, I casually mentioned that I was giving away tickets for an Eddie Money show at the Bottom Line club and might be able to get an extra pair for him and Denise as a thank-you. Paul said he would come by the station the next night to pick up the tickets. He arrived in the lobby, wearing a long coat, I came out of the air studio to greet him, and Paul gave me a big bear hug. A hug! Literally no one had given me a hug in over a year, since I'd been diagnosed. Not that I'd gone around trying to solicit one. Certainly, I appreciated that some people were afraid to hurt me (which was ironic, since I have no feeling on the exterior of my chest). But I had noticed a few people with whom I had constant contact at work who would no longer even shake my hand. I suspected the cancer thing creeped them out, or they thought they might catch it from me. If that was their gut feeling, fine, that's just the way it was, and I couldn't hold it against them or try to change their mind. But I was shocked that the tall, handsome, friendly recording engineer was treating me like just a normal person. And I sensed that things weren't going that well between him and Denise—she would call and interrupt him with problems while he was working.

I had continued to come by the recording studio with Annie, and Paul and I struck up a friendship. Although Annie did not get her recording contract, Paul and I kept hanging out. So here we were, maybe a month or so later, having dinner in the second-floor Indian restaurant near Unique, just being friends, but maybe friends with "interest." In the course of conversation, Paul mentioned his birthday, which was coming up in June. "Which birthday?" I asked. "Oh, twenty-nine," said Paul. So there it was. This guy was twelve and a half years younger than I, and I hadn't had the faintest idea. It was at that point that I shot my driver's license across the table to him, for his inspection. After several moments of deliberation, Paul returned my license. "That's a pretty good picture of you," he said.

When I told my father about my new "friend," Daddy said, "What? He's twenty-eight. He has his whole life ahead of him. What does he need you for? Besides, he's Greek, you say? Well, Greeks don't like you"—Daddy pointed his finger at me—"and they don't like me either."

I pointed out that Paul had mentioned that his family owned some land in Turkey. Maybe they liked us there.

"Nah, he's just fooling around."

"Listen, Pa," I countered, "if he was fooling around, do you think he'd pick an older woman from a different religion who's sick and has no . . . upper deck?"

"Well, you have a point there," my father agreed.

And so I began going out with Paul, whose calm demeanor I found to be a welcome relief from that of my recent drama kings. Although Paul didn't get some of my generational references, his emotional maturity made up for our age difference. He was also dryly humorous, a very talented musician, and like me, a *Star Trek* fanatic. "A match made in the Delta Quadrant," we used to say. Plus, he didn't seem to see my tenuous health situation as a big deterrent. When I finished my nightly radio show, I liked visiting Paul at the big Manhattan recording studios where he mixed hit records and sound tracks for people like Diddy and Tina Turner.

After two and a half years, we were married at the UN Chapel on July 17, 1994. It was just the immediate families. "I always thought I'd get married in my bride's church," Paul had said, and since that wasn't exactly possible, we picked the multinational UN as a setting, and had a Reform rabbi (who threw in a lot of Hebrew for my father at my request). The rabbi explained the symbolism of the Jewish wedding to Paul's parents and grandmother, who'd initially had a little bit of a hard time dealing with the whole thing. Okay, more than a little bit of a hard time. Well, you couldn't really blame them. I wore my sister's wedding gown, which I altered with safety pins, and a pair of my mother's shoes. We had our wedding lunch at the Water Club restaurant on the East River, which is where we go every year for our anniversary.

I say Paul has made some sacrifices by marrying me. After numerous warnings about the return of my cancer from Dr. Norton, and the obvious familial element to my situation, he agreed with my sad wish not to inflict my guaranteed genetic curse on any children, and so we have none. I feel very bad about it sometimes, but still think I made the right decision. It's too late now anyway. And I'm a good aunt, I think, and Paul's definitely a great uncle to my sister's son, Robbie. So why didn't she make the same decision I had? Never crossed her mind. For one, Dr. Jane didn't have cancer, and didn't really think she would get it. She would be totally shocked by the diagnosis in 2008, a recurrence, and mastectomies in 2009 and again in 2010. I wasn't that surprised.

Despite it all, it looked like I had a second chance at life. Maybe catch a breather. Not quite.

40

WNEW-FM hired a new program director in 1994, and on his very first day I had lunch with him and our then general manger, the late Kevin Smith. New management is always a problematic scenario for DJs. It boils down to: Could/would this new person fire me? How much power does he have? Is he going to dislike me and give me a hard time? Does he have any special DJ friends to whom he'd like to give my job? You get the idea.

Coming back to the station after lunch, the new program director very deliberately grabbed my crotch. From behind and underneath. A real grab. In this, or should I say that, day and age, I was extremely surprised. There were laws and company regulations about this kind of thing by then. But if you wanted to keep working, going around complaining and litigating would probably finish off your career. If you just wanted a pile of money, well, maybe complaining and litigating were the things to do. But I've only wanted to work.

What to do? What to do? It was the guy's first day, and getting in a keep-your-hands-to-yourself confrontation didn't seem like a good idea. Especially because it would totally embarrass the general manager who'd hired him, and wanted to show off his good choice to the rest of the station and indeed to his own managers. In retrospect, had the incident happened at a more secure time, I might have mustered a humorous but firmly delivered, "Hey, knock it off. Crotch grabbing is not in my contract." But at the time, I was a little too frightened to pull that off. I didn't want to risk my job. I was also still a bit overwhelmed by my hospital lifestyle. So I pretended to ignore the crotch grab. Maybe that would be the end of it. Of course, it wasn't, but I would always pretend to ignore his way-out-of-line behavior.

Besides all the groping, the program director, who seemed to have a touch of the psychotic about him, asked strange questions about my health, such as "Do you have any sensation on your chest?" I didn't see what this had to do with my broadcasting job, but he insisted that as the director, he "had to know" these things. "No," I finally replied, "I don't." "Well, do you have any sexual feelings down below?" he asked in a rather evil tone. "What?!" I said. "Uh, yeah, would you please stop asking me this stuff?"

One day, as I stood in the hallway of our new WNEW studios on Seventh Avenue talking with three male co-workers, the program director approached me and put his hand on my reconstructed left breast. "What are you doing?" I asked. "Removing a hair from your jacket," he said. "What's the difference? You can't feel it anyway. Here, if you want, I'll put it back," and he did, rather forcefully. I declined to tell my new husband about any of this, fearing it might inspire some kind of testosterone-fueled showdown, which could easily get out of hand and, again, cause my dismissal. My need for AFTRA union employment was now paramount, as they provided my very necessary health coverage.

So I was already up against this employment situation, which included further groping and tonguing incidents in the summer of '95, when the program director in question began to get vindictive with me because I wouldn't "play ball." Concocted reports in my corporate employment file, etc. Was I surprised all this was going on in the new era of political correctness and corporate self-regulation? Not really. It's the oldest story in the business world, but I sure didn't need it happening to me.

More importantly, the program director changed the format of WNEW to "New York's Rock Alternative," which featured a lot of newer and more eclectic music that was generally unpalatable to our core audience, which had traditionally been composed of the twenty-five- to fifty-four-year-old male demographic. Although this particular program director was probably not solely responsible for the switch, he championed artists such as Tori Amos, Blur, certain grunge acts, and most notably Alanis Morrisette, which made absolutely no sense to me. Where had it been shown that our audience demographic had any preference for this music? Especially that of Alanis Morrisette, whose appeal and man-hating lyrics were designed to register with young women, and angry ones at that. I personally got a kick out of her, but will never forget the time her voice first came over the airwaves of WNEW while I was in the car with Paul. "What is that horrible noise?" he said, wincing.

So I began to fear in earnest for my job, which I was afraid would end badly one way or another. I also defended my musical opinions, when asked, as being for the good of the station's survival. Perhaps I should have kept them to myself, but in the end, it wouldn't have mattered anyway. The offending program director got himself fired for offending other people. I never filed any complaint. But I heard he similarly offended another woman while at his next job.

In January 1996, WNEW had a chance to rectify its format change situation but neglected to do so. Classic Rock competitor WXRK, which featured Howard Stern and his team on the morning show, had switched to a younger, harder-sounding alternative rock playlist, leaving the field open for WNEW to return to some of its former glory by reverting to a basically Classic Rock format. In July 1996, WAXQ, also known as Q104.3, switched to Classic Rock. WNEW decided to do that as well, early in 1997, but with all its shifting around, WNEW had lost its credibility. In 1998 the WNEW management began to dispense with much of the longtime staff, including the station founder, the revered Scott Muni. I waited on the edge of my seat to be fired, but I wasn't. I had already agreed to my pay cut.

But later that year, WNEW hired "shock jocks" Opie and Anthony, whose basic motifs were belittling women and scathingly making fun of WNEW's history and DJs. I took O & A out to dinner on their first night there, and figured we'd get along, why not? I generally found them to be funny, and Anthony to be a particularly skilled mimic, but their act was generally not as clever as that of the brilliant Howard Stern, whose well-known interviews and send-ups were legendary. Before going national, Howard had directed some of his humor at fellow New York radio personalities on other stations. There were many times when I would have to laugh along with a cabdriver who was hearing Howard speculate as to the color of my panties that day and making obviously false but all-in-fun claims that he had a stack of naked pictures of me. "Hey, your friend Howard Stern thinks you've got a nice ass," my father had said, just a little too loudly, at a Mothers' Day restaurant dinner. "Whadaya going to do about it?" "Well," said my mother, who took things a little too literally, "isn't it better that Howard thinks she has a nice ass than a ugly one?"

But things took a bizarre turn one day when the latest WNEW program director asked me to stick around the station and interrupt Opie and Anthony's show to disagree with their relentless ridicule of WNEW's Evolution of Rock and Roll feature. "This'll be good radio," the director said. Frankly, I wanted to leave and not bother to get involved, but the director insisted. I was sure that he had told Rick, the producer of O & A's show, that he was going to send me in for this "bit." But the bottom line was that Opie and Anthony were never told I was to make an entrance and disagree with them.

It took me a while to realize that they were really getting angry. By the time I realized they were serious, things were getting out of control, but I figured I should defend myself rather than wimping out and leaving the studio. At one point, I went around the corner to the Duane Reade pharmacy, and purchased a Fleet instant rectal enema Twin Pack, and wrote their names, Opie and Anthony, above the pictures of the two enema bottles. "What do you expect me to do with this?" demanded Opie. "What you usually do with an enema," I replied. "Shove it up your ass." I figured there had to be some humor in this. But Opie was clearly enraged, and threw the enema against the studio wall of CDs. I was amazed. To these guys, it was all-out war. They could dish it out, but they couldn't take it.

The program director, wanting to protect his newly hired "stars," insisted that I wait in the mail room before entering the studio, as my show followed theirs, and he didn't want us to cross paths. This waiting in the mail room business, where there was a telephone extension, afforded me the opportunity to surmise that Anthony was cheating on his wife. I bet money (okay, just a few quarters) with co-worker Eddie Trunk that Anthony was cheating with Lobster Girl, a listener who had volunteered to have sex with one of O & A's side characters if it would prevent the boiling of a hapless live lobster. This is what radio had come to!

In the end, I finally confronted O & A in the hallway in order to end this ridiculous feud. And not much further down the line, the management of WNEW shelved its over thirty-year history as a rock station, in favor of more programs featuring this elevating "hot talk" format. I did my last show at WNEW on September 10, 1999, where I was allowed to present a free-form show of representative songs of my own choosing, and received a glowing dismissal letter from the management. (The "hot talk" format basically didn't really work in any of its varied configurations, and was finally dropped at the end of 2002.)

But now I was really up a creek. I was terribly saddened by the thought of not working after all these years, and also needed the AFTRA union work for my medical benefits. Those bills for surgery and constant hospital visits were piling up. Surely they could squeeze me in somewhere, even part-time, at now Classic Rock WAXQ (Q104.3)? After all, I had been on FM rock radio in New York continuously since 1973 and was well known as a meat-and-potatoes full-timer to that audience. Apparently, that wasn't going to matter. There was evil afoot. Or a giant misconception.

41

Immediately upon my format-dictated dismissal from WNEW, I sent a letter, tape, and résumé over to WAXQ, thinking that was the appropriate way to apply for a job. The program director there at the time had also spent a small spell in that position at WNEW, and I thought I might get a warm welcome. Strangely, I got no response. I asked my representatives at the time, from the Don Buchwald agency, to make contact and investigate. Through them, I was given some dumbfounding information. First, that I had "harassed" the Q104.3 DJs with phone calls to their studio hotline. The only call I had ever put in to that number was for the purpose of congratulating a former WNEW part-time colleague who had gotten a job at the new station. Second, I had "crossed paths" with someone in management at WAXQ and that I would never, ever get a job there. I wasn't sure I knew anyone in management at Q, and was hard-pressed to even come up with a name. But I knew one thing: I would have to come up with some AFTRA union work in short order to be able to maintain my health insurance.

Don Buchwald contacted Mel Karmazin, the president of Infinity Broadcasting (and at the time of this writing, the head of SiriusXM Satellite Radio) on my behalf. I had known Mel back in 1973 when he was a salesman at WNEW, and had spoken to him a bit over the years, including recently, before the demise of WNEW as a rock station. Mel contacted Tom Chiusano, the general manager at K-ROCK, and I was very appreciative to be given a part-time slot at that union-affiliated New York alternative rock station. Although I was quite familiar with the music presented there, I was typecast as a classic rocker and could not hope to attain a full-time position.

Why wasn't I immediately hired at WAXQ? Tom wanted to know. I told him I was stumped by the turndown. I also made the rounds of many of the other top stations in New York, of varying formats, and was identically told at each one that "everyone" knew me as a rocker, there was no way they could put me on the air playing other types of music, the program director in question thought I was just swell, and why wasn't I already on WAXQ? That station's ratings were not yet stellar.

Ironically, I had already been working for a couple of years on British radio, basically for nothing, with a weekly program on XCEL-FM, which had been arranged by the station's director, and my friend, Alan Thompson. When Alan moved back to the BBC, he found me a weekly slot doing live lifestyle news and commentary over the telephone from New York. I would hold this position with various BBC local hosts for several years, and it would be the most interesting highlight of my week, even if it was not financially profitable. Everyone on that end thought I was a newsperson. None of this classic rocker problem.

On the morning of September 11, 2001, it was Alan Thompson who called me from the local BBC and frantically asked me if I was all right. I didn't know what he was talking about. "It's the World Trade Center," he said. "We have the pictures here on the television and it's horrific." As I had a clear view of the Trade Center from my kitchen window, I told him I'd call back and ran into the kitchen. One of the towers was smoking. I woke up Paul, and showed him the fire. When we popped on the TV, we were horrified to learn that a plane had hit the tower, and another one was on the way. Yet another plane was reportedly heading to Washington. "Why can't they stop this?" I yelled, looking out the window as the second plane looped around and smashed into the other tower of the World Trade Center. Watching the towers collapse from the vantage point of my window was stupefying. Later, I would drive down to the area, taking some requested shirts and dog food, and finally get a phone call through back to the BBC with a live report.

I had additionally already been making a long commute up to Hartford, Connecticut, doing a couple of shows a week for their classic rock station, WHCN, which was owned by the same company as WAXQ. The pay was very low, and they were not union affiliates, but it was keeping me in the game, so to speak, and the people were great. No one in management there could figure out why I wasn't at WAXQ either. The Hartford job eventually cost more than it was worth, when I was involved in two serious car accidents on icy Connecticut roads, and twice had to rebuild the Volvo. I soon became a prerecorded voice, for very little money, at the fledgling Sirius Satellite Radio, also not a union affiliate, and so also not helpful for my health insurance.

It was an odd series of events that finally led to my hiring, in 2004, at WAXQ, now the nation's top-rated classic rock station. On Mother's Day, 2001, I came up with the idea of getting the old WPLJ New York's Best Rock crew back together, and I contacted our former program director, Larry Berger, still a dear friend even though he'd fired me, who was now living in San Francisco. At first, Larry was dubious, but we cooked up a concept that was just bound to work, and contacted the main former DJs, some of whom were between jobs. I held a meeting at my place, with Larry making his appearance via the telephone, and came up with a marketing plan. The proposed venture made it into the newspapers, but shortly thereafter our key DJ, morning man Jim Kerr, was hired by WAXQ, therefore putting the kibosh on the WPLJ re-grouping. I hadn't worked with Jim in a long time, but through our proposed project, he again became my friend, this time one of my best friends.

Now that he was at WAXQ, Jim promised to try and find out why I had not been hired there. A new program director, Bob Buchmann, had started at Q the previous year, and under his guidance the station finally began to pick up in the ratings. Why could I not speak to him either? Finally, after nearly five long years, Jim found an answer: apparently, someone who didn't want me there—possibly to protect his own job? I wondered—had told the higher-ups in that company that I had sued my former employer, WNEW, and the company that owned WAXQ understandably did not want to hire a litigious person.

To say I was stunned would be an understatement. I had never sued anyone in my life, nor had I ever filed any official complaints with anybody about anything. Also, Jim reported, it was rumored that I was "difficult to work with." If that were the case, why had I been kept on by WNEW management until the bitter end of the music format and given a glowing recommendation letter? Since Jim had worked with me previously at WPLJ, he attested to the fact that I had never been known there as "difficult." But the rumors had circulated, and I had to rectify this sorry situation.

In April of 2004, I had undergone some more surgery, and had a catheter put in place. On that particular day, I left Sloan-Kettering with my new tube to attend the A.I.R. Broadcasting awards ceremony at the B. B. King club, where Jim Kerr was being honored and introduced by then New York governor Pataki. Shortly after my arrival, I spotted Andy Rosen, the New York market manager for Clear Channel Radio, which owned WAXQ. I approached Andy, said hello, and then told him I'd heard he thought I'd sued WNEW. "I don't know where that came from," I said. I noted that I'd heard of another woman at WNEW who in fact at one time had sued that company, but it sure wasn't me. "You must feel terrible about that," said Andy kindly. "Here's my card; call me tomorrow."

At the awards ceremony, I also met Tom Poleman, the brilliant young New York market-programming director for the company, and asked if he might include me in some of his fact-finding audience research. The next day, I called Andy Rosen and met with him in his office. He then arranged a meeting for me with Tom Poleman and Bob Buchmann. Within a couple of weeks, I had a full-time job back and was thrilled to join the staff of Q104.3 on June 21, 2004. Five years of banishment because of a rumor that was cleared up in roughly thirty seconds!

Right before I joined the Q staff, I paid a visit to Scott Muni, who was, sadly, in a nursing home suffering from either Alzheimer's or the effects of a stroke, depending upon whom you talked to. I had been unable to visit Scott for the month previously because, with a tube running into my chest (a Jackson-Pratt drain), I was advised to keep away from other hospital-type settings. But Scott immediately beamed as he recognized me, got out of bed, gave me a kiss, and asked after my health. I told Scott I would soon be joining him on the Q staff; at that time, he had a daily pre-recorded hourly show running. His ability to speak was fading, but I understood what he was talking about. When I mentioned that I was still recording shows for Satellite radio, Scott said exactly, "It can't be . . . the clicking . . . the future." I knew what he meant, that we'd have to keep live radio up and running, alive and well; the medium could not be reduced to simple clicks of a computer that would assemble a program. When I got up to leave, Scott said, "Please come back soon." And then perhaps strangely, "I love you." Several months later, he passed away. I think about him all the time.

Over the next few years, I would work very hard at Q104.3 on my evening show, where I was thrilled to be talking to the same listener-friends who'd grown up with me over the decades. I would talk to some of these friends and others over the satellite radio, and then again others through my nationally syndicated Led Zeppelin show, *Get the Led Out*. I would even be sent by Q104.3 in 2007 to the Zeppelin reunion concert in London, where I would run into yet other longtime friends.

At the time of the concert, my father was hospitalized with an infection related to his non-Hodgkin's lymphoma, a cancer he would successfully battle consistently with chemotherapy. Paul and I rushed home from England to be with him, and my father soon came home. My sister and her husband, Mario, had already helped to hire a trusted aide, Kojo, to live with my parents, look after them, and drive them to their medical appointments. Daddy seemed to be doing satisfactorily, but toward the end of 2009, he took a turn for the worse. In fact, he was misdiagnosed. He had now developed actual Hodgkin's disease, and it had gone untreated for several months. He was readmitted to the hospital in February 2010 with terrible daily fevers, which would render him incoherent or unconscious, and he was placed on top of a special cooling blanket. Often, when conscious during a fever, Daddy lost most of his ability to speak, and much of his memory as well, which would intermittently return. But I always knew he was "in there," and tried to finish his sentences. I drove out to St. Francis Hospital in Port Washington,

Long Island, almost daily, before deciding that overnight visits would be a lot easier due to the traffic.

One afternoon, Daddy was coherent, but I sensed that he was pretending to remember things he couldn't, to save his dignity. I told him I had to leave to go to work. "Daddy, it's not your fault, it's the fever, so don't feel bad, but you don't remember where I work, do you?" "No," he said quietly, after a pause. "And you don't remember what I do for a living either?" Again an embarrassed no. "I talk on the radio," I said. My father immediately broke into a huge, radiant smile. "You do? That's terrific!" he exclaimed. I was stunned. "That's not what you told me forty years ago, Daddy, but I'll take it," I grinned, both sad and happily shocked at the same time. Much of Daddy's critical edge had gone; his personality resembled more that of his easygoing mother than his more severe father. But I had no doubt that he meant what he said at that moment: he was excited that I was on the radio. That would never erase my feeling that I had been a sore disappointment to him and the family, but it mitigated the pain I always carry around.

I'm glad that my last conversation with my father was about the here and now. He disliked big emotional statements, abstract mumbo-jumbo like "positive thinking." "I hate that crap!" he said once, waking up in the emergency room, after I'd uncharacteristically said something of the sort to encourage him. Toward the end, while seemingly unconscious, he would clutch my hand or wrist to the point where it was painful. One night, as I regaled him with my daily monologue about the Yankee game and other current events, I veered off the road of my usual solitary recitation and became a bit more agitated. "Look," I said, "maybe you're afraid, but no one's dying here! You're gonna get better, so will you come on and snap out of it?"

With that, my father's eyes opened slowly, and a smirk began to creep across the corners of his mouth. "I got a pretty good grip, doncha think?" he said, as if he'd just been pretending to be unconscious all this time. "Of course," I said matter-of-factly, albeit actually flabbergasted that he had become conscious on cue. "Guess what I got for you, Pa," I whispered. "Your favorite—Planters and a seltzer water! I'll give ya a *bisseleh* [little bit]."

"Really?" he said. "Where'd ya get that?"

"Downstairs at the machine," I told him. I had been bringing the non-permitted food and drink with me every night. Carefully, I removed his horribly uncomfortable through-the-nose feeding tube and let him have a tiny sip and bite, which he relished.

"What time is it anyway?" he said, as if just waking up from a normal nap.

"It's three A.M."

"Whadaya doin' here so late?"

"It's free parking at night," I deadpanned.

"Oh yeah?" he said. "Good. And who's that makin' noise over there?" He gestured with his head toward the door.

"That's the nurses. You know you're in a hospital, right?"

"Yeah, sure," as he took another small sip of seltzer. "Okay, honey"— Daddy paused—"thank you so much. I'm a little tired. I have to go back now."

Back to where? I wondered, as he slipped into an unconscious state.

Daddy passed away on May 12, 2010, barely over two weeks short of his ninety-second birthday. The saddest day of my life. My sister and I spoke at his funeral. I don't know how we did it. Probably not an hour goes by that I don't think of him and heed some of his advice: checking the tires, or humorously dismissing someone's ridiculous statement.

After my father was gone, I spent extra time with a dear friend who had become special to me over the last few years: Elaine Kaufman, the renowned proprietor of the famous New York restaurant that bore her name. For decades, she had hosted a nightly table-hopping fest and introduced patrons to each other who she thought would get along, celebrities and neighborhood regulars alike. It's hard to explain, but Elaine was exactly like my father's side of the family—the same mannerisms, same expressions—and she had the same amusingly conflicted background I did, having one foot in the old Yiddish world and the other foot in the twenty-first century. When my father was gone, I would talk about him to her as I always had, and feel like I was sitting with a relative.

Elaine ran a restaurant, not a bar, she would say, even though her bar was a very lucrative and prominent feature. Nice Jewish women didn't run bars, even those women who could curse with the best of them. "Look at dem *nafkes* [whores]," she mused to me in Yiddish one night, observing the patrons at her own bar.

"Yeah, *alta nafkes* [old whores]," I said grinning.

"What kind of a woman gets dressed like that and sits at a bar alone?" asked Elaine.

"I dunno," I said. "I wouldn't do that, would you?"

"No," she said emphatically, and waved her hand.

Sometimes I would visit Elaine alone on my way home from work, or with another friend, like Jim Kerr, if it was a Friday and he didn't have to get up at the crack of dawn for his morning radio show. Then I would drive Elaine home in the Volvo to her apartment near her restaurant. She liked my car. "Take your time, the meter's not running," I would say. Then, as she was overweight, I would help her to the lobby of her building, where Walter would open the door. She would sit down and rest in a chair in front of her elevator, and tell me to leave. "Not on my watch," I would say. "I'm not gonna leave you sit here alone." Then I would stay with her and help her unzip her shoes until she was ready for Walter to take her upstairs in the elevator. Elaine passed away too, in December 2010, but not until after another of my own personal calamities. I miss Elaine very much. Two thousand ten was a very difficult year.

42

"It's bad! bad! bad! It's cancer, and all of it has to come out! I'm your little sister, but this time you're going to listen to me!" Those were the words of Dr. Jane Miller, as I awoke on her operating table around noon on Sunday, September 26, 2010. Talk about bedside manner. Oh well, she didn't have to put on an act for me. I was momentarily nauseated and feverish, but certainly not as shocked as the first time I'd heard the Big C word directed at me.

I had asked Dr. Jane to perform my internal procedure on a Sunday, instead of having it done during the week at Sloan-Kettering, so that I wouldn't have to miss doing my radio show due to the after-effects of the anesthesia. Dr. Brown, my surgeon at Sloan, had noticed something problematic on one of my scans six months earlier, but said that we'd just watch it. I agreed, especially because I was spending all my free time at St. Francis Hospital with my father. Now that he had passed, and with the scan and another test repeated six months later, things apparently looked worse. "We're sending it to the lab," said Dr. Jane, "but I'm telling you now, I know what I see."

It wasn't as if Dr. Norton hadn't urged me several times to have my remaining female organs removed in advance, because of the genetics thing, but really, I'd been busy. In fact, I'd just had surgery at Sloan on August 12, to repeat my right breast reconstruction, and in fact had undergone the scan for Dr. Brown's review, with a plastic Jackson-Pratt tube and drain coming down my right side from Dr. Disa's excellent surgery. A little confusing here? It's amazing how you can get used to things, but still . . . "Yeah, I guess the party's over now," I said, lying on the surgical table, to Dr. Jane and her nurse Carol.

The specimens were sent off to a lab in New Jersey, where the slides would be analyzed. Not a pleasant few days of waiting. On top of that, my sister had just had to put her wonderful dog, Chino, to sleep the night before my procedure. Unbelievable. I actually wished my sister hadn't offered her opinion on my situation, which had just made the waiting worse. According to my father, he had concluded I'd had a problem when he'd seen my mammograms twenty years earlier, but had not wanted to needlessly upset me before the biopsy. Don't ask, don't tell, for better or worse.

The phone call on Thursday was no surprise. "You have grade three uterine [endometrial] cancer." The stage, a different parameter from the grade, at first said to be two, was downgraded to one. So here it was, the second part of the family genetic curse, delivered nearly twenty years to the day after my first. I immediately got on the phone to Dr. Brown's office at Sloan to arrange for the surgery. They would be taking everything out—the whole shootin' match. There was a slot open for the surgery almost immediately, on Monday October 4, but Dr. Brown needed the slides . . . tonight. I jumped into the trusty Volvo and headed out to the lab in Jersey to transport the slides myself before going on the air. Usually the slides could not be readied that quickly, but luckily for me, sometimes it pays to be the evening DJ on a big rock station.

Rushing back to Manhattan and double-parking my car on East Sixty-eighth Street, I bolted upstairs to deposit the slides in Dr. Brown's office. Fortunately, I'd been up and down fast, and not gotten a ticket. On the way down to the radio station, while I was driving on the FDR, my cell phone went off. It was my supervisor from SiriusXM telling me that, effectively, they were taking me off one channel and cutting my pay in half. When it rains it pours.

The surgery began with some difficulty on Monday, due to lung complications, and I first received a nebulizer treatment, under a mask. But then, a most amazing sight. I was taken into the operating room where the surgical team and a huge surgical robot awaited. "What are we having done today, Ms. Miller?" said a nurse, following protocol.

"We're taking out the plumbing," I said using the old Yiddish euphemism.

"You have to be more specific," said the nurse. "Are we taking out the ovaries? What else?"

"Look, if it comes with the package, we're taking it out, okay?" I said, my eyes riveted on the robot, which was standing tall, covered with sanitizing shrink-wrap, and beginning to warm up for action by blinking its lights. It was better than *Battlestar Galactica*. This Da Vinci robot was a real Cylon, who was going to be skillfully commandeered by Dr. Brown and do some pretty intricate surgery.

Da Vinci did his job, and again I thought I'd lucked out—they said the Big C hadn't spread. I returned to work the following Monday, in a good deal of pain, I might add. I kept my promise; I only missed a week off the radio, and was trying to make the best of my recovery. I joked that I'd never be an in-patient on the tenth floor of Sloan-Kettering again, because it was the "women's floor," and all my womanly organs had been removed. Soon a vocal cord infection from the anesthesia tubes set in, coupled with a bad period of asthma, which caused me to totally lose my voice. Paul and I made the best of New Year's Eve 2010 by taking my sister to a friend's bar on Eighth Avenue and then heading up to Elaine's restaurant, even though it had taken on a much saddened atmosphere since Elaine's passing. But I was still alive, and a new year was reason to look ahead. I turned my focus back toward being on the air and finishing this book.

It wasn't so bad, what I'd done with my life, was it? Yes, I was often wistful that I had no children, but reminded myself that I had two talking parrots who called me "Mommy." And my non-traditional radio schedule had made it possible for me to keep working through my periods of illness. Weeks into the new year passed, and ironically, with all of my painful problematic body parts removed, I had never felt physically better. It was as if I were now going to have that chance, even at my age, of finally feeling what it was like to be the pain-free, perennial young person I had always been on the air. And not feel so guilty about choosing the radio career. If only Daddy were here. I zipped out of my surgical follow-up appointment with Dr. Brown on April 13 in an up-tempo mood, which I enjoyed for a whole week.

Until the next phone call from Dr. Brown. The follow-up tests had revealed that my uterine Big C had returned. The doctor was shocked; I wasn't. The only thing I found shocking at this point, I told her, was the price of a gallon of gas. I reported back to Dr. Brown's hospital office for the removal of a small tumor. The good people at Memorial Sloan-Kettering put me through every CAT/PET/MRI scan in the book. I begin five weeks of internal radiation treatments tomorrow; actually, in just a few hours.

But I feel lucky. I'm going to beat the Big C again, no doubt about it, and continue to avenge the fate of my relatives. Hopefully all the re-search data and body parts I've donated will help to eradicate the damn illness. I'm still on the radio, with my friends, the listeners who have been with me for decades, and I hope I've been a good companion to them, playing the music that has kept us going through "Good Times Bad Times." Plus, I have a wonderful husband.

In fact, I feel so lucky that I'm going to give away a thousand dollars tonight to the twenty-fifth caller. With *mein mazel* (my luck), someone's going to be as lucky as me. And it just might be you! Stay tuned.

ACKNOWLEDGMENTS

For assistance and patience during the preparation of this book:

Paul J. Logus, Jr.

Hilda Miller

Jane E. Miller, M.D.; Mario Vizcaya, Robbie Vizcaya Miller

Abigail Holstein

Marilyn Allen

Libby Edelson

Rachel Bressler

Daniel Halpern

Lynn Goldsmith

Jim Kerr

Larry Berger

Lynne Bershad

Larry Norton, M.D.; Carol Brown, M.D.; Joseph Disa, M.D.; Kaled M. Alektiar, M.D.; Diane Stover, M.D.; and all the staff at Memorial Sloan-Kettering Cancer Center

Marc Benhuri, D.M.D.

Dr. David Orentreich, M.D.

Dr. William Rosenblatt, M.D.

Bob Pittman, and everyone at Clear Channel Media and Entertainment and Q104.3

Denny Somach, D.S.P.

Joe Cristiano

Andy Denemark and United Stations Radio Network

Mel Karmazin and SiriusXM

Flavia Salazar and family

Luke and Jeeb O'Reilly